GUILTY

Violent crimes in Ireland

D0368328

STEPHEN RAE

BLACKWATER PRESS

Editor
Margaret Burns

Design & Layout
Paula Byrne

Cover Design
Melanie Gradtke

ISBN
1-84131-594-X

Produced in Ireland by
Blackwater Press
c/o Folens Publishers
Hibernian Industrial Estate
Tallaght, Dublin 24.

CONTENTS

ACKNOWLEDGEMENTS

It is inevitable when writing a factual book on crime and in this instance murder, that the majority of those who helped most in the research would prefer to remain anonymous. I am referring to the members of the Garda Síochána of all ranks who generously gave of their time and knowledge. I was particularly struck by their razor sharp memories for dates and events which showed a great capacity to withstand the eroding effects of time.

My gratitude also goes to my colleagues at the Independent Group for giving me the time and space to complete this project. In particular, I would like to thank photographic editor Declan Cahill and the library staff. Also my gratitude to the Group for allowing reproduction of the pictures inside and on the cover.

My special thanks also to lawyer, Gerry Fanning, for his incisive observations.

Several retired detectives were invaluable when it came to investigating aspects of the murder, including John Courtney, Gerry O'Carroll and Mick Canavan. My appreciation also to Michael Brophy, *Sunday World* Managing Director, who as a young reporter covered the murders of Elizabeth Plunkett and Mary Duffy and who helped fill in detail on the crimes.

Thanks to Margaret Burns, editor with Blackwater Press for her patience and perserverance.

Most importantly of all, my heartfelt thanks goes to Liz, who was always ready with sound advice and encouragement.

My appreciation also goes to those who I have inadvertently omitted to mention. Thank you all.

Stephen Rae, November 2002.

INTRODUCTION

Murder is committed where the accused kills the victim intending by his act or omission to kill or cause serious injury to the victim.[1]

This book chronicles a number of Irish murders and one attempted murder. The cases have been chosen either because I have covered them as a security correspondent or have had a special interest in the progress of the investigations down the years. I trace the last movements of the victims of some of the most notorious killers in Ireland's recent history.

The idea for this book first arose when I learned about the activities of two British men, John Shaw and Geoffrey Evans, responsible for the disappearance and murder of two young Irish women in 1976. As a crime reporter, I have been exposed to the details of some of Ireland's worst crimes in recent years but I had never realised that such barbarism, as committed by these two serial killers, could have occurred here.

I found it strange that although these men committed some of the most appalling crimes ever witnessed in this State, most Irish people had never even heard of Shaw or Evans. I felt that the full extent of their crimes should be put on the record. The two men were archetypal serial killers. Their victims were strangers and the crimes were accompanied by sadistic acts. To most rational people there appears no motive; most would say that these killings were the acts of madmen.

If John Shaw and Geoffrey Evans were serial killers, then two other murderers portrayed in this book, Malcolm MacArthur and Frank McCann were typical sociopaths.

Sociopaths have been described as less capable of forming loyal relationships, are selfish, irresponsible, impulsive, uncaring and do

---

1. Charleton, Peter, *Offences Against the Person*, (1992) Round Hall Press: Dublin.

not tend to feel any guilt. They are easily frustrated and tend to blame others for their bad behaviour.[1] Both men fit this description completely and both have never shown any remorse for their deeds.

In *Guilty*, all but one of the victims are female and in one instance the victim was a young girl. Women are increasingly the victims of violence in our society and this book simply reflects that. You will see that in most cases those who were murdered were just in the wrong place at the wrong time. Without being alarmist, my wish is that by the end of this book you will have learned that there is always a need for some method of personal security. Although, as the case of Joyce Quinn shows, precautions cannot prevent being targeted by a sick individual.

The theme of this book was also guided by the wish to write a book on the crime subject outside of the gangland and drugs area, which has become a common theme.

The dedication and technical prowess shown by the Garda Siochána in investigating these crimes is evident in each case. The work of the Gardaí is charted from first discovery to final arrests and convictions. In one case the murder remains unsolved, but in each case there is an argument that the work of the Gardaí was hindered by a lack of witness evidence.

Upon reading this book, it is my hope that the reader will realise that even in a small and relatively crime-free country like ours, there are dangerous people in our midst.

---

1. Williams, Katherine S., *Textbook on Criminology*, (1991), Blackstone Press Ltd: Oxford.

SERIAL KILLERS

'If a balance is to be struck between one person's right to liberty, for some hours or even days and another person's right to protection against danger to his life, then in any civilised society in my view, the latter right must prevail.'

– Supreme Court Judge Griffin, *The People (DPP) v Shaw*, 1982.

JOHN Shaw and Geoffrey Evans set out on a trail of rape and murder on 28 August, 1976. By the time they were arrested a month later, two young women lay dead and a third had a narrow escape.

This country had never before witnessed the likes of the two Englishmen, whose crimes are all the more despicable because of the high degree of premeditation involved. Most homicides are the result of sudden violent rages but in the case of Shaw and Evans, they set out in each case to rape and then kill. The spate of violence they unleashed is almost impossible to comprehend. Equally mystifying was the accident of the meeting of two such similar minds. Both were hopeless recidivist criminals who spent most of their lives in and out of British jails.

Soon after their release from jail in 1974, they became the focus of a major manhunt by British police. They were sought in connection with the rape of three girls, one of them the 16-year-old daughter of a high-ranking officer in the Greater Manchester Police. As the heat was turned up in Britain, the two wanted criminals fled to Ireland. They set each other one perverse goal – to rape and kill one woman a week.

* * *

John Shaw and Geoffrey Evans came to Garda attention soon after their arrival in Ireland. They were arrested for house-breakings in counties Cork and Tipperary.

On 5 February, 1975, both men appeared before Cork Circuit Court on 16 counts of burglary. The offences had occurred over several weeks. The judge was not impressed by the men's previous convictions.

At the age of 31, Shaw, the father of three children, had already accumulated 26 convictions in Britain. Three of them were recorded against him before the age of 14. Most of the offences related to larcenies, but in 1971 he had received a seven-and-a-half year sentence at Liverpool Crown Court for attempted rape. At Wigan County Magistrates Court a few years earlier he was convicted of indecently assaulting a young boy. There was no doubt that Shaw was a hardened criminal. But his record also revealed him to be a sexual deviant.

Geoffrey Evans, the older of the two by two years, had also been married but was now separated. Originally from Tyldesley, northern England, he had 36 previous convictions, mostly for stealing and robbery, including car theft. Although physically a much smaller man than Shaw, Evans exercised a Svengali-like influence over the former coal miner.

Along the lawyers' bench and amongst gardaí, muffled gasps of disbelief greeted the recital of the defendants' convictions. It was long before the advent of heroin and other drugs in Ireland. For any offender to have accumulated such a string of recorded crimes was indeed astonishing. Having listened to their long criminal record, the judge sentenced each man to two years imprisonment. He said he would find them guilty on one count of burglary and take the other 15 offences into account.

Both men were led away to Cork jail and later transferred to Mountjoy. They later remarked how conditions in the 'Joy were much more favourable than in the countless British prisons where they had served time.

Shaw served precisely 18 months of his sentence. Evans was incarcerated for three weeks more and was released on 26 August, 1976. They arranged to meet up in Fethard, Co. Tipperary, at the home of another Englishman, a friend of Evans called Cliff Outram. Evans got the train from Dublin after storing most of his belongings in the left-luggage room at Heuston station.

Back together again they didn't waste any time planning a most heinous crime.

* * *

On Saturday, 28 August, Shaw and Evans left Outram's house and went into Fethard where they borrowed a car belonging to a local man. They drove to Dublin, stopping off at Heuston station to collect Evans' suitcases. Near the Four Courts, the pair had a few drinks and something to eat in a pub which, on weekdays, was frequented by police and lawyers. That night they set off for Co. Wicklow. Between Wicklow town and Arklow, near Jack White's pub, the two conspirators saw a sign for the turn-off to Brittas Bay.

After several hours drinking at Jack White's they decided to break into caravans at Brittas. But they also had something more sinister in mind. In a manoeuvre they had used a number of times before, Shaw got out of the car some distance down the road to make the offer of a lift from Evans appear less menacing.

'We were talking about girls and Geoffrey said he was going to pick up a bird and have it off with her. He said he wanted a small bird. Geoffrey was driving and we drove around the roads for a while looking for a bird,' Shaw said.

'We saw one standing at a corner. Geoff stopped and asked her if she wanted a lift. I had got out of the car and walked up the road at the time. This girl told Geoff that she was waiting for someone and he picked me up again.'

The woman was lucky. The fact that she said she was expecting to be met was enough to discourage the two. The last thing they wanted was to be confronted by anyone would might be a good match for them. Their next target would not be so lucky.

* * *

Elizabeth Plunkett was 23 years of age and had travelled to Brittas Bay earlier that day with five friends from Dublin. The group intended spending the weekend in a caravan owned by a friend. They arrived in holiday mood at McDaniel's pub shortly before 9 pm in two cars, but when they met outside the front door of the caravan they discovered they had forgotten the key.

Elizabeth's boyfriend, Damien Bushe, volunteered to telephone the caravan owner at home and the rest of the group went to the pub. The group included Damien's sister, Mella Bushe, who worked with Elizabeth in Dublin. Both women had returned from the holiday of a lifetime in St Tropez, France, just three weeks earlier. The two of them had saved up for the Mediterranean trip and looked stunning after their sun holiday.

The group had ordered their first drinks when Damien returned to say that Mrs Iris Turner, who owned the caravan, sited about half a mile away, was prepared to make the one-hour drive from Dublin with the key to the caravan. Someone bought Damien a drink and he sat down to wait for the key to arrive.

Within a short time, however, he got into a discussion with another member of the group about the sale of a car and the conversation became heated. Elizabeth shouted: 'We're here to enjoy ourselves this weekend. To hell with the car until Monday.'

An hour later, when Mrs Turner arrived at the public house, the bickering was still going on and Elizabeth warned: 'If it doesn't stop I'm going home.'

That was the last any of the group heard from her. When the arguing continued, she got up from the corner table and stormed out of the pub which was packed with more than 800 holidaymakers. Among them were two Englishmen who had been scanning the premises for some time. They saw Elizabeth leave the pub and followed her.

She was walking alone along the dark road when Shaw and Evans drove by. 'She will do,' Evans announced coldly.

They first drove past Elizabeth and turned back. Shaw got out of the light-coloured Austin A40 down the road and Evans made the offer of a lift to Elizabeth on his own.

Evans asked Elizabeth where she was going. She replied that she was headed for Dublin. He told her to hop in since that was where he was going. Once she was in the car, Evans drove on and picked up his accomplice, who sat in the back. Although her fate was probably already sealed, Elizabeth Plunkett mentioned that she had just had a row with her boyfriend. It was certainly something the pair wanted to hear. It meant Elizabeth's disappearance would not appear suspicious for a while.

It was 11.30 pm when the two men stopped the car close to the entrance to Castletimon Wood. They suddenly pounced on the young woman, hit her across the face and dragged her from the front seat. When she started to scream they stuffed tissue paper into her mouth. Elizabeth, who had taken judo lessons and was a strong swimmer, put up a fierce struggle. But the 23-year-old was no match for her abductors. Both were physically strong. Evans, before he set out on his life of crime, worked as a builder's labourer. Six-foot-tall Shaw worked in the coal mines as a teenager and had been employed on construction sites.

They tied her hands behind her back and beat her severely. No one will ever know the true horror suffered by Elizabeth Plunkett at the hands of these two debased men. One can only imagine the terror she endured in the long agonising hours which followed deep in the pitch-black forest. The only accounts are those given by Shaw and Evans in their confessions and these only give sanitised versions of what occurred. The statements also have to be treated with some degree of caution insofar as each culprit tried to shift the bulk of the blame onto the other.

'We climbed over a wire fence that was across the road there. We went into the woods with her. We had a hold of her. We told her to lie down and she did so. We took the suitcases out of the car and put them on the ground beside her,' said Shaw.

A good distance into the woods near an old sandpit, away from any possible disturbance, the two men raped her. First Shaw, then Evans.

Evans described the sequence of events. 'We pulled her in the trees. She was saying "Let me go." We took off her slacks, they were a light-blue colour. We took off her panties and John had intercourse with her. He forced himself on her as she didn't want to. I walked away while John was doing this. After about a quarter of an hour I came back. The girl was lying on the ground. John was sitting beside her.'

Evans, who was by all accounts the leader of the two, then raped her repeatedly.

Realising that Elizabeth's friends could be out looking for her and that the car parked on the roadside could attract attention he sent Shaw to get rid of it.

'Geoff told me to take the car away. I went into the car and left Geoff with the girl. I parked the car in a car park on the main Dublin Road at a pub.'

Shaw was gone for a couple of hours and when he returned they both again savagely raped the helpless young victim. During the night it rained heavily but this did nothing to dampen the ferocity displayed by the two men. After the spate of sexual assaults, Evans, the more calculating of the two, told Shaw to kill Elizabeth Plunkett.

'Geoff said he would go back for the car and he told me to kill her while he was away. He said to me "Remember what happened in England." [1] Geoff went off for the car and I had intercourse with the girl again. When Geoff came back he said: "Why haven't you killed her?" He said again, "Remember what happened in England". I took a nylon shirt out of one of the cases. I put the sleeve around her neck and choked her.'

---

1. Possibly a reference to the three girls raped in Britain who were later able to describe their attackers.

* * *

Back at the pub, the group had left within ten minutes of Elizabeth's walking out. By then there was no trace of her in the crowded car park and a check at the locked caravan turned up nothing.

Damien Bushe drove back to Dublin to check with Elizabeth's parents in Pembroke Cottages, Ringsend. They had not heard from her. The following morning both the Plunkett and Bushe families began a search of the sprawling sand dunes which skirt the picturesque Co. Wicklow holiday bay. Elizabeth's disappearance was not reported for another few hours.

As dawn broke, the killers were planning how to dispose of her body. They callously set out to cover their tracks. By disposing of the body where nobody could find it, they thought they would at least buy themselves time.

The crime scene was within walking distance of the coast. The killers made up their minds to dump the body in the Irish Sea.

In the early hours of Sunday morning they broke into a number of caravans on sites in Brittas Bay, taking anything they could carry. They couldn't resist committing a burglary whenever the opportunity arose. They took a portable television set, record player, records, clothes and small amounts of cash. Significantly, they also stole a tent and two sleeping bags. For the rest of the day they laid low.

Around midnight they put the body of Elizabeth Plunkett into the boot of the borrowed car and returned to one of the neighbouring caravan parks. While breaking into the caravans earlier the previous morning they had noticed four rowing boats on the shore. Now under the cover of darkness, they searched for a weight which could take the body to the bottom of the Irish Sea.

In a shed close to one of the caravans they stole a lawnmower. They carried it to one of the boats – 'The Skipper'. Using a rock, they smashed the padlock tying up the boat and pushed the small vessel afloat. Shaw pulled down a clothes line and put the rope into his pocket. They returned to the car and between them carried the body to the beach.

In darkness they rowed out as far as they could. Evans tied the lawnmower around Elizabeth's waist and both threw the body overboard. They watched it sink before returning to the coast about two miles south of where they had set out. There they abandoned the boat and hid for the night.

The following day, the whole dastardly plan almost came unstuck when the Gardaí received a report of two men trespassing on one of the seaside caravan sites.

Elizabeth had been wearing a navy and white T-shirt bearing the words 'St Tropez' and white jeans. Her other belongings such as her purse, overnight bag and rosary beads had been left with her friends. Now the killers had to dispose of her clothing. They lit a fire in a corner of McDaniel's caravan park. Suddenly the Gardaí arrived.

Detective Garda Joseph Neilan noticed a guitar on the ground and a considerable amount of clothing. He recalled that both men were in their early 30s. One was short and fair-haired and the other taller, dark-haired with a thick black beard. The Wicklow-based detective asked their names.

The smaller of the two replied: 'Murphy. John and Geoffrey Murphy.'

The garda asked were they related.

'We are brothers,' said Evans.

When the officer said he was surprised at this as they didn't look like brothers, Evans told him they were step-brothers. They said they were on holidays. Asked about the clothes in a bundle at the fire, Evans explained: 'We got wet during the heavy rain yesterday.' He added that they were 'working on the timber in the forest at Byrneskill, Fethard, Co. Tipperary.'

They gave the detective a false address and telephone number. He told them that as they had no accommodation in the park they had no right to be there and had better leave.

After the close encounter with the police, Shaw and Evans went back to Fethard. Cliff Outram put them up again and loaned them a car he had just bought. They returned the car they had previously borrowed from a local man. Over the next three weeks the two killers criss-crossed the country, carrying out a spate of burglaries.

Shortly after returning to Co. Tipperary, they broke into a house outside Fethard. Homes and pubs in Cork, Mitchelstown, Clonmel and Carrick-on-Suir were all targeted by the pair. While in Cork, Shaw and Evans looked up two women friends they had met in the city previously. But they were already planning their next crime.

On the Bandon Road they stole the registration plates from an abandoned Ford Corsair. They already had a purpose in mind for the plates. In the same way as they had gone to great lengths to dispose of Elizabeth Plunkett's body, they were now trying to create a cloak of deception which would disguise their involvement in the next killing.

*   *   *

On 6 September, the two killers couldn't believe their luck when they burgled a house in Cashel, Co. Tipperary. On the table they found three handbags, containing £500 between them. They tried to take the family's car but were heard breaking into it and made off when they saw a light coming on in the house.

On Friday, 10 September, Outram drove his English guests to Limerick from where they hitched first to Athlone and then Galway. On the outskirts of the city, Shaw and Evans identified a caravan site which they could use as a base. With the cash taken in Cashel they bought a mobile home at the Barna House Caravan Site for £380.

A small crime wave hit houses, pubs and shops across the west of Ireland, as premises in Spiddal, Leenane and Clifden were targeted. The two killers brought all the stolen property back to their caravan. But they weren't finished just yet. They still had to get a car which could not be connected to them. In Clifden, they stole a green Ford Cortina from outside a garage. It had been left there for collection by the garage owner but Evans had a master key for Ford cars. They rigged the vehicle out with tyres they had stolen from another Ford in Leenane. Back at base in Barna they changed the registration plates for the ones they had taken in Cork.

The two criminals returned to Co. Cork. In a wood outside Mitchelstown they painted the Cortina black. The job was badly done. They had purchased paint and brushes in Dunnes Stores but the finished job looked anything but professional. Even a casual glance at the car would reveal the brush strokes.

On 17 September, they broke into seven caravans at Castletown, Co. Wexford. From one of the bays in the caravan park they stole the roof rack from a saloon car. It would come in handy for storing the tent, sleeping bags and other items that they had stolen in Brittas. Everything was now prepared. Evans and Shaw were ready to kill again.

There was just one more thing left for them to do – change their identities. After the disappearance of Elizabeth Plunkett, the Gardaí would probably be on the lookout for two Englishmen, Geoffrey and John Murphy. If they were stopped by the police they would probably be asked for identity. At the County Council offices in Clonmel they applied for, and were issued with, two provisional driving licences in the names of Roy Hall and David Ball. They gave the address of their friend Outram. Their grotesque plan was complete.

* * *

Back in Brittas, Elizabeth Plunkett's family had grown extremely concerned. The pretty 23-year-old Dubliner had not been seen since she left McDaniel's pub at 10.30 pm on the night of Saturday, 28 August. Relatives, friends and other holidaymakers in Brittas Bay organised a search of the area. On Monday, 30 August, she was officially reported missing at Wicklow Garda station. The police issued a description of the young woman and began a Missing Persons inquiry.

As the days passed without any sign of Elizabeth, the anxiety grew for her family. The search area was widened to include the 40 acres covered by Castletimon Wood. On the evening of 4 September, a full week after her disappearance, civilian searchers came across the evidence which would change the course of the investigation.

Close to the entrance to the plantation, near the old sandpit, a woman's blue sandal was found. Elizabeth's family confirmed it belonged to her. There was no doubt it was hers. She had bought the shoes when on holidays in France. Superintendent Tom Neagle, in charge of the Wicklow District, knew that this discovery indicated the worst possible scenario. He took the decision to call in the Murder Squad.

The following morning, Sunday, members of the Garda Technical Bureau arrived on the scene. The team was led by Detective Inspector Hubert Reynolds. Scores of officers undertook the task of combing the area for further evidence. The task was made all the more difficult by a heavy undergrowth of briars and scrub. Using briar hooks and other tools, the gardaí hacked away most of the overgrown vegetation.

Reynolds himself moved along an area of the wood about 12 feet in from the road. After a short time, he found a crucial piece of evidence on a makeshift pathway. It was a piece of cardboard with a hole bored through it and white cord placed in the hole. On the cardboard, written in pen, was the name 'Geoffrey Murphy'.

The police were now able to link the two Englishmen who were questioned at McDaniel's caravan park, with Elizabeth Plunkett. Garda stations around the country were alerted to be on the lookout for the two men. They had given their names to gardaí as John and Geoffrey Murphy, but they might be using other aliases.

*　*　*

A shopkeeper was in his shop at Maam, Co. Galway on the evening of Wednesday, 22 September, 1976. Strangers stood out in the small village in the heart of Connemara but none more so than the two men the shopkeeper was about to encounter.

The shopkeeper was working on his accounts when he saw a car drive up at the petrol pumps. It was a Ford Cortina with a Dublin registration. Even more peculiar was the fact that it had just been painted black. It hadn't been spray painted, somebody had used a brush to change the car's colour. It was enough to arouse his curiosity.

The passenger got out and asked for £3 worth of petrol. 'I expected him to have a Dublin accent and I was surprised to hear him speak with an English accent,' the shopkeeper recalled. He tried to engage the stranger in conversation but to little avail. 'I passed some remark about the weather being suitable for holidays and he made a very brief reply.'

The driver remained in the car studying a road map. Nevertheless, the shopkeeper studied his face. There was something about the two men which just wasn't right. The passenger paid with three pound notes and they drove off in the direction of Leenane. It was now sometime around 7 pm and the shop owner wrote down the car's registration. Back in the shop he dug out the daily paper. He remembered reading about two Englishmen wanted in connection with the disappearance of a girl in Co. Wicklow. He hoped the report had given their descriptions. Unfortunately, it only referred to their ages but those fitted the occupants of the black car.

'After they had left I wondered whether I should get in touch with Garda Whelan in Maam. I also considered phoning Garda Summerville in Leenane as they were going in that direction. I did neither as I thought it would look silly,' he remembered.

Though he could hardly have known it, two of the most evil men ever known in this country had just passed through the village. Next morning he alerted the Gardaí to his suspicions. It was the kind of information they had been waiting for.

John Shaw and Geoffrey Evans had already committed one murder. They were on their way to commit another.

* * *

It was after dark when the two English criminals arrived in Castlebar, Co. Mayo. Around the same time, Mary Duffy, a young cook, was finishing work at The Coffee Shop on Ellison Street. The

24-year-old had been trying to get a lift home but she wasn't having much success.

She tried telephoning her brother who worked at a garage in the town from a kiosk near the café. She was unable to get through and went to another telephone kiosk near the town's railway station at the junction with McHale Road.

It was around 11.15 pm and a brother and sister who were using the telephone remember Mary waiting outside. As they left, the girl held the door of the kiosk open and Mary thanked her. She rang the garage. Patrick O'Donnell, the owner of the garage where Michael Duffy worked, took her call. He said that Michael had left to bring another person home but was expected back. She left a message for him to collect her on Breaffy Road as she was going to walk home. She never got that far.

*   *   *

One of seven children, Mary had dark-brown shoulder-length hair and at five feet four inches in height she weighed just around seven stone. Mary was a hard-working young woman. Her normal working day began at 9.15 am at Stewart's shop in Castlebar, Co. Mayo. She was an assistant there and also cooked for the owner. Her job at Stewart's usually ended at 6.15 pm and on four nights of the week she had a second job as a cook in the local café, known as The Coffee Shop, on Ellison Square. She started there at 7 pm and worked through until 11 pm.

It was a long day for the young woman who suffered from persistent backache caused by a spinal problem. The condition required continuous medical treatment.

Mary left school at the age of 14 and had been working ever since, first as a housekeeper with a local doctor. Later she worked in the kitchens of a number of hotels in Co. Galway. However, Mary harboured an ambition to emigrate to the United States where, like so many before her, she could earn far more money for the time and effort she put into her work.

At 9.30 am on Wednesday, 22 September, 1976, Mary left her elderly parents' home at Deerpark, Belcarra. She was dressed in a red polo-necked sweater, blue jeans, black knee-length boots which were the style of the time and a plaid duffle coat. She lived on a 30-acre farm with her 71-year-old father, John and her 64-year-old mother, Mary. That morning Mary Duffy and her younger sister Christina got a lift from a neighbour into Castlebar. Twenty-one-year-old Christina had a job in a shop on Spencer Street. The sisters went their separate ways to work.

Throughout the day Mary had a bad sore throat, as she had for the previous few days, and she mentioned it to Sarah Fadden when she went into The Coffee Shop for lunch as usual at 12.45 pm. Mrs Fadden, who had known her since she was a small child, had arranged for her to work in the café at night. Just after lunchtime, at around 2.15 pm Christina met Mary at Stewart's shop where they chatted for a short time. At 6.15 pm Mary finished work as usual and casually made her way to The Coffee Shop, arriving there around 6.45 pm. She was still complaining of a sore throat and took four Anadins.

* * *

After leaving Maam, Shaw and Evans travelled on to Westport where they went drinking, following which they drove to Castlebar. On the deserted late-night streets it was easy to spot the young woman on her own at the telephone kiosk. Shaw saw her first and told Evans to stop the car. Shaw got out and Evans drove further up the road, parking the car out of sight.

Shaw began following Mary Duffy at a distance of about ten yards. As she drew near the car, he ran at her dragging her to the ground. Her screams were heard in the houses on either side of the road but most residents thought it was young people playing pranks. None of them thought of telephoning the Gardaí.

Mary did her best to fend him off and in the struggle both of them ended up in the middle of the road. Evans turned the car around and drove alongside, swinging open the back door. Shaw, the former coal miner and labourer, hit the girl a few times across the face and shouted obscenities at her. In the rain of blows, some of her dental fittings fell onto the ground.

Eventually, the physically stronger man won out. He pushed Mary, who suffered from severe backache, through the open car door. Seconds later the struggle would have been seen by a car travelling in the opposite direction but by the time the other vehicle passed, Shaw and Mary were in the car.

The young woman was in agony and said something about losing her teeth. Shaw sat in the back with her head caught between his knees. A man living on the roadway, alerted by the screams, looked out his front window. All he saw was a dark-coloured car speeding off in the direction of Galway.

In the back of the car, the young victim was subjected to the most appalling and horrifying ordeal. They tied her hands behind her back and took turns raping her. The nightmare journey continued for 65 miles as the abductors took turns at driving. One would take the wheel and the other would get into the back.

Several times, the car nearly went into the ditch because of the speed and erratic nature of the driving along narrow and winding country roads. In the early hours, the two killers reached their destination, the old railway station at Ballinahinch. The building had been chosen for its remoteness, away from any major centre and miles from the scene of the abduction. The station building itself, which was about 600 yards from the Ballinahinch Castle Hotel, had been unoccupied since January 1975, when foresters stopped using it.

In a clearing near the Ballinahinch river, Mary Duffy was held captive and raped. The area between the clearing and the river was overgrown with briars and ferns so that it would be out of sight to any passing fishermen. The killers had chosen the site carefully.

Shaw told of his part in the brutal crime beginning with the abduction.

'We headed for some place near Clifden. While Geoff drove the car along the road, I had intercourse with the girl. I took off her pants and jacket. Somewhere along the road I started to drive and Geoff got into the back of the car with her. She didn't scream but said, "Don't do me any harm." We got to a forest and stopped. We pulled her out of the car. Geoff pulled off her clothes. We both had intercourse with her. Geoff gave her some pills to take, he gave her five or six pills. She took them and got a bit dozy. Geoff said they were sleeping pills and he would take her home.'

The two rapists put up the tent they stole in Brittas. Showing absolutely no mercy, they tied their victim to a tree. She was left there for several hours, possibly up to 24, perhaps more. In statements they made later they claimed that they had put the badly-injured woman inside the tent. Their statements conflicted.

Evans then took the car back to Barna to get more supplies. The two men decided that their litany of rape and brutality would continue for at least another day.

Evans arrived back at the caravan site in Barna around 5 am and spent the rest of the morning there. He burned Mary's handbag, underwear and tights which were on the back seat of the car. He kept the small amount of money in the bag and hid two rings which they had taken off her fingers in the caravan they had bought. They would try to sell the jewellery later.

At noon Evans went to the shops in Barna village and bought food for himself and Shaw. Conscious that the Gardaí may already be on their trail, he went into a pub in Spiddal to watch the 6 pm news on television. Evans couldn't believe his luck when no mention of the missing girl was made, he then headed back for the camp.

Unfortunately, the Duffy family had not yet raised the alarm in Castlebar. Mary's brothers and sisters presumed that she had spent the Wednesday night in town and had gone straight to work on Thursday. However, as she had Thursday off, nobody at Stewart's shop was expecting her. It was Thursday evening before any concern was raised about Mary's whereabouts. In that time vital hours would be lost.

It was dark when Evans got back to Ballinahinch and Shaw was in the tent with their victim. She had obviously received another terrible beating from Shaw and had a gash over her left eye. The two brutes gave her a cheese sandwich but Mary was unable to eat it. Her sore throat had worsened considerably after the horrific overnight ordeal.

Evans now took over while Shaw went off drinking in Roundstone. The catalogue of rape and abuse continued in the tent. In the early hours after Shaw returned they decided to murder Mary Duffy. Evans had already picked out a spot where the body could be dumped. After giving her a course of tablets Shaw again did the actual killing.

He described the murder: 'I got a cushion out of the car and put it over her head and put my hands around her neck and killed her. We threw her into the back of the car with her clothes. Geoff said he had picked a spot to dump her.'

With the body in the back of the car they drove the nine miles to Lough Inagh, a huge lake in the shadow of the Twelve Pins Mountains. The area is not far from the popular tourist destination of Kylemore Abbey. On the eastern shore of the lake lies a boathouse. The killers drove up to it under the cover of darkness in the early hours of 24 September.

The lake, three-and-a-half miles long, covers more than 2,000 acres. In places it is up to 75-feet deep. At its widest point it measures almost a mile.

The small pier at which Evans and Shaw arrived with the body of 24-year-old Mary Duffy is where the operators of the lake's fishing rights moored their eight rowing boats. The oars and other equipment were stored in the boathouse.

Evans later confessed: 'We carried her down the steps and put her alongside a boat. I went over to the boathouse and smashed a window, got in and took two oars and took them back to the boat. It was tied. John then took all her clothes off, jeans, coat, blouse and boots. We put her in the middle of the boat. I went back into the boathouse to get some weights.

'The only thing I got was a big sledge-hammer. I went to the car and took a concrete block and took that back to the boat and John tied it round her legs with rope from the car. I tied the sledge-hammer round her waist. John said we wanted more weights so I got an old anchor and a small brick. I put some rope around her body with a spare piece to attach the small brick to but the brick kept falling off. I couldn't manage it.

'John attached the anchor to her I think. We rowed out then. It were [sic] hard to see. We hit a marker buoy, a rock sticking up with a marker on it. John told me to lift the body over the side of the boat but I weren't able, so he done it and I kept the other side of the boat to balance it.

'We rowed back into shore and finished up a good distance from the boathouse. We walked along the road to the car. I walked down with John and collected the clothes and brought them back to the car and put the clothes on the floor at the front passenger seat. I drove down back the road we came, towards the railway station.'

On the journey back to Ballinahinch, Evans spotted that his accomplice's black jumper was soaked in blood and said they would have to get rid of it. At the station they packed up the tent and sleeping bags. In a corner of the clearing Shaw started a fire with petrol siphoned from the Cortina. He threw his own jumper, along with Mary's clothes, onto the bonfire, adding more petrol to make sure they were destroyed.

Now the killers had to return to the lake to return the boat before anybody noticed it was missing. En route they stopped off a number of times to dump the sleeping bags and other items into rivers. A number of motorists noticed this early morning occurrence but did not pay any heed to it. One driver thought they may have been travellers striking camp.

It was almost dawn when they returned the rowing boat to its mooring on Lough Inagh. Evans again crawled through the broken window to put back the oars. They returned to the caravan park at Barna around 11 am, confident nobody would ever discover the whereabouts of Mary Duffy or the scene of her terrible incarceration and murder.

* * *

At 11.45 pm on the previous night, Christina Duffy had contacted Castlebar Gardaí to report her sister missing. She told Garda John Duggan that Mary had not been seen since the night of the 22nd. The family had become worried when she did not return on Thursday night. They had made efforts to locate her and contacted friends and relatives but to no avail.

Garda Duggan took details of Mary's appearance and of what she had been wearing when last seen. The Gardaí built up a profile of Mary.

* * *

On Friday 24 September, the police carried out local inquiries in a bid to discover what had happened to Mary, but made little progress. House-to-house inquiries were commenced the next day and questionnaires issued to residents on her route home. It was only at this stage that people came forward and mentioned hearing screams on the night of the 22nd.

Gardaí in Wicklow were notified of the disappearance and told their colleagues in Castlebar that the circumstances were similar to the disappearance of Elizabeth Plunkett.

Anxiety had been heightened even further on the 23rd when a shopkeeper in Maam notified Gardaí about the two strange Englishmen he had served at his shop the night before. At this stage the Wicklow and Castlebar investigations became closely connected and gardaí in the west were put on alert for Shaw and Evans.

On 26 September, in the course of a search of the roadway at Saleen, Castlebar, where Mary was kidnapped, officers found four pieces of a denture plate. Further pieces were located further down the road. The pieces were matched together and identified by the Duffys as belonging to Mary.

Meanwhile in Galway, the two killers drove around the city looking for another victim. Shaw identified several women but Evans was insistent they get a 'small bird'. Around a dozen women were rejected in this way.

* * *

At 11.15 pm that night, Gardaí Jim Boland and PJ Corcoran were on patrol around Salthill in Galway. They were passing the promenade when they saw a black Cortina parked on the side of the street near the Ocean Wave Hotel. The two officers checked the registration, SZH 562. It was the car the shopkeeper had spotted in Maam days earlier and reported to the Gardaí as suspicious.

The two uniformed Salthill gardaí couldn't believe they had found the car every garda in the country was looking for. Particulars of the Cortina had been issued nationwide earlier that day in connection with the suspected abduction and murder of the two young women.

Boland drove past the black car and parked his squad car up a dark laneway out of view. He got on the radio and called for immediate back-up.

The two-way radio was only connected to Galway Garda Station in the city centre. The patrol car crew had no direct way of contacting their own station in Salthill which was much closer. Garda Corcoran jumped out of the patrol car and ran to Salthill station to get reinforcements.

Corcoran was only gone about three or four minutes when Boland saw two men approach the Cortina from the Ocean Wave Hotel. He got on the radio again and demanded immediate assistance.

Boland heard the Cortina start up and saw the lights go on. The patrol car radio crackled to life and the crew of the Galway car said they were outside Salthill Station. Garda Boland told them to get down to the promenade. He started the patrol car and with the full headlights on he raced out of the laneway and blocked the path of the Cortina. The officer ran up to the driver's door and pulled Evans out of the car.

The crew of the Galway patrol car arrived in the nick of time and arrested Shaw before he could get away. The two most wanted men in the country put up little resistance. It wasn't two against one young woman on a dark road anymore. The two men who beat, raped and then strangled two women didn't fancy their chances against four unarmed gardaí.

Boland searched his prisoner for weapons before putting him in the back of the squad car. He asked Evans, the driver, his name. 'Roy Hall,' came the reply. When the garda asked for verification of this, Evans said he had none. The officer asked if he had a driving licence and Evans said it was in the car.

What the arresting officers didn't know at the time, was that Shaw and Evans had just identified their next victim. They had seen a young woman near the hotel and had decided to abduct her. The police had almost certainly prevented a third murder.

The suspects were taken to Salthill station and later transferred to Galway. Garda Headquarters in Dublin was notified immediately of the capture. The Murder Squad drove through the night to Galway.

Meanwhile, the Galway gardaí found one more interesting piece of evidence in Evans' jacket – a receipt for £380 in respect of the purchase of a caravan at Barna House Caravan Park.

∗ ∗ ∗

Shaw was the first to awake in his cell around 9.20 am. He called out that he wanted to go to the toilet. The guard on duty told him to use the toilet bowl in his cell. Shaw replied that there was no paper and the toilet was broken.

Eventually Sergeant Patrick Guerin and Garda John Leen took the prisoner to another toilet on the ground floor. It had a window measuring about 26 inches by 16 inches overlooking a small enclosed yard at the back of the station. A door at the end of the yard led to Daly's Place, a small laneway off Eglington Street. Leen stood outside the toilet door while Guerin took up a position at a window where he had a view of the yard.

Practically every officer in the station heard Guerin shout out when he saw Shaw wriggle out through the window and bolt for the yard door. A posse of gardaí chased out the back door of the station after the escapee. Shaw got out onto St Brendan's Terrace on Wood Quay pursued by half a dozen men in blue. He got about 200 yards when several of them jumped on him. This time he put up a violent struggle but was quickly overpowered in a rain of blows and dragged back to the cells.

If he had gone any further he would have walked into a team of detectives from the Investigation Section of the Garda Technical Bureau, more commonly known as the Murder Squad. The team, including Hubert Reynolds, who was leading the Brittas Bay inquiry, noticed the commotion as four uniformed gardaí wrestled Shaw to the ground.

* * *

The interrogation of the two suspects took place separately. Teams of two detectives took turns trying to get the two Englishmen to tell them where Mary Duffy was. There was still a hope that the young woman was still alive. Both men, particularly Evans, spoke freely to the gardaí but vehemently denied involvement in abducting the women.

Detective Garda Gerry O'Carroll, who was attached to the Central Detective Unit in Dublin, was a last minute addition to the squad which travelled to Galway. Being one of the youngest members of the team, he was forced to stay in the station on the second night of Shaw and Evans' detention. With no bed, the officer found himself having to sleep on a chair.

All day he had been a member of the teams questioning the two killers. Unable to sleep, he decided Shaw was worth another try. He remembered the Englishman had mentioned being a Catholic earlier that day. O'Carroll took Shaw from the cell to the station's billiard room. He reminded Shaw of the terrible trauma of the families of the two young women. It was time to come clean. The detective, from a rural background in north Kerry, began reciting the rosary and urged Shaw to join him.

The ruthless killer snapped. All of a sudden he said he was willing to co-operate.

Almost immediately, he began giving the officer details of what had happened to Mary Duffy and Elizabeth Plunkett. It took four hours to complete his statement.

Armed with this confession, another team now confronted Evans who also crumbled. At 12.30 pm on 28 September, a convoy of garda vehicles left the station at Eglington Street for Lough Inagh with the two killers. They pointed out where they had dumped Mary Duffy's body and then took the gardaí on the journey back to where they had dumped her clothing, the tent and sleeping bags.

At 8.30 pm that evening the team set off for Brittas Bay.

* * *

On Tuesday, 28 September, the body of Elizabeth Plunkett was washed ashore at Lacken, Duncormack, on the south Wexford coast. The spot is 65 miles from Brittas Bay.

It was 32 days since Elizabeth first went missing.

On Sunday, 10 October, the body of Mary Duffy was discovered in Lough Inagh. It followed an intensive search by Garda, Navy and civilian divers. A young Galwayman, Tommy Mulveen, a mechanic and professional diver, was one of those who volunteered to help in the search.

'At about 2 pm on 10 October, I was a member of a section of divers diving on the far side of the lake and close to the shore on the far side. We were in the water for about 12 to 15 minutes when I noticed a body of a female lying on the bottom. The body was in between rocks in a type of a cave. It was lying face downwards in 25 feet of water.

'When I observed the body I alerted the other divers in my section. They came over to where I was and I got a weight belt and one of the divers marked where the body was with a buoy and rope. When the silt settled around the body I checked the body with my torch and noticed that it was in a crouched position. There was an anchor under her chin and it was tied with ropes to her arms. I also noticed a concrete cavity block tied between her legs in the area between her ankles and her knees and a wooden handle between her legs which I presumed to be a sledge-hammer.'

The body had been perfectly preserved by the lake bog water. It was 18 days since Mary had been abducted in Castlebar.

* * *

Geoffrey Evans and John Shaw fought a protracted legal battle. On 9 February, 1978, John Shaw was sentenced to penal servitude for life for the murder of Mary Duffy. He also received fourteen years for rape and two years for false imprisonment. He leaned forward in the dock and smiled as the judge asked him to stand to hear his sentence. The grin faded when Mr Justice Costello imposed sentence.

On 8 December, 1978, Geoffrey Evans was sentenced to penal servitude for life for the murder of Mary Duffy. Twelve days later he got 20 years penal servitude for the rape of Mary Duffy and Elizabeth Plunkett. During the trial Evans claimed he was ill-treated in Garda custody.

'I think it is a very sorry situation and almost a mockery of our constitutional position that a person who could show such a terrible disregard to the integrity of the person as you have shown these girls should claim that your voluntary statement should be excluded from evidence on the grounds you alleged against the Gardaí.

'The troubling thing about these offences of rape is that you knew nothing about these girls. There was nothing about them or about their personality that could have in any way affected you or put you in any sort of a position of weakness.'

Superintendent Neagle told the court that Evans, who was separated from his wife and children, had lived with his parents in Tyldesley and had been in Ireland since 1974. Mr Donal Barrington SC, defending, said his client had instructed him he did not wish any of his family or friends in England to know of his predicament and therefore he could not call any character witnesses in his defence.

Earlier in the trial, following legal submissions, Evans had been found not guilty, by direction of the Judge, of the murder of Elizabeth Plunkett.

The killers subsequently appealed their convictions. Both argued that their Constitutional rights were violated because the Gardaí held them longer than the 48 hours allowed under the Offences Against the State Act.

The Supreme Court decision in the case of *DPP v Shaw* held that the right to life takes precedence over the right to liberty. The court held that as the Gardaí believed Mary Duffy may still have been alive as they interrogated the two men, they had an obligation to do their utmost to find her, even if that meant holding the suspects for longer than the allowed period.

The Gardaí later learned of a young nurse who had had a lucky escape. Prior to the abduction of Mary Duffy, the nurse had been hitchhiking when she was picked up by Shaw and Evans near Oranmore in Co. Galway. One officer who was on the case takes up the story: 'Obviously they could not believe their luck. They intended to kill her. But the woman got a sixth sense that there was something wrong. They were being polite but she knew something was amiss. At Oranmore she asked them to stop because she said she wanted to go to the toilet. Whatever they thought, they let her out and she went into a pub. Lucky for her she escaped out the toilet window and ran off.'

One of the officers who interviewed the two killers, says: 'Of all the cases I have investigated I am proud of that one. I am proud we caught those evil men.' The detective says that neither showed any remorse, although Shaw, after giving his confession, told them he saw the devil coming for him in the cell on the night they were arrested. The burly ex-coal miner mentally regressed into childhood for much of the period he was in custody.

'They were really the first serial killers. If it had not been for luck on our part they would have left a trail of bodies around Ireland. I often think it was God that led us to their car in Galway that night. After all, the police force was not very sophisticated and we did not have the communications we do now, the radios and mobile phones. It was very difficult to mount a countrywide search, so yes, we were blessed the way we caught them eventually,' the detective says.

Another of the officers who was on the investigation was Detective Sergeant Michael Canavan, now retired from the force. He says 'Evans was the more intelligent. Shaw was the muscle but it was Evans that set the plan in motion. Shaw strangled the two victims on Evans' instructions. It was absolutely horrific the way they left Mary Duffy tied to a tree. I remember the details of the case at the time affected us all and left us sickened. A lot of people don't know how close they came to killing again. They had been watching dozens of women in the Galway area but rejected them for various reasons. They had been driving around looking for their next victim when they were caught.'

* * *

John Shaw and Geoffrey Evans are now the longest-serving prisoners in the State and are incarcerated in Arbour Hill jail in Dublin.

INFERNO

'It was all such a horrible mess. It had to be sorted out.'

— Frank McCann, 1992.

IT was 10 September, 1992. Garda James Murphy was on duty outside the ruins of No. 39 Butterfield Avenue in Rathfarnham, Dublin. Six days earlier the gutted house was the scene of a horrific fire which cost the lives of a woman and the young child she had hoped to adopt. Those who witnessed the blaze described it as an inferno. There was no way anybody could have gotten out alive.

The Gardai were preserving the scene until they could discover how the fire started. Nobody was allowed into the house. It was Garda Murphy's job to ensure that this order was enforced. In the course of the day he was approached by a man who walked up to the front gate and asked, 'Is it still under wraps?'

The garda replied that it was. 'Are you a local Sir?' the garda inquired.

'I used to live here,' replied Frank McCann.

Garda Murphy felt there was something peculiar about the man. He appeared jovial despite the fact that he was visiting the scene of an horrific tragedy.

'Had I gone up in that, she would have been a very wealthy woman, worth £250,000,' said McCann. He mentioned that he had tried to insure his wife for £50,000 two weeks previously. The conversation bordered on the bizarre.

McCann began relating a story about being with a group of friends during the week. He told them he was having a barbecue. He told the garda that his friends had started laughing and that he had spoken without realising what he was saying.

The officer couldn't believe his ears.

'Ah, it's no use to her now anyway,' he said by way of closing the conversation and walking off.

The young garda reported the day's events to his superiors. They were amazed at what Frank McCann had revealed. He was a strange person by all accounts but this was completely outlandish. It was not the type of comment one would expect from a grieving husband and father. Frank McCann was definitely a suspect.

* * *

At about 1.40 am on Friday, 4 September, 1992, neighbours on the suburban estate at Butterfield Avenue were awoken by a series of loud bangs. As they rushed out of their homes to check what had happened they were confronted by a raging fire in No. 39. Flames were licking up the exterior walls through the smashed windows. The place was a complete fireball.

Richard Duggan, who lived opposite, had been awoken a short time earlier by the sound of someone starting a car and taking off at speed. Then he heard a loud bang followed by the sound of breaking glass. He told gardaí that when he looked out the window he saw a 'ball of flame' coming out the front door of No. 39 like a 'rolling ball'. Duggan ran to his phone and dialled 999.

A group of friends returning to Dublin from a wedding in Co. Wicklow had got lost and found themselves driving along Butterfield Avenue. Upon seeing smoke coming from one of the houses, followed by flames, they got out of the car to alert any occupants and get them out. Brendan Dennehy, the driver, tried to get into the building but was driven back by the intense heat and clouds of smoke. In the flurry of activity that followed, as neighbours in their night attire ran to the house, Dennehy noticed a man out of the corner of his eye. He recalled that the man was in the front garden around the time the fire brigade arrived. The man was shouting that his wife and baby were in the house.

Neighbour Marie Daly was awoken by the explosions. The fire was directly opposite her home. In the garden she saw Frank McCann. He appeared to be in an awful state. He kept shouting 'Esther' and 'my baby'. His speech was impaired and he was taking deep breaths. She remembers that he was visibly very upset and distraught.

'He kept on saying "My wife and my baby are up there." He was pointing to both upstairs windows. The flames were coming out through the front door. The door was ajar. In the upstairs room over the hall, there was quite a glow coming from there,' she recalled.

The news spread that Esther McCann and little Jessica, the 18-month-old baby the McCanns had hoped to adopt, were in the house. Neighbours found a ladder and tried to get up to a first floor window but they could not fight the heat. Moments later, fire officers made valiant efforts to get in but they too were beaten back by the intensity of the fire.

Mrs Daly was doing her best to console Frank McCann. He kept making attempts to rush into the fire and she had to hold him back by gripping him around the waist.

'I was consoling him saying the fire brigade are here. I held on to him and tried to reassure him. But it was all too much for him. The next thing he fainted and fell back. His head brushed a branch and his glasses went flying off his face.'

An ambulanceman from Dublin Fire Brigade rushed over to render assistance. Mrs Daly's husband, Joseph, watched as first aid was administered to McCann in the front garden. Within seconds, Joseph Daly saw McCann jump up with such haste that he startled the paramedic.

'I was very surprised that somebody who had fainted should come around in that manner,' he recalled.

The scene was one of utter devastation. The dark residential street was lit up by the huge flames and the dancing blue lights of fire tenders, ambulances and patrol cars. Although it was just another house fire for the emergency crews, there was something about it which was a bit odd. The firefighters found the ferocity of the blaze unusual. They described it as an inferno, far more intense than the average domestic fire.

Garda Kieran Farrelly was one of the officers who responded to the call from the Dublin Area control room to go to a serious fire on Butterfield Avenue. When he arrived he saw Frank McCann with two women. Residents told the garda that McCann had been attempting to get into the house. The officer went over to the distraught husband and father and tried to keep him back from the fire. Something told the garda, however, that the man was 'not making any great effort to get past'.

Within an unexpectedly short time the blaze was brought under control. The firefighters involved were surprised at how the intensity had gone out of the blaze so quickly.

But nothing could have prepared them for the scene of destruction and death inside. Firefighter Paschal Henry from the nearby Nutgrove station found the body of 30-year-old Esther on the landing. Her lower body was still lying in the bedroom. The victim had tried to escape from the badly-burned master bedroom but was beaten back. She was probably trying to rescue little Jessica. Esther had suffered terrible burns all over her body.

Eighteen-month-old Jessica was still in her cot. The infant had apparently died from smoke inhalation. Her blackened body was found in the small nursery. The little girl still had a soother in her mouth.

The firemen continued their inch by inch examination of the debris-strewn house. It took them into every corner of the building. Later they found two smoke alarms hidden in the attic, still in their boxes.

Sergeant Tony Heavey from Tallaght station was among the first gardaí to arrive on the scene. After the firefighters had done their work, he set about sealing off the scene and ensuring that only authorised officers or forensic experts were given access to the site. He was the only uniformed garda to enter the house. Sergeant Heavey noticed that the door from the living-room into the back garden was unlocked and a pair of keys were still in the outside lock. The door itself was badly-charred and an area of carpet just inside the room was also burned away, exposing the floorboards. The rest of the living-room carpet was intact and covered in debris. As the firefighters began clearing up their equipment the sergeant saw a badly-charred small table being taken from the hallway. He noted there was a small gas cylinder on the table along with a blow lamp.

Outside, Frank McCann was apparently totally overcome with grief. Several people had seen him faint a number of times and he appeared to suffer panic attacks. Everyone presumed it was the shock of watching as his wife and child died in the blaze. He was taken to his mother's home where he was put under sedation.

Superintendent Pat King, the local district commander based in Tallaght, and his head of detectives, Inspector Tony Sourke, were awoken in the early hours of the morning to be told of the incident. They were informed there had been a terrible fire in Rathfarnham in which two people died. Both officers travelled to the scene where they supervised the removal of the bodies to hospital.

The chances of the blaze being accidental looked very slim. The loud bangs and the intense heat described by the firemen had all the hallmarks of an explosion. Moreover, Sergeant Heavey's discoveries added to the suspicion that the fire was not accidental.

* * *

Frank and Esther McCann married in 1987. In many ways they were complete opposites. Esther was a loving woman who went out of her way to help others. Frank was a determined but cold individual. He was also ultra-secretive.

The couple first met in the Horseshoe Bar at the Shelbourne Hotel in Dublin where Esther was banqueting co-ordinator and office manager. Frank was out with friends when he first saw her in the bar and immediately fell for her. That was in 1986. They married a year later and moved into the newly-purchased house at Butterfield Avenue.

Esther was originally from Tramore, Co. Waterford. The youngest child of Brigid and Thomas O'Brien, she moved to Dublin in 1973 to study psychology in UCD. While at university, however, her interest in computers grew and she gave up her degree course. In 1976 she joined Scholl footwear as a manageress, leaving three years later to become a trainer with Nexus office systems. In 1984 Esther started work at the Shelbourne Hotel on St Stephen's Green and two years later became a secretary/executive with O'Hare, Barry and Associates accountants. When the company split she joined one of the partners, Bernard Somers, as personal assistant.

Everyone who knew Esther described her as a sympathetic person. She was naturally good with people. Her feeling for people was no doubt sharpened by tragedy in her own early life. In 1979, when she was 23, she suffered great loss when her boyfriend was killed in a motorcycle accident just a few days before she had discovered she was pregnant. Her family supported her through the trauma of the accident and the birth of baby Sarah. They helped her purchase a house in Dublin. Tragedy struck again seven weeks later when the child died in a cot death.

An example of Esther's generosity to others was the free computer classes she organised for local women. She enjoyed watching complete novices develop computer skills under her tutelage. She also helped establish the Conor Farrelly Trust Fund which raised £20,000 to send a friend's child with cerebral palsy to The Peto Institute in Yugoslavia. She was a daily visitor to her sister Marian Leonard's home. Marian's son, James, suffered from bone cancer. The teenager, a top-class rugby player and brilliant student at Templeogue College, was mentioned regularly in a computer diary Esther kept.

The differences between the couple could not have been more marked. While Esther was loyal, Frank would cruelly tell his friends that his wife was infertile and could not have children. It was something he even mentioned in statements to police and in an unsolicited remark to the garda outside his burned-out house six days after the fire. In fact she suffered from an underactive thyroid gland – a medical ailment which, with treatment, could be rectified. In 1989 she cut back on the hours she worked as a busy personal assistant in an effort to rectify the complaint. Within a year, doctors reported that she had succeeded.

The couple's desire for a child was realised in an unusual manner. In March 1991, Frank's teenage sister Jeanette gave birth to a baby girl, Jessica. During the pregnancy Esther was a tower of strength, providing support and advice. It was a situation not dissimilar to the one she had found herself in not so long before. She visited Jeanette at the Coombe Maternity Hospital daily and was present for the delivery. With the blessing of the natural mother, Frank and Esther decided to raise Jessica as their own. To formalise the relationship they applied to the Adoption Board to adopt the infant. Marian Leonard often described how the baby girl lit up her younger sister's life.

Frank's outlook was the total antithesis of his wife's. Born in 1960, to a family of four sons and a daughter, he grew up with his parents, Joan and Frank McCann, at Fernhill Road in Dublin. The family later moved to Wainsfort Road in Terenure and the young Frank completed his Leaving Certificate in nearby Templeogue College. From a very early age, he was an outstanding swimmer and went on to represent his country at underage and senior level. Once his swimming days were over, he moved into the administrative and coaching side of the sport, eventually reaching the top of the Irish Amateur Swimming Association (IASA).

Having finished secondary school, Frank joined Irish Distillers as a trainee cooper. His photograph appeared in several national newspapers as the last apprentice cooper to be taken on by the company. It was another achievement for the young swimming star. The coopers were seen as the aristocrats of tradesmen and it was a difficult trade to get into. But in 1982, he was one of 24 of the barrel makers made redundant by the whiskey company. After losing his job, McCann established his own firm – Irish Craft Coopers – based in Greenhills industrial estate.

In November 1989, the plant was mysteriously destroyed by fire. The Gardaí discovered that the blaze had been started deliberately at two separate locations in the factory. Forensic examination of the scene also revealed that an accelerant had been used. Despite a full investigation nobody was ever charged with the crime and the business was later sold on for £92,000.

With the proceeds from the sale, McCann decided to change direction. He went into the pub business. He joined his brother Bert in purchasing the Mary Rose pub in Blessington, Co. Wicklow in 1991. They renovated the premises and sentimentally renamed it The Cooperage.

But while this was going on McCann was living a parallel secret life, one which revolved around his activities in amateur swimming.

In the summer of 1987, shortly after Esther and Frank got married, a teenage swimmer under McCann's charge gave birth to his child. By any standards it was a scandal – a 17-year-old girl becoming pregnant by a senior swimming official. If the affair was made public, it would destroy his career in swimming. It was agreed that the baby boy would be put up for adoption. But not content with having the affair kept secret, McCann then refused to contribute to the mother's medical expenses. The matter was only finally settled when Fr Michael Cleary threatened McCann with telling Esther of the affair unless he paid over £600. The money was left anonymously in the workplace of the girl's father.

As President of the Leinster branch of the IASA, McCann was due to be the next president of the national association and he wanted to avoid any scandal. Although what could be defined as scandal in the organisation at that time is hard to define. Two of McCann's closest allies at the time were convicted paedophile George Gibney and Derry O'Rourke, both of whom were later exposed as repeat sex offenders who used their positions of authority to interfere with young children.

McCann was also involved with the Olympic Council of Ireland. It brought him into contact with Ireland's budding olympians. He was chaperone and manager to Irish swimming teams that included Michelle Smith and Gary O'Toole at competitions in Rome, Paris and the United States between 1990 and 1992. The family photo album even included a shot of himself and Michelle Smith on such a trip. In 1991 there would be some controversy when he disqualified Gary O'Toole at the Irish national championships in Belfast. O'Toole had just complained to McCann about the involvement of some of his coaching friends in what could amount to sex abuse. McCann did not want to know.

On the domestic front, meanwhile, things were not going well. Within a year of their marriage, members of the O'Brien family began to detect a coolness between Frank and Esther. Frank, once the courteous and attentive boyfriend, was now colder and less interested in his wife. The family's concern with the direction of the marriage was distracted to a large extent when young James Leonard was diagnosed with cancer.

*   *   *

On Saturday, 5 September, the day after the fatal fire, gardaí met in conference at Tallaght station. Present were the two men leading the inquiry, Superintendent King and Detective Inspector Sourke. The blaze had made national headlines and the fact that the fire was being treated as arson had caused widespread interest. Dozens of officers were drafted into the investigation, including detectives from the Serious Crime Squad. At the early morning meeting it was decided that normal procedures would be followed, including house-to-house inquiries, the circulation of questionnaires and the establishment of checkpoints to determine if any passing motorists had seen anything suspicious. It was a murder inquiry in everything but name.

The Gardaí were anxious to get the results of a post-mortem on the bodies. This was delayed because the State Pathologist, Professor John Harbison, was away in Co. Kerry. It was Monday before they got the results.

The team was also keen to see what Frank McCann, the grieving husband, had to say. Had he any enemies? Did he suspect anybody? What was he doing himself at the time of the fire? Already, they had established a number of facts. McCann had complained to the Gardaí in Blessington that he had been receiving threats at The Cooperage pub. It was well-known that pubs were frequent targets of extortion and protection demands. Some Dublin city pubs had been petrol bombed and set on fire when the owners refused to hand over weekly payments to the racketeers. It was a possible motive for the threats to Frank McCann.

On Saturday afternoon, Frank McCann arrived at Rathfarnham station. He had been asked by Detective Inspector Sourke earlier in the day to come to the station 'if he felt up to it' to help focus the energies of the investigation squad. 'Keeping in mind the harrowing loss he had suffered, a sensitive request was made to come to the station,' Detective Garda Pat Treacy later remarked.

McCann was accompanied by his brothers, Michael and Bernard, and a family friend Susan Clegg. They went to another room in the station while Sourke and Detective Treacy put various questions to him. McCann began a long rambling statement which took almost five hours to complete. At times he became emotional and broke down in front of the detectives. At one stage they called for tea to help him recover his composure.

McCann told them he believed the fatal arson attack was linked to a series of threats made to him over the phone and in writing. He said he had already made a complaint about the threats to the Gardaí in Blessington. He described how a slogan had been painted on the back wall of his pub with the words 'Burn You Bastard.' He also described a suspicious-looking man who had been in the pub on the day of the fire and had asked for a telephone directory and enquired about the cost of a local call. After the stranger left, McCann said he became worried and looked through the phone book. He found the word 'Burn' circled near the entry for The Cooperage pub. In his statement he said he then looked up the entry for another Blessington licensed premises, the West Wicklow House, located across the street and found 'Bastard' circled. Someone was obviously out to get him.

He described to the officers how his wife was 'in good form' when he left home on the evening before the fire. They had stayed in watching a film until about 11 pm. He had not mentioned the threatening calls to her because he did not want to worry her. Later he drove to the pub in Blessington. He had a lot on his mind and went out for a scone and cup of tea in a local restaurant, but could not eat.

'My tummy was heaving as I was petrified. I had a bad feeling,' he revealed.

He was back in The Cooperage about 11.30 pm and all the customers had left by about 12.30 am. McCann said he told the barman, Alex McDonnell, he could go home at about 1 am. He counted the cash and prepared a float for the following day. According to the statement he then realised he had not carried out a stock-take in the off-licence and stayed on to do that.

'Now I know that if I had not done that, I would have been home in time and could have saved them,' he told the Gardaí.

The publican said he locked up about 1.20–1.30 am and drove straight home. When he got there he saw people on the street and at first thought there was a party underway. Then he saw his house ablaze and ran into the drive. He shouted that his wife was in the building but was restrained from going in.

On a couple of occasions his brothers looked into the interview room, once joking that he must be giving them his life story. He gave the two experienced detectives every possible reason to think that he was the victim of a protection demand by criminals or subversives. But the police were not at all convinced of his story. His demeanour and tears during his time at Rathfarnham station made little impact on the two detectives.

Nevertheless, the police had to check out his allegations to see if there was any truth to them.

As he left the station he stumbled down the stairs. To family members below, it appeared as if the police had pushed him. Frank was acting again.

On the evening of Monday, 7 September, the pathologist's report was sent to the Gardaí. Professor Harbison found that little Jessica had died as a result of inhaling smoke. He had found soot on her tongue and the back of her throat in her air passages and lungs. The child had a lethal level of carbon monoxide in her blood. There were no injuries other than those due to the fire. The autopsy on the body of Esther McCann revealed the full extent of the burns she received. Her head was scorched all over and the remains of some of her clothing had stuck to her body as a result of the intense heat. She died from inhalation of lethal levels of poisonous carbon monoxide fumes and gas. Her body showed no signs of injuries other than those associated with the fire.

Esther McCann's family were distraught at her death. But still they were left to make all the funeral arrangements. Frank did not get involved.

The remains were brought to the Church in Firhouse where Frank McCann walked to the altar and spoke about his wife. He spoke about his love for Esther and her kindness. He mentioned how she loved to keep a diary on her personal computer. By the time he was finished many of the mourners were in tears. McCann appeared very much the grieving husband.

The following day he travelled to Tramore, Co. Waterford for the burial. Again he spoke from the altar. He told how his heart lifted when he came into Tramore and he remembered all the happy times he had spent there with Esther. He placed Jessica's first pair of shoes on her little white coffin and again moved the congregation to tears with a poem he had written in memory of his lost family. The poem was reprinted the following week in the Munster Express. So touched had her family been by the act that they cut the piece out of the paper and framed it.

It was a remarkable performance. The detectives who mingled with mourners at the graveside were taken in themselves. But the mask was about to slip.

On the journey back to his Blessington pub, McCann showed a completely different side to his personality. He was seen shouting lewd comments out the car window to young women as he passed. The Gardaí got to hear about it.

That night a party to celebrate his mother's 60th birthday was held in The Cooperage and Frank presented a cake to her. He watched as she blew out the candles and he sang 'Happy Birthday'. It wasn't the type of behaviour associated with a man who had just buried his wife and 18-month-old child. Again the police were beginning to build up a profile of the real Frank McCann.

* * *

Within a short time, the detectives based at the incident room set up at Tallaght station began receiving reports that the publican had become involved in a relationship with a girl in her late teens in Blessington. They decided to look into the claims. Detectives were shocked to find there was a basis to the reports and that the teenager even stayed overnight with him in the pub.

Significantly at this stage, the team discovered that a series of gas leaks had occurred at the McCann household over the previous few months. During the month of July there were four leaks reported at the house. The first, on 3 July, when investigated by Bord Gáis, was put down as a false alarm.

Two weeks later a massive leak of gas was found. On 26 July, gas workers were called out again after another complaint from Frank McCann, but they could find no trace of escaped gas. Early on the morning of 28 July, however, while Frank was in his Co. Wicklow pub, the most serious leak occurred.

Esther awoke some time after 7 am to find the house was filled with the smell of gas. It brought on a blinding headache and she got a smell which she described as similar to onions cooking. She knew immediately what it was.

Luckily she had worked briefly for Bord Gáis and knew what precautions to take. Such was the extent of the leak that gas inspectors later said that a massive explosion would have been triggered by a light switch, a naked flame or by starting the car parked outside. Esther, a smoker, grabbed Jessica and ran to their car. She rolled it down the street before starting it. She then contacted Frank on her mobile phone. He was furious. But he directed his anger at the gas board and said he would contact them.

Esther's quick thinking had saved her and the little girl from almost certain death.

An inspection by Bord Gáis showed that the colossal level of gas in the house had been caused by the separation of two gas joints under floorboards beneath the staircase. Those who examined the break told the Gardaí they believed it could only have been done deliberately. There was no way the joints – which had only been installed a week earlier when a new meter was put in – could have separated by accident. The joints had been dismantled. The gas inspectors thought privately that it could have been an insurance scam.

The inquiry team now had a series of events which could only be described as attempts on Esther's life.

They located a friend who visited her at the Butterfield Avenue house on the night before the huge leak. She revealed how Esther appeared 'very dopey,' almost drugged, just before she retired to bed. She did not even say goodnight which was an unusual lapse of courtesy for Esther. The friend was then driven home by McCann.

The Gardaí were now faced with a possible scenario in which Esther was probably drugged, perhaps by her husband who then broke the gas pipes before leaving for The Cooperage. This theory was given added weight by the results of the forensic examination of the gutted home.

Detective Garda Seamus Quinn from the Technical Bureau had searched a recess under the stairs in the kitchen area. The alcove contained tools, shoes and an ironing board. Significantly, some of the floorboards were missing and there were fresh wood chippings underneath the floor – evidence, he concluded, of 'recent work'. He also found an amount of welding solder on the sub floor indicating work on the gas pipes.

The detective also examined the blowtorch and a small gas cylinder on a badly-charred table in the front garden. They had been seen on the night of the fire by Sergeant Heavey. These items were passed on to forensic experts for tests. In the garage, Detective Sergeant Quinn found a tile cutter, two cans of paint, one two-inch, white-handled paint brush and one two-inch, black-handled paint brush.

The Bureau experts also visited McCann's pub. They inspected the rear wall of the premises where the owner had reported someone had written the slogan 'Burn You Bastard.' The writing had been made by a two-inch paint brush.

The detectives from Garda Headquarters took samples of the paint away for analysis and also brought away the 04 telephone directory from the bar, in which the words 'Burn' and 'Bastard' were circled. The book was handed over to a handwriting expert.

As the investigation built up pace, several other strange occurrences in the weeks before the fatal fire began to emerge. Members of the O'Brien family told of a particularly worrying incident at 39 Butterfield Avenue. On the night of 14 August, Esther was suddenly awoken by the sound of the telephone ringing. She found an electric blanket on fire at the bottom of her bed. As Esther fought to dampen down the flames, her husband rushed into the room and pulled the electric plug out from the wall. They brought the fire under control but the incident left Esther badly shocked. Frank seemed unperturbed. A short time later he drove off to the pub and took the blanket with him. It was never seen again.

Esther mentioned the bizarre incident to her family. She said it was very peculiar. The last place she had seen the blanket was in the guest room, where her sister, Sr Monica, was staying at the time. She even remembered that Sr Monica had placed her folded clothes on top of the blanket. She had no idea how the blanket had come to be on her bed.

Luckily for her the phone rang when it did. It had been staff at the pub looking for Frank because the alarm system had gone off in The Cooperage.

At the time, other matters had prevented the family from spending as much time together as they normally would. Esther's nephew, James Leonard (17) who had been in remission from the cancer was diagnosed as having 'secondaries' and re-admitted to hospital.

In Blessington, detectives spoke to Alex McDonnell, the barman on duty at The Cooperage the night before the fire. He told them he left the pub at around 1 am. There was still about 30 minutes' clearing-up work to be done when McCann told him he could go home. Mrs Peig Gethings said McCann had been in her chip shop that night. She asked how Jessica was. 'Not a bother on her,' he replied. He returned to the pub around 12.40 am. She heard the gate between her shop and the pub creak at about 1 am and thought this was McCann.

* * *

In his statement made on 5 September, McCann had also mentioned telephone threats being made to the West Wicklow House across the road in Blessington. A check through Telecom Éireann's computerised records revealed the malicious calls had been made from the phone at 39 Butterfield Avenue. Frank McCann's story was not adding up.

Their suspect was still busy trying to convince the Gardaí that he was the victim of a vendetta. McCann reported to the investigation team that a 'sick' Mass card had been addressed to him at a friend's house, where he was staying. On 18 September, Detective Garda Brendan Gallagher was sent to interview him about the incident. The garda asked if he could see the card but McCann first insisted on bringing him into the kitchen. There McCann collapsed on the floor. He appeared to the garda to be semi-conscious.

A doctor was summoned but when he attempted to administer an injection McCann had fought him off violently. He 'suddenly seemed very alert,' Garda Gallagher reported later. McCann went on to tell him he was receiving threats over the telephone. He handed the detective the card. It read:

'At the request of Ha Ha, the Holy Sacrifice of the Mass will be offered for Francis McCann ... at the request of the Reverend Burn.'

Some of the words were made from cut-out newspaper headlines.

Forensic examination of all the notes received by McCann was carried out by handwriting experts at Garda Headquarters. It showed that they could have been written by McCann himself.

Moreover, the squad had also been conducting tests at the headquarters of the Civil Defence in Phoenix Park to establish if the blow torch and gas cannister found in the house at Butterfield could have caused the explosion. They discovered that they could be used to make an explosive device capable of causing the high intensity fire which killed Esther and Jessica.

On 24 September the Gardaí confirmed officially that the fire was being treated as arson. It was now officially a murder investigation.

*　　*　　*

The garda team based at Tallaght district headquarters had made great progress over the previous three weeks. They now had no doubt that Frank McCann had tried to kill his wife several times before by causing massive gas leaks and trying to burn her in her bed. But what was his motive? Why was he trying to kill her?

The answer came as soon as they inquired about the status of the McCann's application to adopt Jessica. Detectives found the Adoption Board had turned down the couple's application. McCann, who had been so careful to cover up the pregnancy of the young 17-year-old swimmer, had been found out. On 16 April, 1991, the teenager's mother telephoned the board to say he'd had sexual relations with her daughter and made her pregnant. After its own examination of the claims, the Adoption Board decided on 28 July it was not satisfied that he was of good moral character and therefore did not comply with section 13 of the Adoption Act.

This decision was conveyed to McCann's solicitor. The lawyer was also told that the Board wanted him to tell Mr and Mrs McCann and Jessica's natural mother about the difficulties with the application. They wanted a reply from him within one month. But Esther was ignorant of their decision and continued to press them, in letters, for an explanation of their delay.

On the night that the board reached its conclusion the first major attempt on Esther's life was made. Her husband had made the decision she should never know about his secret child. He would kill rather than be found out.

* * *

The evidence the investigation team had accumulated pointed to a well-planned murder. The detectives believed that after McCann had acted normally by buying chips at the local takeaway, he deliberately sent the barman home early. He gave the impression that a good deal of stock-taking and cleaning up remained to be done and that he would carry this out.

Instead, once the staff member had gone, McCann jumped into his Toyota Starlet and took off in the direction of Rathfarnham. On the deserted roads, he would have covered the journey in about 20 minutes. Having parked his car outside the house he walked through the dining-room. He went out through the open patio door into the back garden where he probably picked up the gas cylinder and blow torch which the gas board inspectors had seen him use to strip paint on an earlier occasion. In the hallway, he sprinkled the carpet with an accelerant, perhaps petrol or pure alcohol used by publicans for cleansing.

From their own experiments carried out in Phoenix Park, the Gardaí believe he then put the gas cylinder on the floor and trained the lighted blow torch on it. He then left through the front door and ran to the car. However, in his desperation to get away before the inevitable explosion occurred, he held the key in the ignition a little too long leading to the grating sound which woke up neighbour Richard Duggan. The car heard by Mr Duggan was McCann's, speeding off from the scene.

The Garda experiments with the Civil Defence showed he would have had enough time to get away before the explosion. Then he would have had time to recover his composure and settle his thoughts before returning to the scene of horror.

The Garda theory was helped by the discovery of a rug with scorch marks on it in a skip near the pub. Esther had edged off the leftover piece of carpet from their bedroom. But McCann had taken it and used it to practise setting his house on fire. The Gardaí were able to link the rug with the bedroom carpet in his home.

After the tests, and with the sheer quantity of evidence they had now accumulated, the Gardaí decided it was time for Frank McCann to account for himself. The explosive experiments they had conducted showed that the arson attack was in effect an explosion. Therefore they could arrest him under the Offences Against the State Act which meant he could be held in custody for up to two days. This would become very significant.

It appears McCann had prepared himself for a 12-hour detention period. Normally, where a gun is not the weapon used in a murder, the Gardaí can only use the provisions of the Criminal Justice Act 1984 to effect an arrest. These provisions only allow for a maximum period of detention of 12 hours. McCann felt this was the legislation they were going to use should they arrest him and had mentally prepared himself for it.

* * *

At lunchtime, on 4 November – exactly two months after the double murder of Esther McCann and Jessica – two teams of armed detectives converged on The Cooperage pub in Blessington. One team spread out around the pub and began a piecemeal search. The second team found Frank McCann upstairs. At 1.25 pm he was arrested under section 30 of the Offences Against the State Act on suspicion of having committed a scheduled offence, namely causing an explosion.

The squad arrived back at Tallaght district headquarters just after 2 pm. After processing their prisoner, he was brought to a detention room and his solicitor was notified of his arrest. Within a very short time, the prisoner soon began exhibiting signs of a panic attack. He began shaking in the room and was unable to speak. It appeared he was in a state of shock. A police surgeon and his own GP were called to the station. After examining McCann they concluded he was fit to be interviewed. McCann's theatrics were beginning to fail him.

Over the next 12 hours, the suspect was, as is normal in such circumstances, interviewed by teams consisting of two detectives. The questioning went on into the night but the prisoner insisted on his innocence. He appeared to be treating the interview teams as fools. 'He treated the whole thing as if we were asking for his tax and insurance. He thought the police were not as smart as he was.'

The following afternoon Chief Superintendent Michael Reid, the divisional commander, signed an order extending his detention by 24 hours to the maximum 48 hours.

That night, at about 10.40 pm, two Detective Sergeants, Robbie McNulty and Maurice O'Connor from the Central Detective Unit at Harcourt Square began questioning him. In the course of the interview they told McCann how the Telecom Éireann computer printouts revealed that the malicious calls he spoke about had been made from his own home. They told him to come clean. McCann slowly began admitting making threatening phone calls to the West Wicklow House pub in Blessington.

When it was put to him that he himself had never received any abusive calls or threats, as he had claimed, he became upset. 'I had to make it look that way,' he told the two gardaí. He nodded when asked if he had sent a Mass card to himself. He also nodded in agreement when asked if he had made entries in the phone book in The Cooperage and had daubed slogans on the back wall.

Asked about the Adoption Board's refusal to allow him adopt Jessica, McCann said: 'It was all such a horrible mess. It had to be sorted out.'

Later, McNulty put it to the prisoner that he had started the fire. McCann broke down and cried, then nodded his head. He cried for some time and O'Connor tried to console him. 'It's for the best, we knew all along,' the detective said.

Early the next day he was visited by members of his family.

At around noon he began dictating a confession to Sergeants Pat Walsh and Patsy Glennon. McCann also asked that Detective Inspector Sourke be present. The confession was in the familiar dramatic style the Gardaí had come to expect from the killer over the past two months.

'I burned my fingers. There were flames everywhere. There was burning. It just went whoosh.' Asked why he had brought the cylinder and torch into the house he replied: 'I was going to finish it off. I was going to clear up the mess ... me, Esther and Jessica.' McCann was describing the event as if he was reliving it.

At 1.22 pm, while the double killer was in mid-flow, a uniformed Sergeant knocked on the door of the interview room and said the suspect would have to be released as his 48-hour detention period was up. McCann was allowed to go. He left the station but for some unknown reason returned again a short time later and said he would voluntarily complete his statement. Whether it was conscience, or some other factor, we will never know, but McCann later signed the statement which was witnessed by all three gardaí and his brothers in the presence of his solicitor.

The gardaí decided not to charge him with the murder immediately but to send a file to the DPP to decide on the matter. McCann was free to go for the second time.

He checked himself into St John of God's Hospital in the Dublin suburb of Stillorgan where he underwent psychiatric treatment. It's hard to establish his motive in doing this. Perhaps he was trying to establish a defence of insanity at any forthcoming trial. But the series of attempts on his wife's life, along with the posting of notes after the event, showed a degree of premeditation which would make it extremely difficult to maintain a defence of insanity. At the clinic he began a relationship with another woman who was being treated there. She told friends that McCann's care for her had helped save her life.

When discharged from the psychiatric clinic he moved from Dublin to a mobile home at Ballyboyle, in Stradbally, Co. Waterford. It was here on 22 April, 1993 that a team of four detectives from the Tallaght investigation team arrested him under warrant for the murder of his wife Esther and 18-month-old Jessica. He had been fitting out the caravan, complete with pipework beneath the floor.

He was brought to Tramore Garda station and that evening charged before the local District Court with the two homicides.

In January 1994, when a date was finally set for his trial, the State's legal team and gardaí travelled to an industrial safety centre at Cardington, England, to carry out a series of experiments to prove exactly how McCann had caused the fire.

An exact replica of the house at 39 Butterfield Avenue was constructed at a cost of £70,000. The experiments, watched over by prosecution and defence lawyers, showed that McCann probably caused the blaze by pouring petrol, or another accelerant, over the living-room carpet and setting the room ablaze. This fire then caused the gas cannister to explode, creating the loud bangs heard by neighbours. The experiments were videotaped for later use in evidence.

On 11 January, 1994, McCann's trial began before Judge O'Hanlon in the Central Criminal Court. But on 31 January the trial had to be abandoned when he set fire to himself with deodorant in a cell at Arbour Hill prison.

It was a further two years before a new trial date was set for 10 June, 1996.

'He had to be carried from the witness box, shaking and crying. In the course of his testimony and at other times he sat hunched between two prison officers, his face in his hands or his eyes fixed on the floor. At times of stress the red burn marks left by the flaming deodorant on his forehead and temple turned to an angry crimson,' Brenda Power wrote in the *Sunday Tribune*.

She went on: 'But when the jurors were out he was a different man. Far from being the distraught, bereaved widower accused of nightmarish crime, he was animated, focused, controlled and watchful. He complained about the state of the holding cell in the basement – in reality an exact replica of the press room on the other side of the hall – he explained swimming techniques to the gardaí and most bizarrely while waiting for the jurors to return he sat calmly reading a murder mystery novel, a forensic science courtroom drama about a woman accused of murdering her mother and stepdaughter.'

On Thursday, 15 August, the jury returned a unanimous verdict of guilty. At 48 days it was the second longest criminal trial in the State. Family members saw extra significance in the date of the verdict. Esther had a great devotion to the Blessed Virgin. The 15 August is the feast of the Assumption.

Members of the O'Brien family wept and hugged each other and several whispered 'Yes' as the verdict was read. Mr Justice Carney told McCann he was imposing the mandatory sentence of life imprisonment for both murder counts. He said both sentences would run concurrently.

Afterwards, Esther's mother, Bridget O'Brien said: 'Thank God. He got what he deserved.' She said, however, the guilty verdicts would not bring back her youngest daughter. 'We have been crying for four years. They are gone for four years and this won't make a difference. But maybe it will make a difference, I believe he would do it again. We were blind. Frank killed the two best friends he had in the world. The only friends he had in the world. He killed his baby over another baby.'

When she recalled how they had framed the poem he wrote for the funerals she sighed: 'When I think of it, the lies, the fools we were.'

Marion Leonard will never forget opening the boot of Frank McCann's car on the day of her sister's burial in Tramore. Marion, who from the beginning suspected McCann of involvement in her sister's death, found his chain of office from the Irish Amateur Swimming Association in the boot. 'He had taken it from the house just before the fire. It was more important than either Esther or Jessica. He could have taken Jessica out, but to him the chain of office was more dear to him. He also saved his passport in case he needed to flee the country.'

'It was typical of a man who showed no emotion and could display no loyalty to anybody.'

Detectives involved in the case concur with the families belief that McCann would have killed again.

'He was a complete sociopath. He would have killed any number of people if he thought it would serve his purposes. He had no compassion for anybody. In all my years investigating serious crime he was the worst case I have ever come across,' the officer said. 'He is a very dangerous man. A clinical psychopath, that is the only way to describe him.'

*   *   *

At the Court of Criminal Appeal on 12 March, 1998, McCann's appeal against his conviction for the murders was dismissed. He is currently serving his two life sentences in Arbour Hill jail.

On 9 October, 1998, Esther's mother, Bridget O'Brien, was awarded half the net proceeds of the sale of the £180,000 house at Butterfield Avenue. McCann was also ordered to pay Mrs O'Brien a further £27,900 which had accrued from his share of a life insurance policy on the mortgage.

In linked proceedings, the killer was ordered to pay his mother-in-law £9,300 under the Civil Liability Act for mental stress and funeral expenses.

The decision was a landmark one in Irish law.

Afterwards, Esther's sister, Marion Leonard, said McCann was quite capable of murdering again. 'I would think he has no conscience. He certainly does not have any value on life, especially female life.'

She said the family had taken the action to ensure he did not profit from the deaths of Esther and Jessica. 'It was something that had to be done. It wasn't revenge. It was more a right and wrong thing, looking for a rightness in all the wrong and all the evil.'

'DON'T RUIN YOUR LIFE'

'I felt a bump from the rear wheel of the car.
I think the rear wheel hit the body but I did not stop to find out.'

– Private Sean Courtney, 1991.

AN hour before dawn crept across the city on Saturday, August 31, 1991, a cyclist left his home at the foothills of the Dublin mountains for work. The 46-year-old storeman cycled strenuously against the incline on Mount Venus Road in Rathfarnham. Despite the darkness he had no light on his bicycle. He used the orange illumination from the city below to guide him. The 5.30 am start was not unusual and he had covered this route in the early hours hundreds of times before.

As he reached the top of the hill at the entrance to the GAA grounds at Frank Kelly Park, the cyclist changed gears. Out of the corner of his eye, he noticed what he thought to be a body or a large doll lying on the ground. He tried to stop but the grip of the rubber brake pads was not sufficient to bring the bike to a halt. The bicycle careered downwards to the bottom of the hill. By this time, he concluded that his mind must be playing tricks on him. He continued on to work.

The cyclist had just missed the departure of a white Peugeot 205 car from the same spot just a few minutes before. The two-door car had been parked at the entrance to the sports grounds for several minutes. It had then been driven off at speed towards Dublin.

Later that morning the cyclist became concerned about what he thought he saw and decided to report the matter to the police. By that time a full-scale murder inquiry was already underway.

* * *

At 6.35 am, mechanic Aidan Cullen was driving along Mount Venus Road to work on the Naas Road. As he approached the entrance to the GAA pitch he saw what he took to be a mannequin on the ground. He slowed the car and realised the scene was covered in blood. Shocked by what he saw, he pressed on the accelerator and drove the 800 yards to Pine Valley Golf Club where he saw two golfers unloading their clubs from a jeep. They were startled by the screech of brakes and looked up.

'There's a body of a girl down there,' he shouted across to them.

Both golfers were momentarily stunned. Throwing their clubs aside, they followed Cullen in their own vehicle to Mount Venus Road. The scene that met them on the quiet country road was horrific.

A blonde woman in her late 20s lay naked and bloodied on gravel in the gateway. It was obvious to the three men she had received serious head and facial injuries. Close to the body lay a red brick, covered in blood and hair. The woman's navy blue trousers, a blouse, underwear, belt and other belongings lay scattered around the place.

Despite its proximity to Dublin, the scene was still relatively remote. At that time, the Frank Kelly GAA Park had not been developed and resembled a construction site. The body was found near two gates which led to the grounds. It lay about 10 yards off the roadway which served as a link route between the Rockbrook Road and Stocking Lane/Kilakee Road. The sports park was near Kilakee Forest and Cruagh Wood, both popular locations with walkers and sightseers during the day and courting couples at night.

Aidan Cullen asked the two men to remain at the scene while he alerted gardaí at the nearest station. He sped off towards Tallaght returning at 6.56 am with uniformed officers in a patrol car. They had been delayed for a few minutes because of a difficulty in finding the spot. Gardaí John Hammond and Brian McHale immediately set about preserving the scene and summoned their superiors. The evidence pointed to a murder inquiry.

Traffic along the route by this time was beginning to build up as shift workers commuted to the industrial estates nestling on both sides of the mountain at Stillorgan and Tallaght. One of the gardaí began diverting cars away from the scene along the series of minor roads which criss-crossed the locality.

Most investigators agree that the discovery of a naked body in an open area is one of the hardest categories of murder to solve. The inquiry team are confronted with innumerable problems from the very outset, including identifying the victim, discovering her last known movements, finding out where she is from and then trying to narrow down the list of suspects. Often the body will have been transported several miles from where the crime was actually committed. When a body is found in a house or other enclosed area, at least the police will have some clues as to the possible identity of the victim and often the circumstances of the crime – whether it is frenzied, calculated or arising from robbery.

These problems were crossing the minds of the senior team which arrived at Mount Venus Road on the morning of 31 August to investigate the homicide of Mrs Patricia O'Toole – although it would be almost two full days before they would finally manage to identify her. The large force of detectives and uniformed officers from Tallaght and Rathfarnham stations were joined by a four-person team from the Technical Bureau – a ballistics sergeant, fingerprint expert, photographer and mapper. All of whom would provide essential documentary evidence at any forthcoming trial.

They noted the victim had received severe head and facial injuries. Her face was severely mutilated and what appeared to be the murder weapon, the bloodied brick, lay near the body. There were also signs that the body had been dragged some distance. A drag mark along the gravel was located at the head of the dead woman and went for about four feet towards the entrance to Frank Kelly Park. This was where the investigators concluded the major assault took place.

The first problem the team faced was identifying the victim. Detective Superintendent Gerry McCarrick, who was leading the inquiry, ordered a check on any women who had been reported missing in the previous 24 hours.

The scene was left intact until the body was examined by the State Pathologist. In the meantime, Dr James Maloney was summoned to the scene and at 7.30 am he officially pronounced the time of death. He took a temperature reading on the dead woman, it read 32.2 degrees. He noted that she wore a gold ring on the ring finger of her left hand. The right ring finger bore three silver rings intertwined, typical of a Russian wedding ring.

Ballistics expert Detective Sergeant Brendan McArdle from Garda Headquarters and his team carefully began to collect the deceased's belongings in evidence bags. The bloodstained brick was also collected. Back at the Bureau offices at Phoenix Park, it was found to weigh five-and-a-half pounds. It was late afternoon when Professor John Harbison arrived on the scene. He had been conducting a post-mortem in Ballinamore, Co. Leitrim when contacted by the Gardaí.

While awaiting his report on the nature of the injuries, the police issued a description of the woman to the Saturday evening papers and RTÉ, with an appeal to anybody who may be able to help identify the woman to contact the incident room set up in Tallaght. The press statement gave the essential details. 'Height 5ft 5ins, medium build, auburn hair with blonde highlights. Wedding ring on left hand, a distinctive Russian ring of three interwoven silver rings on the ring finger of her right hand.'

* * *

After a short examination of the site, Professor Harbison arranged for the body to be taken to the mortuary at James Connolly Memorial Hospital across the city in Blanchardstown. With the full Technical Bureau team in attendance he opened the plastic sheeting in which the body had been placed and noted a slight whiff of alcohol. He noted the same smell when he took away a plastic bag used by the Gardaí to cover the head.

The results of the autopsy showed that the victim had died of inhalation of blood as a result of a combination of bleeding from mouth and nose injuries. The victim would have been unconscious for at least part of the attack. The head injuries were consistent with furious blows from the brick found at the scene but there were also signs that the woman's head had been beaten off the ground. The killer blows, however, would have been those inflicted with the brick.

Abrasions on the buttocks and knees suggested that the deceased had been dragged over rough ground. Bruises on the backs of her hands and wrists were sustained when warding off the violent blows.

There was also evidence that the killer had driven over the body before fleeing the scene. Severe pressure abrasions on the left arm suggested that the wheel of a vehicle drove over the deceased. Muddy imprints on the fronts of the thighs had the appearance of tyre marks. Oil marks on the body reinforced the belief that a car had been driven across the body.

Professor Harbison's findings confirmed the Gardaí's belief that the murder had been a frenzied one. They were dealing with a killer who could strike again.

At a hastily arranged conference in Tallaght station, the investigation team was formed. The 40-strong unit consisted of officers from Tallaght and Rathfarnham stations, both of which comprised the 'M' or Mike District, augmented by gardaí from the Divisional Task Force in Crumlin. Assistance was also sought from the Serious Crime Squad at Harcourt Square under Detective Chief Superintendent John Murphy and Detective Superintendent Tom Butler.

Officers almost immediately began to conduct house-to-house inquiries in the area around the scene. The team decided from a very early stage, that the press and television, who had already been notified of the killing, would play an important part in the investigation and were to be co-operated with fully.

Detective Superintendent McCarrick's request for a list of missing women had also come through. It revealed that on the previous day,

Friday, a total of eleven females in the victim's general age group had been reported missing – an unusually high number. Several of the women had never gone missing before and the police would have to check each one out individually.

One woman from Cabra in the north of the city who had disappeared mysteriously was the same age and build as the murder victim. A team of officers visited her family and a relative was brought to identify the body but couldn't make a positive identification.

The woman was later found alive and well in Donabate. Superintendent McCarrick ordered two-person teams to follow up each of the remaining ten cases.

*   *   *

The last time Brian O'Toole had seen his wife was in the car park of the head office of the First National Building Society in Booterstown in South Dublin on Friday, 30 August. The couple had an appointment with a representative of the Accounts Department at 1.30 pm. They met 15 minutes beforehand. After the meeting he walked Patricia back to her car and they spoke for about ten minutes. Patricia said she was due back at work at Consolidated Insurance Brokers on Mount Street at 2.15 pm. He asked her about her plans for the evening as he hoped to play golf. Patricia said there was a farewell party for one of the girls in the office after work in Scruffy Murphys, a pub off Mount Street.

Before they parted he told her that if she had too much to drink she should stay with one of her friends from the office who lived in town. Patricia mentioned that she intended visiting her sister, Anne, the following day in Baldoyle. This was a regular occurrence on a Saturday. Normally Patricia would spend the day with Anne and husband Peter and return home around 10 pm on Saturday.

After the lunchtime meeting, Brian returned to the couple's house at Watson Avenue, Killiney and at 3 pm he was collected by a friend. They drove to Delgany Golf Club but couldn't get a game and continued on to the club at Greystones where a competition was underway. The two men travelled on to a third club, Blainroe, where they got a game but gave up after just three holes because of delays on each tee box. They were refunded their money and had a drink in the clubhouse before heading on to a pub, The Graduate, in Killiney. They remained there until 8.45 pm when Brian got a lift home and got ready for work as a bouncer at a nightclub on Leeson Street. He arrived at Buck Whaley's Club at 10.45 pm and worked through until 6.15 the following morning. He then returned home.

At about 9 am another friend called to his house and they returned to Blainroe where they played golf until 4.15 pm. After the game he fell asleep for a few hours and got ready for work on Saturday night, the busiest night of the week on Leeson Street.

When Brian got home at 5 am on Sunday morning he was surprised and concerned to find that Patricia's car was not in the driveway. There was no point, however, in trying to ring any of her friends that early, so he slept for a few hours on the sofa and woke again at 10.15 am. Since his sister-in-law in Baldoyle had no phone, he first rang a neighbour and got to speak to Peter. Peter told him he had not seen Patricia all weekend.

Brian rang some of Patricia's work colleagues at home and got the same answer. They hadn't seen her since the party on Friday night. They said she had visited several pubs in Mount Street and Ranelagh with her friends and had a considerable amount to drink, up to ten bottles of Budweiser and some wine, over several hours. She was last seen by friends when they left the Pronto Grill Restaurant in Ranelagh around 1.30 am.

While Brian O'Toole was ringing around on Sunday morning, 1 September, a call to the Garda's 999 switchboard at Harcourt Square reported that a white car had been abandoned at Dolphin Road in Inchicore. A couple living on the street had noticed the car the previous morning and when it was still there 24 hours later they decided to call the police. The garda operator at the Dublin Area Communications Centre entered details of the call into the computer system and dispatched the message over the radio to two Sundrive Road officers.

Gardaí Annette Murtagh and Stephen O'Mahony, the crew of Golf Bravo One, the Sundrive patrol car, responded to the call and arrived at Dolphin Road around 11.15 am. They saw that the car in question was a white Peugeot 205, registration 88 D 13968. The two officers checked the vehicle and found that there was no damage or sign of a break-in. The car was not on the 'stolen or suspect list'. The Communications Centre revealed the car was registered to a Patricia Madden, Watson Avenue, Killiney.

Before they had a chance to carry out a more thorough examination of the vehicle, the patrol car crew got an urgent call to go to the Marist College on Sundrive Road where a woman's handbag had just been snatched.

Back in Killiney, Brian O'Toole was listening to the 11 am news when he heard about the murder in Rathfarnham. Despite his anxiety over Patricia, he was initially confident that the victim was not his wife because of the description given out. But his concern mounted when he heard mention of a Russian wedding ring at the end of the news item. He rang the Gardaí at Cabinteely. He told the officer on duty that he had not seen his wife since the previous Friday afternoon and he feared she may have had an accident. Garda James Dillea checked the details of her car on the station console and discovered that a patrol car crew from Sundrive Road station had run a check on the car just 30 minutes earlier.

The officer contacted Sundrive station and spoke to one of the gardaí there who told him the car had been abandoned down by the canal close to the Garda station. Garda Dillea then contacted Brian O'Toole and told him about the car and asked if he wished to officially report his wife missing. He said he did and the garda took a brief description of Patricia.

Suspecting that she may be the woman found murdered in the Dublin Mountains on Saturday, the young garda contacted the incident room which had been set up at Tallaght and asked for a fuller description of the woman's clothing and jewellery. The two rings found on the body sounded similar to the rings Brian O'Toole said his wife had been wearing.

The garda telephoned Brian O'Toole at his home and asked him to come to Cabinteely station. He should also bring some photographs of his wife with him.

In the meantime, Garda Dillea contacted the Tallaght incident room again and informed them of the facts and that Mr O'Toole was coming to the station to report his wife missing. Arrangements were made for one of the senior investigators on the murder inquiry, Detective Sergeant Kevin Tunney, to travel from Tallaght to Cabinteely, a route which passed close to the scene of the killing.

Back at Sundrive station, while dealing with the handbag snatch the crew of Golf Bravo One now heard over the radio that the owner of the Peugeot 205 car had been reported missing at Cabinteely station. They returned immediately to Dolphin Road.

The two officers carried out a visual inspection of the interior and discovered bloodstaining on the inside panel of the driver's door. More bloodstains were visible around the outside handle on the passenger door and on the rear of the car around the boot lock. An urgent radio message passed on by the Tallaght murder hunt team crackled over the radio for the Golf Bravo One crew to remain at Dolphin Road. They were to preserve the scene and not allow anyone near the car.

In the early afternoon of Sunday 1 September, Detective Sergeant Tunney met Brian O'Toole at Cabinteely station. After looking at the three photographs he brought of his wife, the detective knew almost immediately that they had identified the murder victim. He brought Mr O'Toole to Tallaght where he was shown two rings taken from the deceased. The first was Patricia's wedding ring and the second was the Russian wedding ring he had bought her on Grafton Street five years earlier.

The formal identification of her body was made by Patricia's brother-in-law, Peter, at the mortuary in Blanchardstown Hospital at 4.15 pm. Brian O'Toole also identified the body of his wife later in the evening. It was necessary for Patricia's dentist to assist in the identification from dental records because of the degree of violence used.

* * *

Patricia O'Toole was a striking looking woman. Her good looks and quick wit meant she was frequently the centre of attention on social occasions. She was very popular at work where colleagues described her as full of life and good fun. Born on 12 April, 1959, she was the youngest of two girls. The family lived on Brookstone Road, Baldoyle, Co. Dublin.

At school she was very bright and gained four honours in her Leaving Certificate in 1976. After secondary school she took up a secretarial course at Rosse College on Charlemont Street in Dublin and worked at a number of office jobs for the next five years. In the early 1980s she went to Greece to work for a year, and, soon after she returned, she took up a job at Consolidated Insurance Brokers where she worked in the pensions department.

A short time after she joined the firm in 1984, she met Brian O'Toole and two years later they bought the house in Killiney. He had been married before and separated in 1982, divorcing the following year. On 16 August, 1990, Brian and Patricia were married at Hennslaw Civic Centre in London.

Patricia was a popular, outgoing woman and had a wide circle of friends. She was also a keep fit enthusiast and completed a National Certificate in Aerobics Exercise and Fitness Instruction in March 1991 as well as competing in several women's mini marathons. Shortly before her killing, Patricia spoke to colleagues at work about moving to Spain with Brian. She hoped to put her fitness instructor's qualification to work there.

A few days after her murder, the formal results of her fitness diploma exam arrived in the post. She had done extremely well in all her subjects.

After work on Friday evening, 30 August, Patricia joined several friends for drinks at Scruffy Murphy's pub to mark the departure of a colleague for a new job. The group remained drinking together until about 9.50 pm. Patricia was in excellent spirits throughout the evening.

After leaving the pub, she joined friends at Abrakebabra fast food restaurant on Baggot Street where she had a vegetarian kebab. The group continued on to Russell's pub in Ranelagh. Later, because the place was packed, they moved on to O'Brien's public house. They remained there until about 12.30 am when Patricia and one of the couples decided to go to the Pronto Grill in Ranelagh village for a late-night snack. Patricia, who had been drinking bottles of lager during the night, had two glasses of white wine with her food.

Staff at the restaurant were anxious to clear up and at around 1.35 am the three patrons left, walking along Elmpark Avenue and Ranelagh Road. There Patricia said goodnight and headed towards her car, parked near Russell's pub. She mentioned something about going to Sach's Hotel in Donnybrook but never arrived there.

* * *

All of Saturday and Sunday morning had been taken up with trying to identify the body. Now, with a positive identification and the location of Patricia's car, close to the Suir Bridge on the Grand Canal in Drimnagh, the murder hunt team was beginning to make some headway. The fact that the Gardaí now knew where Patricia had been for most of Friday night, allowed them to interview her work colleagues. Moreover, the discovery of the car meant the focus of inquiries shifted to Drimnagh.

The direction of the investigation was being decided by Superintendent McCarrick. He had no prime suspect. He prepared the inquiry team for a long and difficult investigation.

The tall, grey-haired 53-year-old was a new type of detective. In the 1980s he helped form the Serious Crime Squad to tackle the growth in gang-related activity in the capital. Unlike his predecessors, the Sligoman set about actively recruiting informants in the underworld, something which was still viewed with suspicion and cynicism by a lot of his colleagues and peers. But the paid agents soon began providing the squad with tip-offs which helped foil armed robberies and major drug deals.

This network of informants also produced the information which led McCarrick and his men to the kidnappers of Jennifer Guinness on Waterloo Road, Dublin in 1986.

A few years later, McCarrick was promoted from the rank of Detective Inspector to Superintendent and moved to the Border.

In time, McCarrick came back to Dublin, not to Harcourt Square, the centre of organised crime investigations, but as the Detective Superintendent at Crumlin, in charge of detectives in the Southern Division. By this stage his famed underworld network of informants had all but vanished. Nevertheless, he took on the new job with gusto. The divisional Headquarters at Crumlin was at the centre of the home base of many of the city's most notorious villains, most of whom, at one stage or another, ran with the infamous Martin Cahill gang.

The murder of Patricia O'Toole was another brutal crime the Detective Superintendent was determined to solve.

*   *   *

On Monday, the Gardaí circulated photos of Patricia to the press with an appeal for anyone who saw her in the early hours of Saturday to contact them. Forensic examinations of her car and clothes began. There was no evidence of the car having been broken into and gardaí discarded this as a motive. Moreover, there was nothing taken from her handbag which was found in the Peugeot. The only missing items were her car keys.

Fingerprint analysis of the car provided one vital clue. On the steering wheel, experts at Garda Headquarters located a palm print implanted on blood. The fingerprint was not Patricia's. It could only have been the killer's.

The forensic expert who examined the car concluded in his report that, 'I am satisfied that Mrs O'Toole was assaulted in her car. However, I am satisfied the major assault took place where the body was found.'

On the centre of the passenger door six blood splashes he found were all formed in a downward direction. Smears and specks of blood and direction splashes were also found on the rear door of the hatchback. 'These extended from the extreme left rear corner across the rear of the car, the greater blooded area being the left corner.'

Directly below the outside driver's door handle a light smear of blood measuring about two inches long was found. A large area of blood was found on the front passenger seat belt and a clump of hair was taken from the central pillar.

On the floor in front of the passenger seat they found a navy blue lady's jacket, two pairs of shoes and a shoulder bag containing a purse with credit and bankers cards bearing the name Ms P Madden – the victim's maiden name – and a cheque bearing the same name.

By Tuesday, the incident room was getting a flood of callers claiming to have seen a white car on Friday evening or Saturday morning. Gardaí knew that most were sightings of other white cars which were of no consequence. They asked that anyone driving a white car in the Rathfarnham or Drimnagh areas during the relevant period should contact them so that some car sightings could be eliminated.

McCarrick arranged for Garda Noreen MacBrien to dress in clothes similar to those worn by the victim and, wearing an auburn wig which was somewhat shorter than the victim's hair, to parade for press photographers and the TV cameras in the hope that the image would jog someone's memory.

On Tuesday evening, Patricia's body was removed to St Peter and Paul's Church in Baldoyle. Patricia O'Toole's funeral Mass was held the following morning.

By now the appeal for information from people who may have seen a white car in the Drimnagh area had begun to pay dividends. A caller told the Gardaí he stopped his car around 1.45 am on 31 August outside Windsor Motors on the South Circular Road in the Dolphin's Barn area to let a friend out. A small white car driven by a blonde-haired woman who was alone, pulled alongside. She asked for directions to Inchicore. The two men told her to continue along the South Circular Road. They identified the woman as Patricia after being shown her photograph.

The next sighting was made shortly after 2 am on Goldenbridge Avenue, Inchicore, at its junction with Southern Cross Avenue and Stephen's Road. Stephen O'Byrne and Colm Nolan were waiting at the junction when a lone woman driver asked O'Byrne for directions to Connolly Avenue. But instead of following the route he gave her, she continued to drive up Southern Cross Avenue towards the Grand Canal.

Two barmen, Conor O'Leary and Joe Fitzgerald, were cycling home along Suir Road towards Kilmainham around 2.30 am when a small white car came out of Goldenbridge Avenue onto Suir Road and pulled up alongside them. The car was driven by a woman and she was alone. She asked the barmen for directions to Connolly Avenue. They noticed that she was upset. Conor O'Leary directed her back up Goldenbridge Avenue and told her it was at the top of the road. They thought she was very drunk and unfit to drive. Both identified the deceased as the driver from photographs produced to them.

Having given the directions, the barmen saw a man drive a red-coloured Fiat 127 along Suir Road and then stop alongside the small white car. They observed the two drivers speak to one another before cycling off.

John Coloe was the driver of the 127 and told detectives he stopped to complain to the driver of the white car which, he says, was parked dangerously. She appeared drunk and upset and again asked him for directions to Connolly Avenue. He indicated that it was back up Goldenbridge Avenue and he was going in that direction. Coloe drove up the avenue to its end and turned right onto Connolly Avenue. He noticed at this stage that the woman driving the small white car had not followed him. He drove back around onto Suir Road where he had originally met the car but could not find the Peugeot. He did a U-turn and continued on his way home. Coloe identified the woman driver as the deceased from photographs produced to him.

The next and final sighting was made between 3.45 and 4 am on Suir Road but it would be another few days before the investigation team would discover who made it.

Rosaleen Holland says she was walking along Suir Road with her boyfriend, soldier Sean Courtney, when a small white car stopped near them at Hyland's shop. The driver asked for directions 'to some address' which Rosaleen Holland did not properly hear. She says her boyfriend gave directions to the woman but the driver could not understand the instructions. The driver asked the couple to get into the car. Courtney sat in the front seat and his girlfriend sat in the back.

They travelled to the couple's flat on the South Circular Road, near the Wessel Industries factory. While Courtney remained in the car his girlfriend got out. He told her he would return when he had brought the woman to the address. Holland says she went into the flat and looked at her watch which read 4.10 am. She did not go to bed until 4.40 am as she was expecting Courtney to return. He had no keys to the flat. When she awoke the following morning Courtney was waiting on the steps outside.

* * *

Sean Courtney appeared the model soldier. Ever since he was a child, he wanted to join the Army. He hero-worshipped an uncle who served in the Defence Forces and as soon as he finished his Intermediate Certificate at the Crumlin Vocational School, Clogher Road, Courtney tried to enlist. But at 16 he was too young and was rejected. In the interim he used a talent for drawing to get a job as a signwriter in Walkinstown.

Sean's father was a bus driver with CIE and his mother worked part-time as a cleaner. Both were hard working and gave him a secure upbringing. He only got into trouble with the law once when arrested for burglary at the age of 14. The case was dealt with under the Garda's Juvenile Liaison Scheme which meant the teenager got off with a warning and did not incur a criminal conviction.

In 1983 he started going out with a girl named Amanda, who was to later become his wife. The couple were seeing each other for about a year and a half and had their first child the following October. After the birth, the couple moved in with Courtney's parents in Drimnagh. They married in April 1985 and got a house on Drumcairn Drive, Tallaght.

On 12 November, Courtney finally got the chance he had been waiting for and joined the Army at Cathal Brugha Barracks in Rathmines. When he finished recruit training in July 1986 as a three-star private, he joined the Transport Platoon of the 2nd Infantry Battalion where he learned to drive Land Rovers and Armoured Personnel Carriers. His NCOs described him as a good soldier, always on time and turned out neatly and tidily. He even helped one Sergeant out with the scouts and got on well with the youngsters aged eight to twelve.

He remained posted to Cathal Brugha Barracks until April 1987 when he first volunteered to go overseas on UN peacekeeping duties to Lebanon with the 61st Infantry Battalion. It was an uneventful trip and when he came home he and his wife, Amanda, used the few thousand pounds he saved from the Lebanon allowance to renovate their new home in Leighlin Road, Crumlin.

It was a six-month tour of duty for which he would sign up two more times. But he would not complete his third visit to south Lebanon.

The second visit with the 63rd Battalion began in April 1988. That June, Courtney was involved in an incident at a checkpoint when he was forced to open fire at a local Christian militiaman when some of his colleagues were threatened. The private told his superiors the shooting occurred after the gunman had pointed a rifle at his head. As a result of the incident he had been receiving threats from the local Israeli-backed South Lebanon Army fighters. The Irish Army authorities decided to transfer him to another post within the 'A' Company area of operations for his own safety (the Dublin-based section of the battalion).

Towards the end of the mission in August, a colleague of Courtney's, Private Paddy Wright from Ardee, Co. Louth, shot himself. Courtney would later maintain that the discovery of his friend's body had a terrible effect on him, which led to the onset of Post-Traumatic Stress Disorder.

In the meantime, Amanda had given birth to their second child in July. The marriage was not going well. On his return home, Amanda complained that she was never given enough money to run the house. He appeared to be able to buy whatever he wanted for himself but there was never enough money for his wife or the children. Courtney's parents had to intervene to buy clothes and shoes for their grandchildren.

In a bid to repair the marriage and give the couple some time apart he re-volunteered for UN duty and returned to Lebanon a third time with the 67th Infantry Battalion in April 1990. Just two days into the mission, he was admitted to the medical centre at the Irish Army's headquarters in south Lebanon at Camp Shamrock, Tibnin. He was complaining of feeling ill. Seven days later he was repatriated on medical grounds and returned home where he was admitted to St Bricin's military hospital for assessment. He was seen by a psychiatrist and released after a few days.

He returned to Amanda but the couple's marriage was by now in deep trouble. Amanda moved out within a few months and went to live with his parents. In a last ditch effort at reconciliation she returned to him the following January, but the marriage was doomed.

One night he went to a disco in Tallaght and met Rosaleen Holland. Courtney told his wife about the encounter. Two days later he had packed his bags and moved out.

*　*　*

Detectives believe the reason Patricia O'Toole was looking for Connolly Avenue in the early hours was that an old boyfriend of hers lived on the street.

Christy Hoctor had first met her in 1978 and the relationship had been on and off for a number of years. The last time Hoctor had seen her was in September 1990 when she'd dropped up to his house unexpectedly and they had a long conversation, discussing how their lives had turned out.

On the night of 30 August and early hours of 31 August 1991 he was in his house alone. There had been no arrangement to meet Patricia and he told gardaí he was a light sleeper and if she had called to the house he would have heard her. Why she decided to call on him that night, nobody knows, but it is possible that it may have had something to do with the amount of drink she had consumed during the evening.

It was Sean Courtney's weekend off and he had gone with his girlfriend Rosaleen Holland to the West County Hotel in Chapelizod to meet a group of friends. The soldier played with a soccer team from Rosaleen's workplace called the National Medical Care Rangers football team. A disco was being held in the hotel in aid of the club which played its games in Phoenix Park.

The couple were the first to arrive and they ordered a drink. She had a 7-Up and Courtney ordered a pint of Carlsberg. They were joined at the function by Stephen Stack from Walkinstown, Una Madden, Inchicore and Vincent and Yvonne McArdle from Ballyfermot. There is some confusion about the amount of drink the soldier consumed during the night. Courtney claims he had between 12 and 13 pints while Rosaleen told gardaí that, 'he drank about six pints. He gets drunk easily because he doesn't drink very often.'

She went on to say: 'He was in great form and was up dancing with all the gang. He is shy and he doesn't normally dance.'

The party lasted until about 2.30 am when Stephen Stack, Una Madden, Sean Courtney and Rosaleen Holland got a taxi to Una Madden's brother's house on Devoy Road. Her brother was on holidays and she was looking after the house for him. They arrived there around 3 am and sat around watching a video.

Una Madden remembers: 'The four of us went into the house and into the sitting room. I then went into the kitchen to make tea. Sean wanted coffee. When I came back to the sitting room, I saw that Sean was fast asleep on the chair. I didn't wake him up. We had a video on but we weren't really watching it. We were all tired and Rosaleen wanted to go home.' She says that Courtney had been drinking lager 'but he did not appear drunk'.

Around 3.30 am, Stephen Stack woke the sleeping serviceman and walked with the couple some of the way towards their flat as they weren't very familiar with the area. He brought them out onto Suir Road where he left them at the bus stop just beside Hyland's shop and returned back to Devoy Road.

Not long afterwards a white Peugeot 205 car pulled up alongside the couple. The passenger window was wound down and Patricia O'Toole reached across from the driver's seat. She told them she was lost and was looking for Connolly Avenue. Courtney replied that he had a fair idea where it was and offered: 'I'll show you if you want.'

'Okay, get in,' the driver replied.

Courtney asked that his girlfriend be dropped off first and they continued to the South Circular Road where Rosaleen Holland got out. Courtney directed Patricia O'Toole along Suir Road and they turned right at the end of it for Connolly Avenue. Courtney claimed that she stopped the car at a junction of five roads and a conversation developed. Patricia asked the soldier about himself and what he worked at. He told her he was separated. 'I was drunk and was telling her all about myself,' he said.

Then it is alleged that she told him: 'You never know who you pick up in a car at this time of night … I could get you done for attacking me if I went to the police. It would only be your word against mine.'

Courtney claims Patricia was laughing at him 'and seemed to think it was a big joke. I didn't know what to think. I just blew a fuse and went mad.'

He punched Patricia, who was still drunk, several times in the face, knocking her out cold. She slumped over on top of him. Courtney then got out of the car and pulled Patricia across into the passenger seat. He then walked around to the driver's side and switched on the ignition.

'I didn't know what to do. I drove off in the car with this lady in the passenger seat,' he later told gardaí.

He nevertheless appeared to have some plan in his mind and took off in the direction of the Dublin Mountains. He drove along the South Circular Road and across Herberton Bridge towards the southern suburbs. In the early hours the roads were virtually empty and he made steady progress.

On the deserted and pitch-dark Mount Venus Road, Patricia started coming to and, realising her predicament, began screaming. Courtney pulled the vehicle over into the entrance of Frank Kelly GAA pitch and grabbed her by the throat. The passenger door flew open as she tried to get away from him and Patricia fell out. Unfortunately both her legs got stuck in the floorwell and Courtney jumped across onto her. During the struggle both of them fell out onto the ground.

'She was screaming and trying to get away. She was lying on the ground and was kicking and struggling. I just went mad,' Courtney said.

He grabbed the brick from the building works and started hitting his victim across the head and face with his two hands. In the rain of blows, Patricia's screams petered out. In a weak voice she appealed to him: 'Don't ruin your life.'

It was probably her last breath.

'She was barely breathing and then her breathing stopped. I got the key out of the ignition and opened the boot with it. I was going to put her in the boot and leave the car somewhere. All types of thoughts were going through my head. I then took all her clothes off and threw them in the field so as to make it look as if she was sexually attacked. Her shoes were on the road and I threw them in the passenger door window which was open,' the killer admitted later.

With the naked body lying on the ground, Courtney hopped back into the driver's seat and put the Peugeot into reverse, driving over his victim.

'I felt a bump from the rear wheel of the car. I think the rear wheel hit the body but I did not stop to find out,' he said.

The killer headed back into the city, eventually abandoning the little Peugeot on Dolphin Road at around 5.45 am. As he crossed the road, a Garda patrol car raced by but took little notice of the slight figure in the shadows, whose clothes were bloodied. Courtney skulked along the canal towards Suir Bridge where he threw the car keys into the water. He stepped over the wall and walked down the banks to wash the blood off his hands. After cleaning himself he continued on to Rosaleen Holland's flat.

When she awoke later in the morning he was waiting outside on the steps. Rosaleen asked where he had been. He told her he had slept on the steps. He got undressed, managing carefully to put his bloodstained trousers and shirt under the bed and got in beside her. The killer slept until about 3 pm when he put his clothes into the washing machine – something he would normally leave for his girlfriend to do. Significantly, he overlooked the paisley tie which he had been wearing and which was covered in blood spatters.

He watched a game between Everton and Liverpool on the television and went out for a curry later. On the way home he bought an *Evening Herald* and read about the murder in the mountains.

The couple remained in for the evening. Rosaleen remembers emptying the washing machine and getting extremely annoyed. When she took the clothes out 'I saw that the dye had run from his navy trousers and that everything was blue. There was a pink shirt belonging to me which was now navy. My underwear was ruined.'

The killing seemed to have had no adverse affect on Courtney. The following day, Sunday, he played with the National Medical Care football team in a game against a Cardiff club. Other players remember him carrying on as normal and attending training the following Thursday. He was scheduled to play with the team again on Sunday, 8 September.

* * *

The progress of the murder inquiry meanwhile was followed intensively by the media. The investigation team was making regular appeals for information and McCarrick had shifted the focus to the Drimnagh and Inchicore areas where the car was found. He was convinced the killer must have returned here because he knew the area. McCarrick ordered door-to-door inquiries and also had checkpoints set up to question drivers about anything suspicious.

Everybody had their own theory on the savage killing. The gossips had a field day. Prurient curiosity grew and there were reports that Patricia and her husband Brian were in financial difficulty. These baseless rumours did nothing to ease the pressure on the families directly involved.

Later Brian recalled how, only a week before the murder, the couple had sat down and discussed an offer to move to Los Angeles where she could have pursued her interest in aerobics. 'I said I wouldn't fancy going to LA because it had so much violence,' he said ironically.

The case was front-page news and any new angle was pursued by the papers. Patricia's final hours were examined in minute detail on radio and television. Days after the body of his wife was found, Brian told reporters: 'Whoever killed Patricia, if they are caught and convicted, will, some day, under any legal system walk out – be it 10, 20 or 30 years. Patricia will never walk back – her sentence is permanent.'

The distraught husband, trying to come to terms with the death of his wife added: 'Patricia was in the wrong place at the wrong time.

Five minutes later and she would be alive today. The hardest thing for me is to wake up in the morning and face another day and she isn't here.'

But the wide coverage in the papers was in its own way of enormous help to the investigators.

On 8 September, the *Sunday World* ran a front-page piece about the murder with a full-colour picture of Patricia. The paper, following the Garda concentration of efforts on the Drimnagh area, prophetically asked if Patricia's killer was somebody the victim had asked for directions.

The pressure was, by now, piling on Courtney. He began to feel the Garda net closing in on him.

On Saturday, 7 September, he called on his ex-wife, Amanda, and took their two children out for a few hours, returning around 6 pm. At first they discussed the future of their children and to which school they should send them. But Courtney began to extend the conversation.

Amanda recalled. 'Sean knew that I had gone to see the film called *Silence of the Lambs* a few days before that. He asked me what it was about and I told him it was about a fellow who went about killing people and then used their skins to make clothes for himself. He asked me why I was so interested in murders and I said that I just found them interesting. He asked me what I found interesting about them and I said that the Moors murders happened 24 years ago and people still found them interesting.

'He knew that I had written to Myra Hindley and Ian Brady a few years ago. I just wanted to get a letter back from them to put in my scrap book but they never answered my letters. He asked me would I ever write to anybody else in prison if they had committed murder. I said no. He then asked me what did I think of the girl being found murdered up the mountains, referring to Patricia O'Toole. I said it was terrible.'

By Monday, 9 September, the pressure was increasing even more. Courtney rang Rosaleen Holland at work and said he had something to tell her which would make her leave him. Rosaleen didn't know what he was talking about but she mentioned this to some of her work colleagues. She remarked that Sean hadn't been himself lately and appeared depressed.

At 3 pm, Courtney drove into the industrial estate where Rosaleen worked and collected her and a colleague, Elizabeth Abbey. During the journey the radio news came on and broadcast a report about the murder. Ms Abbey noticed how Courtney turned off the radio and seemed to drive a bit faster. It also appeared to her that he had been crying.

Back at the flat he shared with Rosaleen, the soldier was acting very peculiarly. He asked her to 'go out and get the newspaper from under the driver's seat of the car and don't read the front of it until you come back in.' She returned with the *Sunday World*.

At this stage he was crying and blurted: 'I killed her. I really made a fuck of it this time.'

He was shaking and told her he didn't mean to do it. She asked if he had raped the woman and he said: 'Look in the paper, I didn't rape her.'

Peculiarly, Courtney was anxious to return to work at Cathal Brugha Barracks where he was on duty and pleaded with Rosaleen not to tell anyone. He would return that evening and they would talk about it.

'He told me not to worry, that he would do all the worrying. He gave me a hug and went off to work.'

Rosaleen read the Sunday paper and went out and bought an *Evening Press* and read more about the brutal killing. She sat on her own crying until Courtney returned again around 7 pm.

'Don't be shaking, you'll be alright,' he told her.

'We'll have to tell somebody. We'll have to tell your ma.'

'No, it will only break her heart,' he replied.

Soon afterwards Courtney returned again to his base in an Army Land Rover and asked Rosaleen to ring him at the barracks. Instead she rang her work colleague, Elizabeth Abbey, and asked her to call down. But before she could say what was wrong, the friend replied she already had a good idea of what was wrong. Courtney's mannerisms in the car earlier had aroused the woman's suspicions.

A group of friends arrived at the flat around 9.30 pm and took Rosaleen to one of their houses in Ballyfermot. Rosaleen filled them in on what her boyfriend had told her over the previous six hours. The group decided they would have to tell the police. One of the group remembered seeing gardaí on duty in the area earlier in the evening and thought it was in connection with the murder.

Detective Garda John Maunsell and Garda Thomas Flynn from the investigation team at Tallaght were carrying out door-to-door inquiries on Goldenbridge Avenue, Inchicore, around 9.45 pm when they were approached by two men. The men said they had vital information about the murder in the Dublin Mountains. It was the vital breakthrough the Gardaí had been looking for over the previous ten days.

Detective Maunsell immediately contacted the incident room at Tallaght to tell them of the developments. Along with the two men and more officers who had arrived on the scene as a result of his call to base, he visited the house on Kylemore Road where Rosaleen was staying.

Back in the incident room, Detective Superintendent McCarrick, Superintendent Pat King and Detective Inspector Tony Sourke were now preparing to go to Cathal Brugha Barracks.

At 12.30 am, Maunsell travelled with Rosaleen to the flat on the South Circular Road where she pointed out the clothes that Courtney was wearing on the night Patricia O'Toole was murdered. The clothing, including his paisley tie, were handed over to a forensics expert from Garda Headquarters.

Within ten minutes, McCarrick and the two other officers arrived at the Army barracks, situated just off the main Rathmines Road at the end of a tree-lined avenue. They met the officer on duty, Lieutenant Paul Murphy of the 2nd Cavalry Squadron, and asked if

Courtney was on duty. Lieutenant Murphy checked the records and told the gardaí he was in the barracks. At 12.55 am the officer brought them to the Transport Section of the 2nd Infantry Battalion where Courtney, dressed only in his underwear, answered the door.

The gardaí allowed him dress. Detective Superintendent Gerry McCarrick put his hand on the killer's shoulder and said he was arresting him on suspicion of murdering Mrs Patricia O'Toole on 31 August, 1991, at Mount Venus Road, Rathfarnham. He cautioned him: 'You are not obliged to say anything unless you wish to do so but anything you do say will be taken down in writing and may be given in evidence.'

The suspect had no reply to make. Instead he turned to Lieutenant Murphy and asked what he should do. The young officer told him he would have to go with the police. The gardaí and their prisoner arrived at Tallaght station around 1.20 am. Courtney waived his right to rest and began making a full statement.

His confession began with his telling of how he joined the Army and went on to describe his experiences in Lebanon. Then he described the night of the killing and how he and Rosaleen had been given a lift by Patricia O'Toole. He claimed he went crazy when he thought she was laughing at him. He knocked her unconscious with a punch and drove to the Dublin mountains.

'I just went mad. I grabbed some type of a rock and started hitting her on the head and face with it. I hit her several times, sometimes holding the rock with my two hands. She was screaming at first as I hit her. She went silent.' Courtney went on to tell the police how he drove her car back to Dublin.

The following day, he agreed to show the Gardaí along the routes he had taken before and after the murder and where he dumped the car keys and other items.

* * *

On 22 January, 1993, Sean Courtney was sentenced to life imprisonment for the murder of Patricia O'Toole. Mr Justice Kevin

Lynch had to order part of the gallery of the court cleared when screams and cheers greeted the jury's 10–2 verdict. The decision took five hours and 46 minutes to reach.

Courtney sat white faced and rigid as the jury announced its guilty verdict. No emotion showed on his face when the judge said the decision carried an automatic life sentence. The minute the judge left the court, however, the killer snapped and shouted: 'She was only a f...... tramp.'

It was in total contrast to the reaction of Patricia's 68-year-old father, Patrick Madden who, in a newspaper interview the following day, said: 'I feel sorry for his mother and father and also for his poor children and his wife and girlfriend.' He cried softly as he spoke of the memento of his daughter he would always cherish – the clock he lovingly crafted for her wedding. He told how he returned home after the early morning court verdict and could not sleep as he wrestled with his memories and sat alone in the dark of the family sitting-room.

* * *

In July 1994 the Court of Criminal Appeal rejected all grounds of appeal by Sean Courtney against his conviction.

HOUSE OF HORRORS

'It's just a misfortune and pure bad luck. But I had nothing to do with it.'
— Michael Bambrick, 1991.

THE home of British serial killer Frederick West at 25 Cromwell Street in Gloucester, where he murdered 12 young women and buried the bodies, became known as the House of Horrors. West and his wife, Rosemary, subjected their victims to unspeakable torture and rape before killing them and burying the dissected remains in the house and garden.

No. 57 St Ronan's Park, in the Dublin suburb of Ronanstown, was to bear witness to similar horrors. The nondescript local authority house, situated just 400 yards from the local Garda station, was the scene of the killing of two women within the space of less than one year.

The victims, Patricia McGauley and Mary Cummins were totally defenceless when Michael Bambrick, a man they both trusted, choked them to death. Both victims had their hands tied behind their backs in sex bondage and were unable to fend him off. After the killings, Bambrick hacked their bodies into pieces.

On 26 July, 1996, Bambrick stood motionless as he was sentenced to 18 years imprisonment for the manslaughter of his two victims. Mr Justice Paul Carney described the case as one of the worst to have come before the Central Criminal Court. 'The five years which I have spent in this court have demonstrated to me that each case gets worse,' he said.

The judge believed that even after 18 years, Bambrick would still pose a threat to the public and he was sorry that legal constraints prevented him sentencing the killer to life imprisonment. 'The problem from the community's point of view is that Bambrick will be subject to no controls on release with remission ... The probability is that he will have a pent-up appetite for this form of bondage fuelled by group fantasising with other sex offenders in Arbour Hill prison.'

But while the Garda file into the deaths of the two women is now closed, the file on Bambrick remains open.

* * *

In the early hours of 12 September, 1991, neighbours on St Ronan's Park were awoken by a violent row in No. 57. They could hear screaming and shouting emanating from the house. It continued for two hours.

One resident, Mary O'Neill, remembered 'all hell breaking loose' next door. 'I heard her [Patricia] screaming and roaring curses at an awful rate.' The row continued until about 4 am when neighbours heard the couple's two children, Adrienne and Louise 'screaming and roaring crying'.

In any other case, the other residents would probably have telephoned the police but in St Ronan's Park it was well known that Michael Bambrick and Patricia McGauley were always fighting, usually after a few drinks. One minute they would be at each other's throats and the next they would be off down to the pub together. What neighbours could hardly have known was that this time it was a lot more serious.

The couple met nine years earlier. They both had failed marriages. Patricia, one of a family of four, was born in Dublin on 19 December, 1948. She went to school at George's Hill Convent in the north city centre and in 1962 went to work at Burtons Associated Tailors on New Street where she remained for five years. Between 1969 and 1978 she worked at a variety of jobs, including Creens Soap Factory on North King Street and in a clothing factory on Bridgefoot Street.

While employed at the soap factory she met and married John McGauley. The ceremony took place in the Registry Office on Kildare Street in 1976 and the newlyweds took up residence at a flat in Wellington Street. From the outset, however, relations between them were not good. Both were heavy drinkers and there were frequent rows.

After just a few months they split up and found separate flats. There was a further attempt at reconciliation but the rows continued and the marriage was finally doomed when Patricia moved in with her mother. They never kept in touch after that.

On 14 February, 1981, when Patricia was drinking with friends at the Legal Eagle pub, opposite the Four Courts, she and John McGauley had a chance encounter. Both had been drinking heavily and an altercation developed. Patricia fled the premises to get away from him. Not far away, as she walked along the street, she was grabbed by two men who dragged her into a laneway and raped her.

Gardaí later arrested and charged two men in connection with the attack. The prosecution was forced to drop the charges, however, when Patricia failed to turn up in court to give evidence and both accused were set free.

A year later she met Michael Bambrick. Like Patricia, he had been married and separated. He had returned to live with his parents in Ballyfermot.

When his parents died, he got a flat in St Teresa's Gardens, one of the many flat complexes built by the Corporation between the city's canals in the 1960s. St Teresa's Gardens lies just off the South Circular Road on Donore Avenue and had seen its share of hardship down the years, particularly the scourge of drug abuse.

Within a few months of beginning to see each other, Patricia moved in with Bambrick. On 21 August, 1984, Patricia gave birth to her first child, Adrienne. The birth of the baby girl made them eligible for a new house and two years later they moved into No. 57 St Ronan's Park in the expanding local authority suburb of Ronanstown. In 1990, a second child, Louise, arrived. Those who knew her said the arrival of the children helped Patricia cut down on her drinking and she took more responsibility for her life. All said she was a loving and caring mother.

Most people who were acquainted with Michael Ba... hesitation in describing him as strange. From his youth he... those individuals who never completed what they set out to d... career in the Defence Forces was a perfect example.

In June 1974, at the age of 22, he enlisted in the Army and after basic training was assigned to the 2nd Infantry Battalion at Cathal Brugha Barracks in Rathmines. But after less than two months in the Defence Forces the young Private Bambrick went absent without leave (AWOL), fleeing back to his parents' home. A year later, on 20 March, 1975, the young deserter had a change of heart and surrendered himself to Military Police. He was returned to his unit. This renewed enthusiasm for military life was short-lived, however, and he absconded over the barracks wall the same night. Bambrick, to this day, remains a deserter from the Army.

He was born in England in 1952 the youngest of three boys to William and Edith Bambrick. His father was a native of Kilkenny and had been married before in a union which produced three daughters. William Bambrick's first wife died when the girls were small. After her funeral, he put them into the care of the religious and emigrated to Britain. There he met a young Londoner, who was to become the second Mrs Bambrick. They had three sons, Mervin, Kevin and Michael.

In 1957, William Bambrick returned to Ireland and found a home at Keogh Square in Dublin where the family remained until 1968 when they moved to Rossmore Avenue in Ballyfermot. Soon afterwards, the eldest son, Mervin, returned to Britain while Kevin and Michael continued to reside with their parents.

The difference between the two boys could not be more marked. Kevin was always the more ambitious of the two, coming across as more energetic and enthusiastic about life. On the other hand, Michael was unruly and disruptive, causing no end of problems for his parents. On one occasion, in a fit of anger he savagely attacked his own mother, leaving her seriously bruised.

r led to serious rows in the household and
ie a number of times, smashing furniture

e complicated by the fact that he was lazy.
most of the day or sat in and watched
it night, he might venture out to go as far as
eaving school, unlike his brother, he never

At the age of 20, Michael met a young woman called Marie Hayes. They started going out with each other in July 1972. The relationship blossomed fairly quickly and that December they got married. The ceremony took place in the grand surroundings of the Pro Cathedral on Marlborough Street, situated almost directly opposite the headquarters of the Department of Education and not far from O'Connell Street in Dublin.

The young couple moved into a flat on Rathmines Road. Although predominantly a middle-class area, Rathmines in the early 1970s also played host to hundreds of students and hippies and to the less well-off who were attracted by the area's large reservoir of budget accommodation and bedsits. This social mix made the urban village a happening place in the still largely Church-dominated State. Rathmines was one of the places where drug use first raised its head in Ireland around that period. But even the most liberal of Rathmines' residents at the time would have been shocked by the tendencies being exhibited by Michael Bambrick.

Soon after the couple moved into their new home, Marie discovered she was pregnant. Sick of living on the poverty line and depending on social welfare allowances, the newly-married couple decided that Michael would have to find a job. It was at this stage that he decided to embark on what was to become his short-lived military career.

On 30 August, 1973, Marie gave birth to their first child, a son they named Alan. Just before she went into labour, Marie tried to convince her husband to get a job so her child could have a father he could look up to and who would bring home a weekly wage. But her appeals fell on deaf ears. Apart from a few brief periods working as a caretaker in a convent, Bambrick would never again hold down a steady job.

In or around April 1974, Marie Hayes returned to the flat and was horrified to find her husband wearing women's clothes. The young mother discovered him peering into a mirror wearing a dress, high heels and applying lipstick.

It came as a total shock to her. Cross-dressing was not a subject which was discussed much in the Ireland of the early 1970s and certainly not something for which you could turn to many people for advice or help. Marie told him he would have to seek professional advice for his transvestism. He agreed to see a psychiatrist at the Mater Hospital.

Bambrick kept his weekly appointments with the psychiatrist for only three visits. Soon after he stopped going to counselling, he woke his wife in the middle of the night. He was standing over the bed. He was dressed in a blouse and skirt and held a pair of tights in his hands. Bambrick wrapped the tights around her neck and stuffed the ends of them down her throat. The woman was unable to get away from him as he was kneeling over her and had her pinned down. He pulled hard on the ends of the tights, causing his wife to black out.

When she recovered, Bambrick demanded sex with her, despite the fact that she was bleeding from the mouth. She asked her husband for a drink of water and was dragged down to the kitchen where he filled a cup of water and forced her to drink it.

The incident was enough to convince her that she would have to leave. Shortly afterwards she moved out with her son and never again contacted Michael.

At the time, she did not report the vicious attack to the Gardaí. However, officers would have reason to track her down more than a decade later as they checked into his background while investigating two more violent crimes against women. His ex-wife would tell the detectives she felt he wanted to kill her that night. She thought she was going to die.

Soon after the split Bambrick's luck ran out. He decided to call unannounced on a friend of the couple who lived in a north city flats complex. The woman was surprised by his appearance at her front door at 9.30 am. She told him she was going out but would make him a cup of tea.

After he finished the tea, Bambrick was showing no sign of leaving and the woman repeated that she had to go to the Rent Office with her baby son. As she got up to go he grabbed her by the shoulder. She told him to stop but he started to kiss her. He warned that if she screamed he would kill her and the baby. He placed his hand over her mouth and dragged her into the bedroom where he stripped off her clothes and indecently assaulted her.

Before leaving the flat he threatened that he would kill both mother and child if the matter was reported to the Gardaí.

However, the police were informed and he was arrested and charged. At Dublin District Court No. 4, on 30 July, 1975, Bambrick was convicted of the charge of indecent assault on a female. He was given a suspended six-month sentence and bound to the peace for 12 months. This was his second criminal conviction – he had been found guilty of burglary and bound to the peace for 12 months in 1972. With one marriage already behind him he now moved back in with his parents in Ballyfermot.

For the most part he managed to keep out of trouble over the next few years. He certainly did not appear in court again for another 12 years. While at his parents' home, Bambrick's lifestyle centred around the television and drinking in local pubs.

In 1978 his father died. That same year, when his brother Kevin got married and moved out, he was left alone in the house with his mother. Edith Bambrick died in 1980 and Michael was transferred by the Corporation to a flat in St Teresa's Gardens. Soon after this he met Patricia McGauley and they began living together, first in his flat and later in St Ronan's Park. What was to follow was one of the most bizarre and violent episodes in the annals of Irish crime.

* * *

On the evening of 11 September, 1991, Michael Bambrick and Patricia McGauley decided to go drinking at a local public house, The Advocate. They left their two young children, Adrienne and Louise, off at the home of Patricia's mother, Mrs Julia O'Connor. They remained drinking until about midnight. Michael Bambrick consumed six pints of Guinness and Patricia had four pints of Tennents lager. At 12.30 am they collected the girls at their grandmother's and returned home in a taxi to 57 St Ronan's Park.

It would appear the couple had been fighting in the pub over Michael's drinking. Patricia had wanted to collect the children earlier but he insisted on having a few more pints. The arguing had subsided when they got to her mother's home but flared up again back in their own house.

She told him she had run out of cigarettes and asked him to go and get some. He replied that they had passed a garage on the way and why didn't she ask for them then. The row was so heated that neighbours could hear the strident exchanges. Finally, he found one cigarette in the living room and gave it to her. The argument subsided and both went to bed.

The sequence of events after this time is uncertain and the police had to rely on Bambrick's version of what occurred. A lot of what happened was corroborated in statements made by neighbours.

According to Bambrick, the couple had sex and he tied her hands behind her back with a pair of tights. He then put the tights in her mouth and tied them around the back of her head. He stated that she allowed him to do this sometimes but that she didn't like it all the time.

In the middle of the bondage session he heard her gasping for air. But his first reaction was not to pull the tights out of her mouth. Instead Bambrick claims he panicked. He says he didn't know what to do. The most obvious act would have been to release the tights and untie Patricia but this did not occur to him. According to Bambrick, Patricia died almost instantaneously after a few desperate gasps for air.

Leaving the tights around her, he ran downstairs and got a scissors. Then he came back and cut the tights. Despite the fact that she had stopped breathing, it never occurred to him to summon help or call for an ambulance or doctor.

Indeed, Bambrick's protestations that he panicked hardly seem likely since he said he regularly engaged in this type of sex. Moreover, his denial runs contrary to the evidence of the previous attack on his wife, Marie, two decades earlier.

He took the body from the bed and dragged it feet first into the small front bedroom or boxroom. The killer walked back into the hallway and locked the door behind him. He now had to come up with a way of disposing of Patricia's body.

The following morning, apparently unperplexed by the death of his partner, Bambrick tried to act normally. He took the two children to their school at Warrenmount as usual and he carried out his normal day's work there, as a caretaker on a FÁS course. After work he collected Patricia's social welfare money from her mother and went home with the children.

By the next day, Friday, Bambrick had decided to get rid of Patricia's body by chopping it into pieces. He used a paper knife to cut the skin and took a hacksaw to sever the bones. Both breasts were also removed using the knife, another act which would appear to belie his later protestations that rather than carrying out an act of perversion he acted in panic.

The butchery all took place in the boxroom where he placed the head, arms and legs into a refuse sack and the remainder of the body into another plastic bag wrapped in a towel and some plastic the body had been lying on. That night he took the bag containing her head, arms and legs into the back garden and dragged it along the ground to the rear wall. Using all his strength he threw the refuse sack over the wall onto the footpath on the other side, not far from a bus shelter.

He had already parked his bicycle at the spot and jumped over the wall himself. He transported the body bag on the bike to Balgaddy dump, approximately one mile away. At the rubbish tip, he removed the body parts from the bags and covered them with clay.

The next day he returned on his bike to the Corporation dumping ground with the bag containing the torso and placed it deep in a rubbish pile. Gathering other refuse bags from nearby, he used them to hide the butchered limbs.

By now, he was worried somebody would notice Patricia's absence. On Sunday, in an effort to cover his tracks, Bambrick went into the city where he reported Patricia missing to Gardaí at the Bridewell station. He told the officer on duty that he had not seen his partner since the previous Thursday, the day after the killing, when he claimed she had left their home on foot to go into town at about 8.30 pm.

*   *   *

The police carried out a routine Missing Persons investigation which failed to throw any light on the horrific end she had met. Later in the month, the Gardaí carried out more inquiries when Patricia's mother, now very worried about what may have become of her daughter, asked them to circulate details of her description. Two sergeants were appointed to investigate the matter, one in the Bridewell area of the north city centre near where Mrs Julia O'Connor lived, and another in the Ronanstown area.

For the most part the inquiry consisted of interviewing Patricia's ex-husband, John, one of her neighbours in Ronanstown and Michael Bambrick. John McGauley, who was now living in Charlemont Street near the South Circular Road, was unable to help the police. He had not seen his estranged wife for more than six months.

A sergeant from Ronanstown then visited 57 St Ronan's Park, just around the corner from the station, and spoke to Bambrick. In a statement to Sergeant John Gillan made on 13 October, more than a month after the homicide, Bambrick claimed that he and Patricia had gone for a drink on the night of 11 September and returned home around 1.30 am. They had a bit of an argument over cigarettes but after he had found her one, she smoked it and fell asleep. The next day he got up, did the shopping and went down to her mother's to collect Patricia's Deserted Wife's Allowance. Although he had the children with him, he went to The Advocate pub, had a few pints and returned home.

Patricia, he claimed, was at home when he arrived back. At about 8 pm she went upstairs and got ready to go out for the night. She came down at about 8.45 pm, wearing a mustard-coloured mohair cardigan with black dots, a black skirt and white sandals. She told him she was going out and left. He had not seen her since, he told the officer.

He was not worried when she had not returned home as he thought she may have stayed with her mother, something, Bambrick pointed out, she did quite often. The next day he again went to The Advocate pub and met a woman there and enquired if she had seen Patricia. On Saturday, the day he dumped the final body parts in the rubbish tip, Bambrick said he was visiting pubs in the city centre trying to locate his partner but without success.

'On Sunday when she had not appeared, I got worried and decided to report her missing,' he insisted.

Meanwhile, the Gardaí had also decided to check out his neighbours to see if any of them could shed any light on Patricia's whereabouts or supply any possible reason for her disappearance.

Mary O'Neill, who lived in No. 59, said she remembered the early hours of 12 September very clearly. She said 'all hell broke loose' next door in the Bambricks around 1.15 am. She heard very loud screaming and roaring. It lasted until about 4 am or so when all finally went quiet.

The next morning she did not see any of the Bambricks. That evening at about 8.45 pm she heard footsteps outside. Ms O'Neill looked and saw somebody she thought to be Patricia passing the gate.

She remarked to her daughter: 'There she goes again and not a bother on her.' The person was wearing a black skirt and a mustard-coloured cardigan with black spots on it. It appeared to check with Bambrick's story.

Despite further inquires carried out at that time, the Gardaí could find no trace of Patricia McGauley. They checked with bus crews on routes from Ronanstown to the city centre who were working on the night of the 12th and with bus passengers who had travelled from the suburb, but to no avail.

What neither Mary O'Neill nor the Gardaí could have known, however, is that the person in Patricia's clothes who walked past her house on that night in high heels was in fact Michael Bambrick.

He had dressed up in Patricia's clothes and casually walked along the avenue. Some neighbours who heard the clatter created by the high heel shoes peered out their windows. In the dark it was impossible to tell that the person was not Patricia.

But at that same time, Patricia was dead and her body dismembered in the boxroom. The father of her two children was already weaving a web of deceit to convince people she was still alive and had simply vanished into the night.

In the weeks and months that followed Patricia's killing, the Garda investigation into her disappearance was gradually wound down. She seemed to have disappeared without trace. However, Michael Bambrick's cover up came very close to being detected one afternoon.

During 1992, officers called to 57 St Ronan's Park on routine inquiries. One of the uniformed Gardaí noticed what appeared to be blood on a mattress in an upstairs bedroom. When questioned about this, Bambrick said that Patricia had had a miscarriage a year earlier. At that stage the officers had no reason not to believe his story. His explanation was accepted and nothing further came of the discovery.

One of Patricia's relatives visited the house soon after her disappearance. She was struck by how clean the place was. The home was normally in a state of disarray. Bambrick had obviously done a spring clean to hide any evidence. The visitor was surprised but didn't take it any further.

The killer's luck was holding out. He was free to strike again.

On 23 July, 1992, Michael Bambrick went drinking in Dublin's south inner city and took his seven-year-old daughter, Adrienne, with him. He liked to keep his daughter close to him. He feared she knew what happened to her mother and might tell someone. It made him anxious to know her whereabouts all the time. He ended up going to Carr's pub on Francis Street where he bumped into a woman by the name of Mary Cummins. The two hit it off and as it was a Thursday, when Mary usually collected her social welfare payments and went out for the night, she decided to spend the evening with Michael Bambrick. It would be a fatal mistake.

* * *

Mary Cummins was one of life's unfortunates. Born on 21 December, 1956, she spent the first four years of her life in St Patrick's orphanage on the Navan Road in Dublin. In 1960 she was fostered by a couple, Robert and Bridget Cummins, whose name she took. Home life would never be a very happy one for the young Mary. Robert Cummins was very fond of alcohol and after a bout of heavy drinking had been known to assault his wife. Once he even cut her wrists. This turbulent and unsettling environment would inevitably impact on Mary who, as an adult, also came to have a reliance on alcohol.

Her foster mother died from cancer when Mary was just 15 and four years later Robert Cummins died of a heart attack. Their home in Oscar Square was left to Mary and an adopted daughter and both received £2,500 from the sale.

Mary moved into a succession of relationships with different men, some of them married. In 1978 she set up home with a man in Finglas. His wife had just left him and taken their two children with her. The relationship lasted for six years and in that time Mary had three children by the man. During this period she also intermittently lived with another man, who had a house nearby in the same north Dublin suburb.

In 1984, the father of the three children died. Prior to his death, however, he made a will in hospital and left his house equally between his estranged wife and two children and Mary Cummins and their children. As a result, Mary received a total of £5,285 in September 1986.

She lodged the money in a Bank of Ireland account but through a combination of heavy drinking and ill-advised loans, the account was down to just 86 pence two months later.

She continued a string of short relationships which were mainly with older men. This lifestyle led to the neglect of her children. The sale of the house in Finglas meant they now had no permanent home. The children had no sense of security as their mother dragged them from one boyfriend's home to another. The problem eventually came to the notice of the Eastern Health Board and social workers were forced to take action. All three children were taken into care.

By the time she met Michael Bambrick, she had another child, a young girl, and was living in a flat in Nicholas Street, close to St Patrick's Cathedral in the Liberties area of Dublin.

* * *

On the afternoon of 23 July, 1992, Mary had collected her Single Mother's Allowance and used the money to visit a number of pubs in the south inner-city area. She had her five-year-old daughter with her during this traditional Thursday pub crawl. Around 6.30 pm that evening she had a chance encounter with Bambrick, who was also in the company of his eldest daughter, Adrienne.

The two children played while their parents drank. He consumed three pints of Guinness and bought one pint for Mary. During the course of the evening two of Mary's friends arrived in the lounge section of the pub to collect her daughter to babysit for the night. Mary liked to be free on Thursdays.

Not long afterwards Bambrick and his daughter, along with Mary Cummins, left the pub and went back to her flat. She stacked away some shopping she had bought during the day and they chatted for a while. He invited her to come to Ballyfermot. She agreed and they grabbed a taxi in the Christchurch area and first headed back to his house. There he got a neighbour to look after the child while he and Mary went to pubs in Clondalkin and Ballyfermot. It was after closing time when they got back to 57 St Ronan's Park and, after giving the babysitter some money, Adrienne was put to bed.

The sequence of events which followed were almost a mirror image of the terrible fate of Patricia McGauley. Unfortunately, there were no witnesses to the awful events and the only account is the one Michael Bambrick has given. Here too, Bambrick claimed the outcome to be a tragic accident.

He claimed he and Mary went into the sitting room where they started kissing and petting. He says they engaged in sex games. He tied her hands behind her back with a belt and stuffed tights into her mouth, tying them around her head. During the bondage, as he carried out a number of sex acts on her, she choked on the gag.

Bambrick later told the Gardaí that when he realised she was dead he again panicked, although his version of events are deeply suspect given his history of violent attacks on bound and gagged victims, unable to put up any struggle.

Again he took the body into the boxroom where he locked the door and left it for a day.

On Friday, using a hacksaw, he cut off Mary Cummins' legs and put them into a refuse bag. He put the rest of the body into another large bag. This time he used a wheelbarrow to transport the dismembered pieces to a large field close to Balgaddy School during the hours of darkness. The open ground is about half a mile away from where he disposed of Patricia McGauley's body.

Before discarding the body, he took off Mary's clothes which he burnt later in the fire at home. He then hid the body under a television set and some dumped furniture.

Later, when Adrienne noticed that the visitor had left her shoes after her, Bambrick burned them too. In his confession to Gardaí three years later he would claim: 'I don't know what came over me on either of these occasions. I don't know how to explain it. I got enjoyment out of stuffing the tights in their mouths. I now realise the danger of what I did on these occasions.'

* * *

It was three days before Mary Cummins' disappearance was reported to the police. A male friend called to Kevin Street station, not far from Christchurch, on the evening of Sunday 26 July, to say she had gone missing. The case was handed over to the local District Detective Unit (DDU) at the station and they took statements from several of Mary's friends. Officers searched her flat at Nicholas Street in the company of the man who reported her missing and took a number of items away for examination.

A peculiar aspect of the case was that one witness from Carr's pub reported Mary being in the company of Michael Bambrick on the night she was last seen and that they both went off together at around 7 pm.

Gardaí, assisted by the Dog Unit, carried out several searches in the Liberties area. The search included wasteground around a derelict church, a site on Francis Street and the grounds at Dublin Corporation's Civic Offices on the city quays. They found nothing.

One local garda, Detective John Cribbin from Kevin Street station, who was investigating the disappearance, followed up the information about Michael Bambrick being in the pub. Within a short time, he discovered that Bambrick's common-law wife, Patricia McGauley, had also gone missing.

It was too much of a coincidence to ignore. The detective decided it was time to look into the background of Mr Bambrick and see what type of character he was. The check was enough to worry officers that the two women could well have been murdered.

* * *

Two months after Mary Cummins' disappearance, Bambrick was summoned to Kevin Street station. He was interviewed at length by Cribbin and his colleague, Detective Mick Mellon, about Mary's disappearance. Bambrick put up a stout defence. He admitted to meeting a woman answering Mary's description on the night in question. Bambrick insisted they had parted company outside the pub and he returned to Ronanstown on the bus with his daughter. He had never seen her after that.

'Isn't it strange the way two women in your life have disappeared?' one of the gardaí asked.

'Yes, isn't it a terrible coincidence,' he replied. 'It's just a misfortune and pure bad luck. But I had nothing to do with it,' he added.

During the interview, Bambrick, who had lost his sense of smell in an accident, took off his shoes. The smell nearly suffocated the two officers. Later, the Kevin Street team learned that Bambrick was a frequent visitor to city dumps where he scavenged for scrap metal. Others involved in this activity told them Bambrick would search around rotting animal carcases oblivious to the stench.

Despite their worries and the fact that Michael Bambrick had now been linked to two missing women, the Gardaí had nothing to go on but a hunch. The fact that both women had gone missing in a period of less than 12 months, and the man connecting the two of them had a conviction for indecent assault and burglary, was not enough to even consider bringing a case to court.

After his questioning at Kevin Street, officers from Ballyfermot and Ronanstown also visited his home in a bid to put pressure on Bambrick. They put it to him that he was involved in the women's disappearance. He had to have something to do with it. Bambrick again insisted it was a total coincidence.

*   *   *

A series of events occurred during 1994 which would cause the police to review the way they handled the two missing persons cases. The first came when a brave nine-year-old girl walked in the door of Ronanstown station in a very distressed state. The little girl was accompanied by a man, a neighbour of the child.

Garda Mary Bushell comforted Adrienne Bambrick and got the impression the youngster was very unhappy with her father.

The officer noted that the girl cried continuously and spoke erratically. The garda would later tell her superiors that the young child spoke quickly and in a confused manner as if she wanted to tell everything at once. She told of a number of experiences she had suffered at the hands of her father. He had killed her pets and beaten her. On one occasion the child was left alone in 57 St Ronan's Park for a period of four days.

The little girl, who showed a maturity and strength of character way beyond her years, told the garda she was not fed on a regular basis and sometimes had to steal food from the kitchen and hide it in her bedroom. Her father would bolt the door to the kitchen to prevent her from getting food.

It was a tale of abuse which shocked the local gardaí. The child was obviously terrified of her father and the matter would have to be fully investigated. The officers called to the house immediately afterwards but there was nobody at home. It was decided to take the child to her aunt, who was already looking after the little girl's younger sister. A little later the gardaí brought her to her godparent's home where she was looked after.

At this stage the police were well and truly horrified. The officers attached to Ronanstown had seen their share of bad conditions, poverty and neglect down the years but what they had witnessed when they visited No. 57 left them in no doubt that it was a house of horrors. Any child being brought up there would have to live in conditions of extreme hardship.

They found a distinct stench of urine in the hallway of the two-storey terraced building. When Garda Bushell looked in the kitchen window she saw dirty dishes laid across the worktops. The sink, floor and walls were filthy. She was left with no doubt that it was not a safe place to store food let alone prepare or cook meals. Gardaí at Ronanstown decided they would have to contact social workers.

The Health Board was only too well aware of the problems at the house. The local Social Worker's Office already had a file on the Bambricks with suggestions of abuse and neglect in the family. The police decided to dig deeper.

They discovered that Michael Bambrick had once beaten his child because when she was hungry she had taken some bread from the kitchen. They also found out that he had locked her in the garden shed over some trivial transgression. In a fit of rage he killed her pet cat and dog in the cruellest manner, by hitting them off the kitchen wall. The degree of neglect, including the locking away of food, was outlined by 13 different people who had come into contact with the family.

The courage it took the girl to go to the police impressed local officers who now took a very active interest in 57 St Ronan's Park. As the investigation into the abuse continued, the child also told the police that she was six when her mother 'went away'. The reference by the child to her mother aroused no small interest in Ronanstown Garda station where the file in relation to her mother was now reopened.

The Gardaí were at last beginning to draw a more tangible link between Patricia McGauley's diappearance and that of Mary Cummins. The version of events being given by the little schoolgirl on the night Mary Cummins vanished was amazing in its detail. It was almost as if she had memorised the sequence of events knowing it would be important in the future. Moreover, it was providing evidence which totally contradicted her father's version of events on that night.

The girl told officers how her father regularly drank in Carr's pub. She even named some of the friends he would meet there.

'Once, I remember he was drinking with a woman there. It was about two years ago. She had a daughter, Samantha was her name [Mary Cummins' child], she and I were playing in the pub,' she revealed. She went on to inform the gardaí that when Samantha was collected by a woman in a blue van, she remained playing on her own. Her father continued drinking along with the woman, until all three of them went back to the woman's flat.

The woman stacked away some shopping, including eggs which she put in the fridge. The child also remembered that the woman changed her clothes and travelled with her father to 57 St Ronan's

Park in a cab. The little girl was able to recall that the woman had given her a Coca Cola flask.

This was a critical piece of information because it definitely linked her to Mary Cummins' flat. Inquiries by the Gardaí revealed that Mary Cummins had been given promotional Coca Cola flasks by a nephew some months before she disappeared. The type of flask Michael Bambrick's daughter had was one of only a limited number and was of the type Mary Cummins was given.

The youngster was still up when her father and the woman returned. He was a bit 'grumpy' at the time. The following morning the woman had gone but had left her runners behind which her dad then burned. Gardaí couldn't believe it when the little girl picked out Mary Cummins' photo from an album shown to her.

This information left members of the local force in little doubt that Bambrick played a part in the disappearance of both women. The 1992 visit to the house in which a uniformed officer had spotted blood stains on the bed was also added to the equation and the prospect that both women had been murdered was now considered a very distinct possibility.

Parallel to these developments, the inquiries into physical abuse and neglect were also continuing. The Gardaí now had enough evidence to arrest him in connection with these offences. At 2.20 pm on 23 January, 1995, Garda Mary Bushell arrested Michael Bambrick at the Four Courts in Dublin. He was put into a patrol car and brought straight to Ronanstown station.

While the arrest was in relation to the allegations of physical abuse of his daughter, he was also asked about other important matters.

Detective Inspector Joe McGarty and Detective Sergeant Tom Mulligan questioned him in relation to the disappearance of the two women. He told the two District Detective Unit (DDU) officers he had not seen nor heard from Patricia McGauley since the night he claimed she walked out of the house to go into town. As for Mary Cummins, he said they left the pub together and went as far as the Iveagh Markets. She went towards Christchurch and he turned right towards Thomas Street and got the bus home with his eldest daughter.

The detectives asked for permission to search his house. They were delighted when he gave them the okay.

At the time, the force had no power to search a building where they believed a murder had taken place, unless the murder weapon was a gun. If the victim was strangled or stabbed there was no power to search. Moreover, the police had no specific legal right to search for bodies. They may suspect or have reasonable grounds for believing a body was hidden on private property but they could not legally go in and search for it.

It was one of the peculiar anomalies of the criminal law. The police had the power to search for narcotics under the Misuse of Drugs Act but if a murder victim was buried in the same house they had no legal right to search for the body. It was vital therefore that Bambrick give his consent to a search.

Now, finally, they would get to the bottom of what had occurred in No. 57, just a short distance away from where they were interviewing Bambrick.

But their optimism was short-lived. Bambrick had sublet the house to a neighbour and his wife and child. It meant the Gardaí would now have to formally seek that family's permission before searching for bodies. It was another setback. The investigation would be at a standstill until they were allowed into the house. Three months later, on 10 April, 1995, when the family moved out, Dublin Corporation (which owned the house) officially declared the address abandoned. The local authority set about changing the locks on the doors and on the following day the Corporation's housing estate supervisor gave permission to enter and search the house and gardens.

In the meantime, the Gardaí were in contact with Gloucestershire Police in England who had searched Fred and Rose West's house in Gloucester. The British team gave them tips on what to look out for and the type of equipment to use. They also told the Gardaí the legislative powers they used to get into the house. Unfortunately, similar legislation was not available here and even now is not in the statute books.

On the morning of 12 April, detectives from Kevin Street, Ronanstown and the force's Technical Bureau began tearing the house apart, searching for clues. A close relative of Bambrick's who knew him very well warned the squad in advance that the chances of finding any bodies were slim.

'You've gotta remember Michael is a very lazy person. He has never lifted a spade in his life. He is just a streak of laziness and I don't think he would bury a body. He would find a much simpler way of disposing of it,' the relative surmised.

A small mechanical digger was lifted into the back garden and started scraping up earth looking for graves. The high level of activity attracted the whole neighbourhood to the house.

The search coincided with the second day of the annual Association of Garda Sergeants and Inspectors conference in Dublin attended by all the newspapers' crime reporters. Nevertheless, within a very short time, the papers and RTÉ had been tipped off. That night, the *Evening Herald*, which had received information about the unusual investigation in Ronanstown weeks earlier but abided by a Garda request on a blackout on the inquiry to avoid alerting the suspect, led with the story of the search for two women's bodies.

The following day's papers were full of column inches on the dig, complete with photographs of gardaí in grey boiler suits and shovels sifting through every corner of the tiny terraced back garden. On the 13th the *Herald* led with a story on the Garda belief that both Patricia McGauley and Mary Cummins had been strangled and their bodies mutilated. The story was followed up by the Pat Kenny radio show later that morning.

It drew a critical response from the police – the Garda Press Office denied the story outright. A senior officer went on RTÉ Radio One's media programme *Soundbyte* the following Saturday to accuse the evening paper of 'sensationalism'.

Much to the dismay of everyone involved, the two-day search of No. 57 drew a blank. Nothing of any evidential value had been found during the intensive dig. In the back garden, officers had found some bones, but on forensic analysis they were found to belong to a dog, probably the pet killed by Bambrick.

Bambrick's relative's words turned out to be an accurate description. The killer had been too lazy to dig a grave in the back garden and instead took the bodies to two separate dumps some miles away. The police had once again drawn a blank. Nevertheless, the inquiry was now very big news and journalists had heard about the link between Michael Bambrick and two missing women. The pressure was mounting on the Gardaí to come up with results.

* * *

One week after the fruitless search of No. 57, the case was given new impetus. Detective Inspector Michael Byrne had been appointed to take charge of the Detective Unit at Kevin Street a few months earlier. On taking over the job he was handed two large files on the cases of missing women, Patricia McGauley and Mary Cummins. It left him in no doubt that Michael Bambrick had been responsible for their deaths.

He met with his colleagues in Ronanstown. The result was that a file on the case was sent up the line, landing on the desk of the new head of Operations – Deputy Commissioner Pat Byrne.

On receiving the report, Pat Byrne summoned Inspector Mick Byrne and Superintendent Mick Carolan, in charge of Ronanstown, to his office and said he was worried about the contents of the report. The Deputy Commissioner said he shared the view that both women had more than likely met violent deaths. It was a matter of such serious importance that he asked what their view was on appointing an overall commander to the case. There was no objection.

On 18 April, 1995, a conference was held at Crumlin station in the Dublin Metropolitan Area (DMA) South division where many of the officers involved in the investigations of the past three years had gathered. The high level meeting was attended by the two Chief Superintendents from DMA South, which included Ronanstown district, and DMA South Central, which covered the Kevin Street area. Also in attendance was Detective Chief Superintendent Kevin Carty, the man Deputy Commissioner Byrne had appointed the previous night as overall commander of the two Missing Persons inquiries.

Up to now, both investigations had been led by two different teams. Carty, the head of the force's Central Detective Unit (CDU) would now be in charge.

One of the youngest officers to reach the rank of Chief Superintendent, he was a respected investigator who had spent the bulk of his career in the Special Branch. Carty specialised in the secret world of gathering intelligence on the Provisional IRA, helping to locate dozens of their arms dumps around the country. With a reputation for getting the job done, the Garda Commissioner had earlier in the year appointed him to take over the investigation of organised crime, particularly in Dublin, which many observers argued was getting out of control. As commander of the CDU he had overall charge of the Serious Crime Squad and the then Drugs and Fraud Squads, all based in the Dublin Area Headquarters at Harcourt Square.

Two other detectives, Detective Superintendent Austin McNally from the Serious Crime Squad and Detective Inspector Mick Byrne from the Kevin Street District Detective Unit (DDU) would assist Carty in the investigation into the mystery of what happened to Patricia McGauley and Mary Cummins. The team, which was able to draw on manpower from around the city, including CDU detectives, immediately set up an incident room at Lucan station, ordering in a new computer database.

* * *

The inquiry soon got underway with gusto. Conferences were held every morning initially and subsequently every two days to analyse the evidence coming into the case. But it was not without its initial hiccups.

Carty was angry one morning to discover that he could not hold a conference of his 20 detectives because the room they were using as an Incident Centre had been taken over to hold a totally unrelated internal disciplinary inquiry. The Detective Chief Superintendent ordered his officers to pack up and head for his own CDU Headquarters at Harcourt Square.

When senior officers heard about what happened, the internal inquiry was quickly found alternative space and the Missing Persons Incident Room was moved back to its original location.

The team began pursuing more than 300 different lines of inquiry and took over 400 statements from people. Carty was particularly impressed with the testimony of Michael Bambrick's daughter. Adrienne's statements touched everybody involved in the search and made them determined to find out the fate of the two women.

With the negative results drawn from the search of No. 57, the team knew that they could not dig up the whole of west Dublin looking for bodies.

The force had received a lot of negative publicity some time earlier when a search for two bodies during a murder investigation in Cork City saw the police digging at several sites. At one stage it was alleged that suspects had managed to take a body from a field during the night because of a ban on overtime. The Lucan team wanted to avoid this type of situation at all costs. They knew they would have to get specific information about the general area where the two women's bodies were buried before they could start digging.

Carty's team looked through all the information that had been gathered by their predecessors, with whom they still liaised. The visit to No. 57 by the garda who spotted blood on the mattress in July 1992 was now reassessed and acted on. It was deemed a critical part of the investigation and pointed to the possible use of extreme violence in the house.

On 19 May, a team of scientists from the Forensic Science Laboratory in Phoenix Park carried out a thorough examination of the interior of the house. Doctors Jennifer Ryan, Louise McKenna and Fiona Thornton visited the address armed with chemicals to detect the presence of blood on furniture, floors and fittings in the house. Two garda photographers were on hand to capture the search on film. Their photographs would provide evidence of the sequence of the operation in any upcoming criminal trial. A member of the Ballistics Section from Garda Headquarters provided lighting for the scientists as they worked through the night. Their work took place over three days and would turn up significant findings.

Positive reactions for blood were found on a large number of the floorboards, 50 in all. It was now obvious that great violence had been used in the house at some stage or over a protracted period. The wood lifted from the boxroom in particular told its own story. Blood had seeped right through the depth of the wooden floor.

All of the floorboards were taken up and brought to Garda Headquarters. On 19 July, Detective Sergeant Donie O'Sullivan took the floorboards to Britain where they were handed over to a Doctor Joan Lygo at the Home Office Forensic Science Laboratory at Aldermaston in Reading. Her tests confirmed the positive reactions for blood on many of the timbers. The investigators were finally onto something tangible.

* * *

In the meantime, Michael Bambrick had moved away from the Ronanstown area and was living with a new girlfriend. She was pregnant by him. It was decided to approach this woman, who already had two other children, to see if she could help in the police inquiry.

On 9 June she was interviewed by Detective Sergeant John Melody from the CDU. She told how she met Bambrick earlier that year at a house in North King Street where she was staying with two friends. She became involved in a relationship with him. She revealed that he liked to dress up in women's clothes and wanted to tie her up and have kinky sex. The woman also told the officer that Bambrick had once said he murdered a girl in Clondalkin. She had asked him how he did it and he said he could not remember. It was too disgusting, he told her. He was crying at the time over what he had done. The statement was another leap forward for the inquiry.

Worryingly, the investigation team was now receiving reports that Michael Bambrick had begun interfering with children. The 15-year-old daughter of a woman who knew Bambrick reported that he had indecently touched her. The teenager said the first time she met him was through a friend. She was mitching from school and was invited in to No. 57 because it was cold. She played chess with Bambrick and he showed her some family photos.

Some time later she was sitting on a wall with a school friend when Michael Bambrick walked up to them and grabbed their breasts. She also outlined that about the time of the World Cup in 1994 she was in the house. On a few occasions she went there on the 'hop from school'. It was on the second visit that she went upstairs and sat on his daughter's bed reading a book. The girl claimed that Michael Bambrick came into the room and caught hold of her hands, pushed her back onto the bed, took off her trousers and underwear, took off his own clothes and molested her.

She concluded the statement by claiming that Bambrick then told her: 'You can get dressed now 'cos I'm finished with you.'

At the time, detectives from the Domestic Violence and Sexual Assault Unit at Harcourt Square also investigated allegations that he indecently assaulted a two-and-half-year-old girl in Dublin's south inner-city. Claims were also made that he touched a four-year-old boy in an indecent way.

A report was received from a prostitute who worked along the Benburb Street strip just across the Liffey from Heuston railway station. The street is one of the capital's seediest red light districts where heroin addicts from the very young to the very old sell sex 24 hours a day. The woman said she had been beaten by Michael Bambrick after having sex with him. But she also told how he paid £20 for her black leather miniskirt!

As the inquiry attracted more publicity, information came into the incident room that their double murder suspect was in possession of a shotgun and a speargun. He had told several people about the weapons and loaned the speargun to one man. Armed with this information and the statement from his new girlfriend that he had killed a woman, the investigation team decided it was finally time to move on Michael Bambrick.

He was put under 24-hour surveillance by CDU officers to monitor his movements and patterns.

Then, early on the morning of 24 June, 1995, at Father Matthew Hall on Church Street, not far from the Four Courts, Detective Sergeant John Melody and three armed detectives arrested him under the Offences Against the State Act on suspicion of possession of firearms. Bambrick was put in the back of a patrol car and brought to Kevin Street station. It was now almost four years after the disappearance of Patricia McGauley.

*   *   *

Within the Garda Síochána, a small number of detectives, many of whom served with the old Murder Squad, have developed the skill of interviewing suspects, particularly those wanted for homicide. It is a skill which only a handful possess and is not something which can be taught very easily. Often it involves gaining the confidence of the suspect, posing questions in a particular way or simply knowing when to remain silent.

The first few hours of Bambrick's custody period were taken up with fulfilling legal formalities. Later during the day the prisoner kept to his story about being totally ignorant of the fate of the two women. Around 7.30 pm on the evening of the 24th, two officers – Detective Sergeant Pat Lynagh and Detective Garda Gerry Dillon – took over the questioning. They read Bambrick over his rights and kept a written note of what was being said.

They remarked to Bambrick that he had a chequered history. They were even able to tell him about the assault on his mother and the way he had trashed the family home. The suspect seemed to be shocked that the police knew so much about him.

Half an hour into the questioning, the two officers made the breakthrough the investigation team could only have dreamed about. Bambrick admitted to the two gardaí that both women were dead and that he had killed them.

At about 8 pm the double killer began outlining the details surrounding the homicide of his victims, including the dismemberment of the bodies and their disposal in Balgaddy.

During the course of the questioning Bambrick agreed to show the detectives where he had hidden the bodies.

Just before 10 pm a convoy of squad cars left Kevin Street station as they escorted the prisoner to Balgaddy School. In the closing light of day, the group walked across a piece of wasteground where he pointed to a ditch, bordered by a whitethorn hedge where he said he had buried Mary Cummins' dismembered body. Bambrick told the officers he had hidden both bags, one containing the trunk of the body and the other the legs, in the ground.

The Gardaí and their prisoner then travelled the half mile to the area known as Balgaddy Dump. Bambrick told the driver to travel down a lane close to a travellers' halting site and right at the entrance to the dumping ground. Just inside the entrance he told the driver to stop and the group got out and went to a drain on the right of the lane. There he pointed to a spot close to a dead tree where he told the detectives he had hidden the severed arms, legs and head of his common-law wife, Patricia McGauley.

A few seconds later he pointed to a spot about 20 yards closer to the entrance where other body parts had been secreted. During all this time the detectives found it remarkable that the killer retained his composure. Throughout the tour of grave sites he never once exhibited any signs of remorse.

Before the killer was brought back to his cell, uniformed gardaí were posted to guard all the areas pointed out by Bambrick. On the return journey he pointed out Carr's pub and Mary Cummins' flat on

Nicholas Street to the Gardaí. The next day an extensive search began at both sites in Ronanstown.

Detectives were still interested in discovering a motive for the killings and the interrogation continued. The following evening, Bambrick confessed a further ghoulish act to Detective Gardaí Bernie Hanley and Thomas Byrne. He told them that, having buried Mrs McGauley, he went back to the spot, only to discover the head was sticking out from the ground. He outlined how he went into the ditch and grabbed the severed head, put it on the ground and dropped a four inch concrete block on top of it. It was an act he repeated, smashing the skull. Bambrick said he then put the head back into the drain and threw some soil over it.

That night the Gardaí returned to the area they had visited the previous evening where their prisoner pointed out the area where he re-buried the skull. A painstaking search of the two burial sites continued for more than a week, attracting widespread media attention.

But for an inquiry which had been hampered from the beginning by numerous setbacks, there was one more final blow.

The area where Mrs McGauley's body had been dumped had been extensively cleared by Dublin County Council almost two years after she was killed. The refuse was taken to Dunsink Dump in Finglas during the months of July and August 1993. Estimates by local authority officials indicated that the material from Balgaddy would be scattered over a three-acre area and buried at a depth of eight feet. The chances of finding any of the body parts in Dunsink were nil.

It was therefore remarkable that small fragments of skull and one human rib were recovered at the spot pointed out by Bambrick at Balgaddy. DNA analysis of the bone pieces revealed they belonged to Patricia McGauley. The find was a relief to her family and young daughter and allowed them to finally bury their daughter and mother in a cemetery. The victim's family later published an appreciation of the Garda work in a national newspaper.

The dig for the remains of Mary Cummins was more successful and several body parts were found, including her left tibia bone. It was positively identified against an X-Ray taken of her years earlier. Pathologist Dr Margaret Bolster found that two femur or thigh bones found at the scene had been cleanly cut through with a saw and the lower limbs placed separately in the ditch. Dr Bolster also found fragmented pieces of black nylon around the leg bones and a purple-coloured suspender belt with the remains. Dental charts were used for positive identification against a mandible also found at Balgaddy while a DNA match was also made.

* * *

Those who investigated the two horrific killings of Patricia McGauley and Mary Cummins are in no doubt that Michael Bambrick could kill again and may have killed other women before. For this reason, the file on Bambrick will remain open for some time to come.

Officers involved in the case point out that had he been able to drive, the toll of killings could have been a lot higher. He was constrained insofar as he relied on public transport to get around and used his bicycle and a wheelbarrow to dispose of body parts. Had he been able to get the use of a car, who knows how many other women he would have killed or where he would have buried the remains?

Michael Bambrick's young daughter, now a teenager, was the real hero of this case. It was her belief that her mother had been killed and that the woman visitor to her home had met a similar fate which gave Gardaí the vital lead. She is now living with relatives on Dublin's southside and is said to be making a good recovery. She is often visited by Detective Mary Bushell who helped the young girl tell her story and free her from the horrific life she led at 57 St Ronan's Park.

Michael Bambrick meanwhile is incarcerated at Arbour Hill jail.

The two sites where the body parts were found have since been built upon. If the investigation into the missing women had been delayed by even 12 months the graves may never have been found.

GUBU

'Wait for a while to ensure death is final. During this time take a few very important items into my possession. Make an inventory of other important items.'

– Malcom MacArthur, 1982.

IT was approaching rush hour on Thursday afternoon, 22 July, 1982, when Bridie Gargan stopped off in Dublin's Phoenix Park. The 29-year-old nurse had just finished work at St James's Hospital on the other side of the River Liffey where she was doing a course in midwifery. Her one-bedroomed flat at the Elms in Castleknock was close to the expansive park.

It had been a glorious summer's day in the city. It was extremely hot. Close to the entrance to the US Ambassador's residence she turned off the main road onto the grass verge. About ten metres in from the road, she parked the silver metallic Renault 5 she had bought new two years earlier. It was close to 5 pm when Bridie took advantage of the warm evening sunshine to lie out on the grass beside the car.

Around the same time, a man desperate for money was on the prowl. Malcolm MacArthur walked along the Cricket Grounds in the park, searching for what he was to describe later as 'easy prey'. He passed a row of trees. He saw somebody lying in the long grass to the left of the trees. The person lay next to a car. He could not be sure whether it was a man or woman. Checking that the coast was clear, he walked past the Renault and then decided to make his approach.

He put a shovel wrapped in a black plastic bag on the ground beside a tree and approached the car. He carried an imitation handgun, crafted from a crossbow, in his right hand and a blue holdall bag in his left. He came to within a few feet of the sunbather before he realised that it was a woman. He pointed the weapon at her and told her to get into the car. She was calm.

'Is this for real?' she asked.

'Yes, it is,' MacArthur replied.

Bridie Gargan tried to remain cool in the circumstances. 'May I put my clothes back on?'

He nodded and she put on her blouse. Following his motions with the gun, she got into the back seat of the car. He assured her that he only wanted the car and told her to lie on the back seat and said he was going to tie her up. At this, Bridie began to panic and refused to lie down on the seat. MacArthur reached into the holdall bag and took out a lump hammer. He struck her several times 'because the first blow did not do what I expected it to do.'

Close by, Patrick Byrne, a gardener, who worked in the American Ambassador's residence, was following events closely. Byrne had immediately become suspicious when he saw the bearded MacArthur looking around before approaching the car. He also saw that he was carrying a holdall bag as he walked around the front of the car towards the driver's door. The gardener stooped forward in a semi-crouched position and saw the girl get up off the ground and move towards the driver's door.

Both got into the car and the next thing he saw was the little Renault rocking up and down. He could see through the rear window that the man was hitting the girl with a black object in his right hand. The assailant then caught the girl by the hair and continued to hit her about the head.

Byrne ran towards the car to check what was happening. He looked through the left-side window and saw that the man was now at the back of the driver's seat. He had opened out a newspaper over part of the back seat.

'Do you own this car?' Byrne enquired.

MacArthur partially opened the driver's door and pointed the gun at Byrne. 'Fuck off you,' Mac Arthur said in an English twang, 'or I'll put a bullet through your head.'

Byrne, concerned for the woman's safety, didn't back off. He pulled at the driver's door and grappled with the gunman's hand trying to take the pistol from him. MacArthur got out of the car and pushing Byrne off, levelled the imitation gun at him and again told him he would put a bullet into him.

Later Byrne told gardaí: 'I remained where I was as this man kept the gun pointed at me. The girl then got up on the back seat and I saw that her face was matted in blood. Her hair was also full of blood and there was blood streaming down the front of her clothes. She then slumped back into the corner of the back seat.'

Byrne stood back as the man drove off at high speed in first or second gear along a pathway used by joggers towards the city centre.

The gardener furiously tried to flag down several passing cars in an effort to raise the alarm but no one stopped. By chance, he finally managed to hail a neighbour from Blanchardstown who drove him to the front gates of the Ambassador's residence. He told a security man to telephone the police.

Meanwhile, the Renault was getting a 'blues and twos'[1] escort through the city. Ambulance crew members Martin Jackson and Martin Fox had a near collision with the little car when it pulled in front of them as it raced out of Phoenix Park. It then tried to overtake another white car. At the Islandbridge gates to the park the vehicle turned left. A short distance away they caught up with the car while it was stuck in traffic. The paramedics noticed the woman sitting in the back seat holding her head with her hands. They also saw blood on the rear side window. Martin Jackson shouted at the driver to pull in and ran towards the car to see if he could help but MacArthur drove off.

The car turned right up the South Circular Road and the ambulance men again managed to catch up with it. Spotting a parking

---

1. Blues and twos refers to the blue flashing lights and two-tone siren on emergency vehicles.

permit for St James's Hospital on the windscreen they now presumed the driver was a doctor rushing a patient to hospital and signalled for him to pull in behind them.

He followed them along the South Circular Road to the Rialto entrance to St James's where he stopped at the gateman's hut. The ambulance driver stopped and beckoned him to come on. MacArthur began to follow again but when the ambulance crew arrived at casualty they realised he had not come after them. They reckoned he had gone into another section of the hospital and decided to return to their base.

MacArthur, however, had left the grounds and headed towards Rialto, where he abandoned Bridie Gargan's car on a laneway near Harold's Cross Bridge. He left the critically injured nurse in it, along with the hammer he used to bludgeon her.

Increasingly agitated, he ran off along the South Circular Road, stopping off to dump his bloodstained crew-necked jumper in a laneway and his tweed hat under some wire. Hurrying along the South Circular Road, he unsuccessfully tried to wave down a bus.

Desperate to avoid police attention, he walked into a travel agent's shop, Odyssey Travel. Sweating and out of breath, he asked the assistant for a glass of water, eventually drinking three glasses. He inquired about getting a taxi to Blackrock and tried to draw attention away from his breathlessness. He said he had been running in the heat. The woman behind the counter found this surprising. MacArthur, who spoke with a posh accent, was not dressed like a jogger. The visitor also inquired about the 'Magicbus', a mystery tour service which had been discontinued years earlier. Eventually, she directed him to a bus stop where he hopped on a double decker going in the opposite direction towards Ballymun. The travel agent found the visit a little perturbing. As soon as the man left, she immediately washed the glass he had used and with it his fingerprints.

The northbound bus stopped off outside one of three shops on Glasnevin Avenue. MacArthur bought a packet of disposable razors and went into the nearby Fingal House pub where he went straight to the toilets. Without any soap or hot water he slowly took off the beard. When he emerged, he ordered a soda water and asked the barman for change of a 50 pence coin and phoned a taxi. It was now two hours since the attack in the park. He asked the cab driver to take him into the city centre but when they got there he told the taximan to continue on to the ferry terminal in Dun Laoghaire.

A 13-year-old boy working in a sports trophy shop was the first to find Bridie Gargan. At around 6.10 pm the youngster saw the driver's side window covered in blood. He then spotted the woman in the back seat. 'I think she had a white dress on her. She was all covered in blood. She kept pushing her hair back with her hand. Her hair was soaked in blood,' he told the Gardaí. The teenager ran to the shop where he alerted his workmates. Within a short time the laneway was alive with paramedics and gardaí.

Bridie Gargan was rushed to the Richmond Hospital, where she was put on a life support machine. She died four days later.

Within hours of the vicious attack, Malcolm MacArthur had made his way to Dun Laoghaire where he was booked into a guesthouse. But the lodgings were only temporary. He had it on his mind to move in with an old friend.

* * *

The senseless murder of Nurse Gargan was the first chapter in a series of events which Charles Haughey would later describe as 'grotesque, unbelievable, bizarre and unprecedented'. The Taoiseach's phrase would gain more popular currency when commentator Conor Cruise O'Brien referred to it as GUBU.

In the weekend that followed Bridie Gargan's murder, three more people would meet their deaths violently. On Saturday, 24 July, Robert Belton, a member of the well-known Fine Gael family died in hospital after being assaulted and shot in the leg as he resisted armed raiders six days earlier at his post office in Donnycarney, Dublin.

In the early hours of the same day, 20-year-old Patricia Furlong was strangled at the Fraughan Festival at Glencullen, in the Dublin

Mountains. It was a case which would later feature prominently in the courts for the best part of two decades.

There would also be the murder of 27-year-old farmer, Donal Dunne, killed by a shotgun blast near Edenderry, Co. Offaly.

The killings were unprecedented in recent times and left the Garda Síochána reeling and wondering how to cope. The spate of violence also had the effect of splitting up the force's Murder Squad, based at the Phoenix Park headquarters, with small teams of detectives now assigned to investigate each homicide. But the motiveless murder of the young nurse from Dunshaughlin, Co. Meath, would be the one that most traumatised the Irish public.

*   *   *

Malcolm MacArthur was the only child of Irene and Daniel MacArthur, wealthy landowners who farmed at Breemount, Trim, Co. Meath. The couple married in 1943 and had their first and only child three years later. With the income from 180 acres of good farmland and a private quarry, the family should have been able to live very comfortably. Mrs MacArthur told friends that she spent her life hunting and gardening.

But the family lost a lot of money in the 1970s and could not afford to live lavishly. The electricity was once cut off because of unpaid bills and their son had to study by candlelight.

The young MacArthur was educated privately at home by a governess until he was about ten or eleven. He then went to the Christian Brothers School in Trim where he remained until he completed his Leaving Certificate and Matriculation examination for the National University of Ireland in 1963. In July of that year, he went to California where he lived with his uncle JD MacArthur, a Labour Court judge.

In the United States he spent a year in Diabolo Valley College before moving to Oregon State University for a year and a half. He spent another 18 months in Davis University, a constituent college of the University of California, from where he graduated in 1967 with a degree in Economics, Anatomy and American History. Later that year he returned home to Breemount. His father wanted him to take a job with Roadstone, which had rented the family's quarry. But Malcolm MacArthur had other ideas and went to Trinity College where he studied for a Masters degree.

Relations in the family were not good. There were constant rows between his parents. At one point, his mother claims that MacArthur Senior bit his teenage son on the hand. The wound required five stitches.

The couple eventually got a legal separation and Mrs MacArthur moved to Mullingar while their son stayed on at Breemount where the arguments continued between father and son. Malcolm was regularly thrown out of the family home. After one particularly serious row, he left for several months but returned again in the summer of 1971. At that stage his father, who was suffering from angina, had become very ill. That August, his son took him to the Portobello Nursing Home in Dublin where he remained for about six weeks. In the meantime, Malcolm was enjoying life alone in the house. Relations deteriorated further when his elderly father returned on 22 October. Three days later his father died.

The death would leave Malcolm a very wealthy man. When the farm was sold in 1973 it netted the colossal sum of £175,000. The money was split between mother and son, with Malcolm getting two-thirds of the sale price. Eight years later he would again come into money when his grandmother died and he received £10,000 from the sale of her home at Iona Drive, Glasnevin in Dublin.

The large inheritances allowed MacArthur to live a bohemian lifestyle in the capital where he frequented fashionable pubs and rubbed shoulders with the city's academic and arty set, who were enjoying something of a renaissance in the late 1970s. A favourite pub was Bartley Dunnes, where he drank with friends, many from nearby Trinity College. Coincidentally, the pub was also a favoured watering hole with leading barrister Patrick Connolly, who was later to become Attorney General.

To those who met him, MacArthur came across as intelligent and well qualified, rarely indulging in small talk. Although he never actually said it, he gave the impression that he had studied in Cambridge. This added to his reputation as a scholar. There were other more obvious characteristics that made him stand out from the crowd. Many of those who met him remarked on his accent, which some described as upper-class English while others thought it was that high-pitched Anglo-Irish twang, often heard in academia. The air of mild eccentricity was topped off with foppish mannerisms and unusual clothes, including bow ties and cravats.

There is no evidence that Connolly or MacArthur ever met at that time, although they mixed in the same circles. Their paths were to cross, however, when MacArthur began living with a woman by the name of Brenda Little. She was a well-known figure in the art and theatre set in south city-centre pubs. Ms Little originally came from the working-class suburb of Finglas and worked at a variety of part-time jobs. At the age of 18, she and a few friends went to London where they earned a living painting pottery before returning to Dublin after a year.

In 1972, she was working in a variety of places including a builders' providers and a hairdressing salon. Another venture which helped her get by was the selling of raffle tickets for underprivileged children. Ironically, this meagre employment would bring her into contact with one of the country's best-known barristers.

Brenda Little first met Patrick Connolly on a city-centre street when she asked him to buy raffle tickets. He expressed an interest in the charity and commented that the money she was helping to raise would build a recreation centre in his native north county Dublin. Over the next few months they became good friends and she was invited to meet his mother and family. It was an entirely platonic relationship. They often went to the opera and cinema together and became members of the Dublin Film Society.

In October 1974, Brenda met Malcolm MacArthur in a pub off Grafton Street. He invited her out the next day and they went for dinner. The relationship quickly developed and after Christmas they both went to London where they began living together.

The following March they returned to Dublin and moved into MacArthur's rented flat at Fitzwilliam Square. During the day, the area is the heart of the city's financial district. At night, it transforms into Dublin's red light district, where prostitutes loiter.

Brenda became pregnant in January. They both decided to remain single and bring the child up together. On 22 October, 1975, the child was born at Mount Carmel Nursing Home. The baby boy was named Colm Malcolm William MacArthur.

In September 1981, Patrick Connolly offered them his rented flat in Donnybrook. The Senior Counsel refused to consider taking rent from the couple, citing a clause in his lease agreement which prohibited sub-letting. Connolly now moved into his own newly-built apartment at Dalkey. He had just acquired a luxury penthouse at Pilot View enjoying unsurpassed views across Dublin Bay to Howth Head.

MacArthur and his friend did not stay very long in Donnybrook. On 26 May, he and Brenda decided to move to the Canary Islands. They told friends that the baby was suffering from a serious skin complaint which needed exposure to the sun. They booked a package holiday to Los Cristianos, Tenerife, and were seen off at the airport by Connolly.

By this time money was beginning to run low. The couple had enjoyed an extravagant lifestyle but it had come at a cost. MacArthur had by now squandered close to £100,000. He was desperate to raise more cash.

On 8 July, MacArthur arrived back in Dublin. The country had just been through a period of intense activity by the paramilitaries. In the Canaries, MacArthur had read how the Provisional IRA had been responsible for a large number of major bank robberies and security van heists. The Provos had netted tens of thousands of pounds in the daring raids. To the desperate MacArthur it seemed the perfect solution. He resolved to carry out a large copycat raid. But first he would need a gun.

* * *

Several police officers have remarked to me that MacArthur had the mind of a killer but not the instincts of a criminal. He would prove this point clearly by the way he attempted to obtain a gun.

Criminals who do not have a weapon ready at hand will usually hire one from any number of underworld suppliers. The gun cannot be traced back to them and may well have been used in several other unrelated crimes. In other cases, they will steal a shotgun from a remote farmhouse and subsequently use it in crime. The extent of Malcolm MacArthur's homicidal state of mind is exhibited by the means he used to acquire a weapon.

As soon as he arrived back in Ireland, he booked into a guesthouse on Upper George's Street in Dun Laoghaire. Later that day, he went into a sports shop and bought a crossbow over the counter. Unlike the sale of firearms, there was no prohibition on the sale of these deadly weapons and no licence requirement. He also bought a shovel in the event that he killed somebody during the planned robbery and had to dispose of the body. Back at his lodgings he sawed off the barrel and stock of the crossbow to make it resemble a gun and painted it black. But it still was not realistic enough. He would have to acquire a real weapon.

For the next eleven days MacArthur laid low, careful to avoid any place where he might be recognised. He grew a beard and purchased a fisherman's hat and glasses to complete the disguise.

On Saturday, 17 July, he took the No. 41 bus from the city centre to Swords, a satellite town in north county Dublin. His destination was a clay pigeon shoot where he hoped to steal a shotgun. Passengers on the bus stared at the man dressed in a tweed jacket, hat, glasses and white open-necked shirt on a hot summer's day. Some thought the shovel wrapped in plastic was a rifle.

Residents tending their gardens were also curious about the stranger walking on the road out of Swords towards the shooting grounds at Balheary. He arrived at the shoot sometime around 1.45 pm. One participant, a doctor, immediately thought there was something odd about him. The doctor watched the man walk over towards his car, prompting him to lock the vehicle.

'It's a grand day,' the shooter said, 'are you interested in shooting yourself?' MacArthur responded that he was and had participated in the sport previously. For the rest of the day, the doctor kept a close eye on the stranger. He noticed the way the man stared at the scoreboard.

'He had a vacant look about him and he moved slowly when walking,' the doctor told police when reporting the suspicious person a couple of days later. Moreover, he told the Gardaí about one of the man's peculiar characteristics. 'He was wearing a pair of glasses which he had positioned on the middle of his nose but he seemed to hold his head down and he tended to look over the top of the glasses or through the top portion of the rim.'

Despite spending almost the entire day at the shoot, MacArthur never got near a gun. A similar venture the following day at Ashbourne, Co. Meath, proved equally unsuccessful.

Donal Dunne, a young farmer from Co. Offaly had advertised a shotgun for sale in the *Evening Press* around this time. MacArthur, who had been buying *The Irish Times* and an evening paper every day, followed up on the small ad. He decided he would need a car to travel there. He rang the Dunne's house several times to make an appointment but cancelled it twice saying his brother was ill. In fact he was having trouble getting a car. He would keep his final appointment.

The killer's attempts to get a vehicle ended in disaster in the Phoenix Park. But the needless murder of Nurse Gargan on 22 July did nothing to stop MacArthur from going ahead with his plan to get a gun.

*   *   *

Three days after the terrible killing of Nurse Gargan, a Dublin couple and their four grown-up children from Dublin went on a Sunday outing to Edenderry, Co. Offaly. The family thought the trip to the country would be good for their father who was recovering from a stroke. Somewhere along the route, as they searched for the Grand Canal, they got lost. The group pulled in off the road at a scenic spot and decided to have their picnic there. A lot of spent cartridges lay around the area and it appeared to be the site of a clay pigeon shoot.

A few family members went off looking for raspberries. One of the sons, aged 23, spotted blood on the ground. He bent down to have a better look. In the undergrowth he saw a large pool of blood and coins lying around the place. He bent down to pick up the coins and turned over a cardboard box, to find a pound note. Another brother and his sister arrived. One of them spotted a hand sticking out from under a box. The first son pulled back the box, revealing a man's arm. It was the body of the farmer, Donal Dunne.

The body was found lying face down. The left side of his head had been shattered by a shotgun blast just a few hours earlier. The sons alerted the rest of the group and they drove to Edenderry where they alerted the Gardaí.

*   *   *

Having failed to get a car, MacArthur had hitchhiked to Edenderry where he had arranged to meet Donal Dunne, who had advertised his shotgun for sale. Late on Saturday, 24 June, MacArthur arrived in the town and slept under a bridge. The following morning he met Donal Dunne in the town and travelled out to bogland off the Rathangan Road to demonstrate the distinctive Italian-made Miroku under-and-over type shotgun.

Dunne gave MacArthur the gun. MacArthur fired a shot at one of the targets. Then he turned to Donal Dunne. 'I'm sorry old chap,' he said as he shot him in the face. He left Donal Dunne's body in the bog hidden underneath cardboard boxes in bushes. He took Dunne's Ford Escort car and drove it back to Dublin.

Meanwhile, a group of Offaly people travelling to see their county's hurlers compete in Croke Park got lost on the way into the city. They spotted the Offaly registered Escort and thought that by following it they would end up at the stadium. Instead, MacArthur abandoned the car on Temple Lane, off Dame Street in the heart of the city. The hurling fans would not easily forget the eccentrically dressed man who led them astray.

Gardaí found the car on Monday and appealed for anyone who saw it being driven to Dublin to contact them.

*　*　*

The force was now dealing with an unprecedented number of killings – Bridie Gargan, Patricia Furlong, Robert Belton and now Donal Dunne. Could they be connected? Or were they all the work of different individuals? The Gardaí were under enormous pressure to come up with answers from a public unused to such a spate of murders.

Murder Squad chief, Detective Superintendent John Courtney was told to pay particular attention to the Gargan murder. His superior, Detective Chief Superintendent John O'Driscoll, had a hunch that this killer would strike again. O'Driscoll was particularly concerned at the discovery of the wrapped shovel in Phoenix Park which he considered odd and sinister.

Soon after the killing of Nurse Gargan, the police had a suspect in mind for her death. He was eliminated from their inquiries when forensic evidence ruled him out. Now Courtney was faced with another murder and he began to see a link. The common denominator in the slaying of Bridie Gargan and Donal Dunne was the use of both the victims' cars by the killer. The descriptions offered by witnesses at both locations also had a lot in common. Although he would not admit it in public for some time, he believed he was looking for one suspect. Courtney's theory about a double killer would be proved correct very soon.

'A stranger had been spotted lurking around Edenderry before the murder of Donal Dunne. The man had purchased a newspaper and a carton of milk from a shop and had then walked towards the canal. He sat near the water, staring into space. Some local people were able to provide details of his mannerisms,' Courtney recalls.

'One struck a chord. Some time earlier a doctor had alerted us about a man acting suspiciously during a clay pigeon shoot in Balheary in Swords. He thought he could be the fugitive we were hunting. A particular mannerism he had noticed was that the man peered over his glasses when speaking. So did the stranger spotted in Edenderry.' The Edenderry suspect, however, did not have a beard – but a beard is not a permanent characteristic and could easily have been shaved off.

Fingerprint expert Detective Sergeant Martin Hogan, based at the Technical Bureau, provided a major break when he discovered a match between prints left on the black plastic used to wrap the shovel in Phoenix Park and marks found on the newspaper and milk carton in Edenderry. The Gardaí were now definitely looking for one person, and he was back in Dublin. The Offaly supporters, who were discovered after a painstaking trawl, told the police about the man with the foppish manners they had followed.

The killer of Nurse Gargan had taken a taxi to Dun Laoghaire – the last known place he was seen. The Garda team now began to concentrate their search for the double killer in the south Dublin harbour town. Courtney put three of his most trusted detectives on the Dun Laoghaire trail, Detective Inspector Noel Conroy and Detective Sergeants Tony Hickey and Denis Donegan. It was vital the killer be caught before he could strike again.

* * *

Elizabeth Plunkett is pictured here during her holiday in St Tropez. She was brutally raped and murdered in 1976.

Michael Bambrick was convicted of the manslaughter of both Patricia McGauley and Mary Cummins.

Balgaddy dump, the area where Bambrick hid the bags containing Patricia McGauley's remains.

A mechanical digger in Bambrick's back garden searches for graves.

Marilyn Rynn was attacked
and murdered on her way
home at Christmas in 1995.

David Lawler was arrested for
the murder of Marilyn Rynn
after he voluntarily gave a
blood sample to the Gardaí.

Private Sean Courtney on duty in the Lebanon. He killed Patricia
O'Toole after offering to show her directions.

Patricia O'Toole pleaded
with Courtney, 'Don't ruin
your life.'

Esther McCann and 18 month-old Jessica were burnt to death in a
fire started by Frank McCann in Rathfarnham.

Frank McCann set out to murder his wife to keep
his sordid past a secret.

Wife, mother and popular local shopkeeper Joyce Quinn was brutally murdered by Kenneth O'Reilly.

Ray Quinn and his son David carrying Joyce's remains from St Brigid's Church in Kildare town.

Kenneth O'Reilly lay in wait for Joyce Quinn before attacking and killing her.

Larry Murphy was convicted of attempted murder and has been questioned about a number of other crimes.

John Cullen, the vindictive pimp who set fire to Dolores Lynch's house killing her and two members of her family.

Malcolm MacArthur arriving at the Central Criminal Court on 12 January 1983.

MacArthur now had a gun, but his financial problems were no better. He was getting even more desperate. He had spoken to Brenda Little in Tenerife over the phone a few times. Perhaps it was the calls to Brenda which prompted him to rack his mind for any old acquaintances who would have ready access to cash. It led to a bizarre development in the case on Wednesday, 4 August.

Harry Bieling, a former United States diplomat, lived in a small mock castle, called Camelot, in Killiney, County Dublin. His home enjoyed a fantastic view directly over Killiney Bay and further south along the coast to Bray Head and the Sugar Loaf mountain. The house, built of granite, was once the gate lodge for a much larger residence further down Victoria Road. Just before 6 pm he answered a knock on the front door to find a stranger standing there.

'Hello, do you remember me? I was at the party here about eight years ago,' said Malcolm MacArthur.

Bieling was indeed surprised. He could not place the man at all. MacArthur, who was carrying a suitcase, said he was a photographer and wondered if he could take some shots of the stunning view.

'If you have company, I will come back another time,' he offered.

The 48-year-old Bieling, embarrassed in case the visitor was somebody he ought to remember, said he was alone and allowed the man into his home. MacArthur mentioned a couple of people that they both knew. Suddenly he appeared to hesitate.

'I presume you have a sense of humour,' he said as he opened the case and took Donal Dunne's shotgun from it. Sitting on a chair directly opposite the retired diplomat he aimed the weapon.

'What kind of nonsense is this?' asked a terrified Bieling.

'It is no nonsense. I expect to get a lot of money from you,' the unwelcome guest replied.

Bieling, who had served in the US military, asked MacArthur if it was alright to pour himself a drink for the shock. MacArthur said it was fine as long as there was no gun in the drinks cabinet. He followed the householder as he made himself a large vodka.

A nervous Bieling said he had only £23 in the house. MacArthur said that he was surprised.

'I used to spend £500 or £600 a week when I had money,' MacArthur ventured.

He asked if the American had a cheque-book. Bieling said he had but there was very little money in the account. Disappointed, MacArthur, still gesticulating with the gun, stated: 'I expected at least £1,000 from your bank account.'

MacArthur said he would phone a friend as he intended staying the night. Bieling said this would be impossible as he was expecting his housekeeper, Bridget, back to wash the dishes after dinner.

'Oh, that is a complication,' MacArthur said.

Trying desperately to defuse the dangerous situation, Harry Bieling asked if the man had been doing this for long.

'A little over a year as there is very little money coming from my patrimony and I dislike working,' MacArthur said.

'Isn't this dangerous?'

'No, you would be surprised how easy it is to change identity. The only danger is the physical recognition but you can change that somewhat. When I first started doing this it was with a young guy who was very nervous but my accomplice now is much better.'

The gunman then asked for the cheque-book and Bieling said it was upstairs. MacArthur, with the gun to Bieling's back, followed him but they could not find the book. 'I think you are playing games with me,' MacArthur said ominously.

'It must be downstairs,' Bieling replied playing for time.

The American went down first, a few steps ahead of his captor. At the bottom he seized his chance and bolted for the door, banging it shut behind him. Out on the street, he ran to a nearby shop and telephoned the Gardaí. MacArthur ran in the opposite direction, hailing a lift from three men going towards Dalkey. He told them a friend had an accident and he wanted to alert the injured man's mother who lived in Pilot View, Dalkey. They thought the situation highly strange and informed the police after the hitcher got out near Bulloch Harbour.

The nature of the incident intrigued Detective Superintendent Michael Sullivan based in Dun Laoghaire. He thought it fitted a pattern. He rang his colleague Detective Superintendent John Courtney. 'I think I have your man out here,' he told him.

* * *

Running out of ideas and in need of some place to lie low, MacArthur turned to his old friend Patrick Connolly. He showed little sign of distress when he called to the Attorney General's apartment a few hours after the incident with Bieling. The Attorney General's home at Pilot View, just a short distance from the town of Dun Laoghaire and right on the coast, was the perfect hideaway for the double murder fugitive. Who would think of looking for him here?

The lawyer was delighted to see his old friend. He was even able to pass on a message. Brenda Little had been looking for her boyfriend a few days earlier wondering where he was. She thought he might be in Belgium looking after some stocks and shares. Connolly, who kept in regular touch with Brenda, had telephoned her the previous day and indeed earlier that day as well. The Attorney General asked what MacArthur was doing back in Ireland. He said he was sorting out some financial affairs. The barrister took this to mean his grandmother's estate.

Connolly asked if he had a place to stay and offered his guestroom. After a little feigned hesitation MacArthur took up the generous offer. Despite the sanctuary he had just found, MacArthur's homicidal impulses were still raging.

* * *

The following morning the Gardaí got their first substantial break. Between 9.30 and 10 am, a groggy Harry Bieling, who had had a few stiff drinks the night before to ease the shock of his terrifying experience, answered the telephone.

'This is your friend from yesterday,' the male voice said.

'Yes,' said Bieling immediately recognising his unwelcome visitor.

'Why did you run away?' inquired MacArthur with Beethoven's 7th Symphony playing in the background at the State's chief law officer's home. There was no reply.

'You must have been scared.' Still no response. Then after a few chilling seconds –

'A stupid joke gone sour. Did you ring the police?'

'Yes.'

'Will you ring the police or should I?' asked MacArthur, inquiring who should tell the Gardaí it was a joke. Bieling said the caller should.

'May I stop around at your house some evening to see you?' the caller ventured.

'Telephone me first,' answered Bieling before putting down the phone.

Around noon, Sergeant Patrick Fitzgerald was on duty in Dalkey station when he answered a call from a man who gave his name as Malcolm MacArthur. He said he was a freelance journalist and mentioned the incident at Bieling's house the night before. It was a joke which had gone sour, he said. The Sergeant asked him for his address but he said he had none and had stayed in Gardiner Street that night.

This was the first time the name Malcolm MacArthur had come up in the case and Sergeant Fitzgerald passed on the details of the call to the investigation team.

By this time, the murder hunt team were making steady progress in the case. The concentration of inquiries in Dun Laoghaire had turned up some leads. Now the Bieling incident was a source of hope amongst the Murder Squad.

The robbery attempt bore similar characteristics to their suspect's previous actions. As in the phone call to Donal Dunne's home when he said his brother was sick, again he had introduced a third party to Bieling when he mentioned an accomplice. He also talked about a third person to the men who gave him a lift outside Bieling's house. A further break for Detective Superintendent Courtney's men came on Friday, 6 August, when a newspaper vendor, John Monks, walked into Dun Laoghaire Garda station to tell of his suspicions about one of his customers.

Monks, who ran a news stand on Marine Road, said he first became suspicious of the man about a month before. The man just looked out of place: 'He was wearing a heavy jumper and a tweed hat while everyone else was going around in tee-shirts.' The newspaperman also mentioned how his customer, who would buy an *Irish Times* in the morning and either a *Press* or *Herald* in the evening wore bow ties and cravats.

'The first time I saw him, he had begun to grow a beard. He always wore glasses – either sunglasses or heavy-rimmed, square, brown glasses. I am sure he could not see through them as he always seemed to be looking out over them and when reading the paper he lifted them up and rested them on his forehead. I also saw him once on a red racing bike. The bike had a red luminous flash on the front wheel and an orange one on the back wheel. This was on 1 August last and his beard has been shaved off since then. I hadn't seen him for a number of days prior to this and when I saw him on that date he reminded me of the description of the man who had killed the girl in Phoenix Park,' Monks said.

He had also seen the man in the local bank. Police discovered later that MacArthur had opened a bank account under a false name and told the official that he was a freelance journalist. In fact, he hoped to use the account to lodge money when he eventually carried out an armed robbery.

The Garda murder investigation team immediately mounted a surveillance operation around the newspaper stall on Saturday. There was no sign of their suspect.

Unknown to them, MacArthur was finding his newfound lodgings very agreeable, sending for his morning and evening papers by taxi.

On Sunday, the Attorney General, who was a keen hurling fan, invited MacArthur to join him and members of his family in Croke Park. Kilkenny and Galway were playing in the All-Ireland semi-final. The most wanted man in the country was chauffeured across the city in a State limousine, driven by a garda. The group had some of the best seats in the park – Connolly sat in the VIP box which also held Garda Commissioner, Paddy McLaughlin. MacArthur sat a short distance away from them.

Connolly asked how the two murder cases were going. Speculation that a double killer was at work was now being aired in the media. Connolly told McLaughlin that somebody must know who the killer was. He said it was obvious that the murderer was a man who had shaved off his beard in recent days.

* * *

The net was closing in however. The mundane and unglamorous part of police work in a murder inquiry, as in any major investigation, is house-to-house inquiries. The Bieling incident had concentrated discreet police activity in the Dalkey/Killiney area. Detective Sergeants Kevin Tunney and Tony Hickey decided to concentrate their part of the inquiry around the Pilot View apartments. After all, the men who gave the Bieling suspect a lift said he had mentioned something about Pilot View. They questioned several of the residents. Many of them asked what the Gardaí were doing wasting their time asking mundane questions when a double killer was on the loose.

Tunney thought he was on to something when he stopped a foreign couple in a Daimler car at the entrance to the development. They acted suspiciously in the presence of the police. Tunney's suspicions were correct but they were nothing to do with the double murder. In fact, the foreigner they had stopped was one of the world's top international drug traffickers. Tunney was amazed to discover this information when he checked out the man's details with Interpol. He passed the file onto the Drugs Squad. A few weeks later, they would raid the address, but their suspect escaped through the roof of his penthouse in his pyjamas. It would become known as the Pyjama Case.

On 12 August, Detective Sergeant Hickey spoke to 76-year-old Alfred Solomons who lived at Pilot View. The officer asked if there had been any strangers in the area in the recent past. Solomons, who was head of the Residents Association, quickly remembered a rude gentleman staying in the Attorney General's apartment next to his own. The man, whom he thought was the lawyer's nephew, was a frequent visitor. He had not seen him for about 18 months but he was back now. The detective was told how the man lacked manners.

'Although I met this man on the stairs on a number of occasions, he never spoke to me. On one occasion either in late 1981 or earlier this year, I saw that man in difficulties with his car, a Mini Minor. I sprayed his engine wire with some damp start liquid and the car started and he drove away. I think the most he said was "thank you". There was no conversation,' the elderly resident remembered.

One detail in particular about the description rang a bell with Hickey – he wore a cravat. Back at Dun Laoghaire station, Hickey's discovery was greeted equally with disbelief and excitement.

For the Gardaí, it was a highly unusual set of circumstances in which to find themselves. A search team does not simply barge into an Attorney General's home on the basis of the statement of an elderly man. Courtney decided to get some background information on the Attorney General and any possible connections with somebody called Malcolm MacArthur.

The intruder at Bieling's home had mentioned that he attended parties there. Bieling could not remember everyone who attended, but he told detectives his caterer would. A number of detectives were sent to track down the caterer. Yes, she remembered Malcolm MacArthur. After all, she told the police, he had once proposed marriage to her. It was a very peculiar proposal. He said they should have a child and raise it to the age of seven and then abandon the infant. He wanted to do this because he claimed he was abandoned by his parents at that age. The Gardaí were amazed at what she was able to tell them about this Malcom MacArthur. Although she had not seen him for several years she had the name and address of one of his friends, an elderly accountant in Mount Merrion.

The 70-year-old man, who acted as a sort of unofficial information officer for Dublin's gay community, told them how he used to drink in Bartley Dunnes pub with Patrick Connolly. It was there he met Brenda Little and Malcolm MacArthur. He filled the Gardaí in on private details of MacArthur and Little's life. He thought they both liked living their separate lives although he did not suspect MacArthur of being homosexual. 'I never knew him in any way to be interested in men.'

He had met MacArthur on the day of Connolly's appointment as Attorney General with Brenda Little and their child. He occasionally arranged to go for drinks in the Shelbourne Hotel with MacArthur.

'When I first met Malcolm he didn't work and sometimes he wrote articles for the *London Times* History Supplement. He was a very wealthy person at this time,' the old man recalled.

The detectives couldn't believe their luck. It was the break they had been looking for. With a little more discreet digging and with an address supplied by the elderly accountant they discovered that MacArthur had previously lived in the Attorney General's Donnybrook apartment.

It was time to move. There was no time for the niceties of informing the powers that be what they had discovered. There was a double killer on the loose who showed all the signs of striking again. Outside No. 6 Pilot View, the team which had been hunting the killer of Bridie Gargan and Donal Dunne began to gather.

Led by Detective Superintendent John Courtney from the Murder Squad, the unit was supplemented by officers from the fledgling Serious Crime Squad. It was a handpicked team.

Courtney's second in command was Detective Inspector Noel Conroy, who was based at Cabra station and had been with the inquiry from day one. The brutal assault on Bridie Gargan on 22 July occurred in his police district. Conroy is currently the force's second most senior officer as Deputy Commissioner in charge of Operations. Detective Sergeant Tony Hickey, who was attached to the Murder Squad, is now an Assistant Commissioner and led the inquiry into the murder of journalist Veronica Guerin. Also at the scene were: Detective Sergeant Denis Donegan, now Detective Superintendent in the Dublin South division, Detective Garda Brian Sherry and Detective Garda Frank Hand from the Serious Crime Squad who was murdered while escorting a post office cash consignment at Drumree, Co. Meath some years later.

Hickey and Donegan, in a Renault 4 van, were first at the scene in the afternoon of Friday, 13 August. MacArthur had returned to the apartment just ten minutes before their arrival. He had just disposed of the imitation handgun made from the crossbow in Bulloch Harbour.

Both officers kept a keen watch on the Attorney General's second-floor penthouse. They couldn't believe their luck at 4.45 pm when they saw their suspect peer through one of the upstairs windows. It was time to move in.

Armed with a search warrant signed earlier by Courtney under the Offences Against the State Act, they went to the front door of the block known as Carnsore and pressed the intercom to apartment No. 6, announcing that they were gardaí, but they got no response.

By this time other detectives began rushing to the scene. One of them, Frank Hand, was directed to cover the back of the building. Fifteen minutes later Courtney and Conroy joined their men in the foyer as they tried to plan a way of capturing the man they had been hunting for the past three weeks.

At 5.15 pm, a taximan, Niall Cooney, pulled up at the building and blew the horn. He was bundled away by the detectives who discovered that he was delivering two hacksaw blades, a bottle of Perrier water and *Town and Country* magazine to apartment No. 6. Ironically, Cooney was the taxi driver who had picked up MacArthur in Ballymun just after the Gargan killing and taken him to Dun Laoghaire. MacArthur had rung the taxi rank at Dun Laoghaire and given instructions for the blades to be purchased in one of two local hardware stores. It was a way of having messages delivered which he had frequently used over the previous days.

The tense standoff continued for another hour and 15 minutes until the Attorney General returned home in his chauffeur-driven State Mercedes. Courtney spoke to Connolly and said they wanted to question his house guest in connection with an aggravated burglary at the home of Mr Harry Bieling in Killiney. He made no mention of the fact that the visitor was also wanted for two of the most brutal murders ever committed in the State.

At the request of the Superintendent, Attorney General Connolly tried unsuccessfully to contact MacArthur on the intercom. They then moved to a neighbour's apartment where Mr Connolly rang his home telephone number but there was no reply.

The barrister agreed to hand over the keys to the penthouse. Hickey and Detective Garda Sherry both drew their official Smith and Wesson .38 revolvers and crept down the corridor. Hickey placed the key in the mortice lock and turned it, but the door remained shut, it was secured from the inside.

He heard a sound inside and shouted: 'We are gardaí, please open the door.'

The voice inside replied: 'I will not, is Mr Connolly there?'

Superintendent Courtney asked Connolly to come from the foyer to the top of the stairs outside his apartment. Connolly then called to MacArthur: 'Open the door.' Within seconds, the Yale lock was opened, the safety chain released and the door eased open.

The detectives stormed in and bundled the fugitive to the ground, searching him for a concealed gun. The Attorney General entered soon after. He told his old friend: 'You are on your own on this.'

The police now turned their attention to finding out where MacArthur had hidden any guns.

'Where's the gear hidden?' one of them shouted.

'I have a shotgun hidden upstairs,' he volunteered.

He then led them to an alcove door on the landing, 'It is in there on the left behind the old papers.' One of the detectives crawled into the storage space and removed a black refuse bag and placed it on the landing. One end of the plastic bag was partially open, exposing the butt end of a shotgun.

When gardaí asked him to account for the weapon he replied: 'I found it under some bushes while walking on Killiney Hill. You will find a bag of cartridges, possibly ten beside where you found the gun.'

The officer returned to the alcove and, slightly to the right where the gun was hidden, he removed a white plastic bag containing the ammunition. Weeks of painstaking inquiries and following up of hundreds of leads finally came together when they checked the serial number on the gun. It was the Miroku gun, one of just three in the country, stolen from and used to murder Donal Dunne.

The detectives carried the sawn-off shotgun and cartridges into Connolly's room where they laid them out on the bed. Detective Superintendent Courtney asked Connolly if he had any knowledge of the gun and he replied: 'I never saw it in my life.'

MacArthur interrupted: 'Mr Connolly knows nothing about it.'

The Gardaí at last had their suspect for the double murder. But there was no power of arrest and questioning for a homicide. Instead they arrested him under section 30 of the Offences Against the State Act for possession of firearms at Camelot – Harry Bieling's house. It gave the detectives a 48-hour period to interrogate MacArthur.

In the patrol car on the way back to Dun Laoghaire station, Courtney asked his prisoner about the incident at Camelot.

'That was a joke I was playing. It was only a practical joke that turned sour,' MacArthur explained.

'It was a funny joke,' Courtney retorted.

* * *

At Dun Laoghaire Garda Station, a former convent in the centre of the town, MacArthur was taken to an Inspector's Office where he was questioned by teams of two officers into the early hours. Conscious that they were dealing with someone who was in a very volatile state, he was treated cautiously. He first denied any knowledge of the two murders.

Eventually, when asked again and again about the slayings he said: 'I wish I could get my thoughts together and tell you what happened.'

The detectives switched their line of questioning. They engaged MacArthur in general conversation. He outlined his family background for them. He told them he was a humanist but could also be described as an atheist or agnostic. His life since he graduated from university had been taken up with travel, study and recreation. He had a deep interest in philosophy and astro-physics.

After a meal of tea and a hamburger, the Murder Squad began to close in on their subject with more intense questioning about the killings. What was his motive? Was it robbery? Soon MacArthur began to outline how he had spent all his inheritance and was now in serious debt. 'I handled this inheritance unwisely having attained my academic qualifications. Money or position meant nothing to me. All that money meant was that it gave me the ability to buy time to think and discover myself. It bought me freedom and the time for study and research, but I now find myself in financial difficulties and in debt to the tune of £600.'

'Is that why you had the gun, to commit robberies?' one of them asked.

'Yes.'

'Because of your present financial difficulties?'

'Yes, desperate situations require desperate remedies.'

Continuing the momentum, the interrogators again asked about the two murders and were surprised by the next reply.

'I want to compose my thoughts, I will tell you the truth in the morning.'

A mattress was brought into the office from one of the cells and MacArthur slept there overnight, watched over by two armed detectives who stayed on duty outside. The following morning, MacArthur began to make a lengthy statement in which he confessed to the killings of both Bridie Gargan and Donal Dunne and to the incident at Bieling's house. It was an experience any of those involved will never forget. MacArthur gripped the table in front of him so tightly his knuckles went white. His eyes began spinning out of control in their sockets, his tan vanished from his face.

'I am regressing,' he told them. 'I want to get my thoughts in categorical order.'

Then he began his confession: 'I affirm that I am responsible for the deaths of the nurse Bridie Gargan and farmer Donal Dunne ...'

* * *

Amazingly, most of the newspapers had not yet caught on to the significance of the arrest or the fact that the killer had been held in the Attorney General's home. Nevertheless, the storm clouds were beginning to gather over Connolly. It wasn't until after his house guest had been taken into custody that he learned from Detective Superintendent Pat Doocey of the Serious Crime Squad that MacArthur was wanted for murder. The news came like a bolt from the blue for the Attorney General and he was deeply shocked. He had absolutely no idea what MacArthur was up to.

As more police officers began entering the apartment, sifting for evidence and checking for technical clues, the enormity of what had occurred was beginning to sink in. Connolly summoned some family members to the apartment and it was decided he would have to ring the Taoiseach at his holiday home on the Blasket Islands to inform him of the impending crisis.

The line to Charles Haughey's private island, Inisvickileaun, was crackly when he finally got through at about 10 pm. The Taoiseach did not appear to understand the significance of the events.

'Do I know this MacArthur?' the Taoiseach asked.

'No,' the Attorney General replied.

Some believe Haughey simply thought Connolly was informing him of an arrest in the double murder case. Connolly, who had made long-standing arrangements to go on a citywide tour of the United States, told the Taoiseach that he intended to continue with his plans and fly out the following morning, Haughey didn't prevent him.

'Have a good holiday,' the Taoiseach said.

Relations between the Connolly family and the Gardaí, however, were strained that night. One family member launched a verbal attack on the investigation chief, Detective Superintendent John Courtney for not tipping the Attorney General off. Courtney said he was just doing his job as a policeman and was not in the business of playing up to anyone, however elevated their position.

The following morning, Saturday 14 August, Courtney and Detective Inspector Noel Conroy returned to Pilot View, seeking a statement from Connolly – but he was in no mood to talk to them. Tempers flared and the Attorney General told the two detectives in no uncertain terms that he was an innocent party and intended to continue with his holiday plans. He would make a statement when he returned from America.

By now, the frightening significance of what had occurred was finally sinking in at Government level, although the press was still lagging behind. There was consternation when it was learned that Connolly had flown to London for a connecting flight to New York in the midst of the crisis. Charles Haughey rang Connolly at his London hotel and demanded that he return immediately but he refused, insisting he would continue with his holiday plans. Haughey got the impression that Connolly was about to board a plane to New York and did not press him.

Sunday morning's papers were full of news of the arrest and the fact that the double murder suspect had been staying as a guest at the Attorney General's home. It was by any standards a sensational story. The Taoiseach's experienced advisors counselled that this was only the beginning. In New York, meanwhile, Connolly could have seen for himself the embarrassment he was causing the Government. On Monday, the *New York Post* carried the headline: 'Biggie Flees Here After Slay Scandal.' The rival *Daily News* said: 'Irish Lawman in shocker.'

Government officials were finally able to persuade the Attorney General of the necessity to return and made arrangements for him to fly by Concorde to London, enabling him to arrive back to Dublin by Monday night. At Heathrow airport, newspaper reporters and a BBC television crew pursued the barrister as he hurried to a waiting Air Corps Beechcraft, which had been sent specially to pick him up. A State car took him from Baldonnel Aerodrome straight to Haughey's mansion at Kinsealy. Outside, a media pack was already in place and anxious to report any new developments.

The meeting in the Taoiseach's palatial home lasted half an hour and both men were of the one mind. The Attorney General would have to announce his resignation. As they chatted about the events of the last 72 hours, a secretary typed up his resignation statement.

※　※　※

The technical examination of No. 6 Pilot View took a few days. Forensic and fingerprint experts from Garda Headquarters searched for vital clues which would further cement the prosecution case against MacArthur.

Officers looked into every nook and cranny of the flat. It consisted of an entrance hall, a large lounge area on the left with a kitchen-cum-dining-room just off it. There was a bathroom and toilet further to the left of the hall. To the right of the stairway was the guestroom where MacArthur stayed. It overlooked the entrance to the Carnsore apartment block and the car park. It provided the occupant with a full view of comings and goings in the small complex. This room was subjected to minute scrutiny.

The Gardaí were to find several extraordinary and bizarre items. These shed new light on the case and revealed how Malcolm MacArthur may have planned to kill again.

In his suitcase, stored against the wall at the end of the bed, they discovered a brown envelope. It contained two books, one was *A Materialist Theory of the Mind* by DM Armstrong, the other was *Forensic Medicine* published by Arnold. Inserted in the pathology book in between pages on Dying Declarations were two handwritten notes. The notes set out how to commit a murder using a contrived electrical device and make it appear accidental. There were also references to the preparation of the murder scene both before and after the killing. MacArthur had also noted passages relating to disguising guns and the use of rubber gloves in committing crime.

From these notes, investigators were left of the opinion that MacArthur had planned the death of a woman, perhaps a female relative.

The notes carry diagrams and drawings of how to wire up an electric fire which would administer the lethal shock. The reminders are meticulous in their detail. For example, he refers to bringing 'two black bags for taking equipment away.' There is also a reference 'wear gloves always – no prints.'

> *Electric fire with faulty plug attached. Adaptor left in wall perhaps or fused adaptor ... plug pulled out. None of my finger prints – make sure hers on handle. Take away one of her fuses if it appears there are too many with ... and body of fire. Fuse to be left behind unplugged.*

Other parts of the memo to himself refer to bringing 'leather straps or tape (cloth to be put between tape and cloth dividing it in two) ... A gag, A blindfold, Additional rope for tying up across chest.' The most incriminating notes come in the following page, which leave

no doubt about his intended target. The text of his crime plan goes
as follows:

> *Wait for a while to ensure that death is final. During this time take a few
> very important items (certain small photo) into my possession. Make an
> inventory of other important items too so that I can check on their
> presence when I arrive for the funeral.'*

> *Letters from me left in prominent place – on table or in or beside her
> address book or telephone directory (if an envelope then tear out the
> stamp) – put her prints on the letter & envelope – giving my address &
> telephone number for a certain length of time, etc.*

> *Return to that address & wait for message. Or if necessary ring up on
> a pretext.*

> *Then give instructions to [named person] & hurry over to take charge.
> (Death Cert) (New suit, paper – Times, undertaker & grave flowers,
> cleric at grave?) Inform a few of her friends [named people] (Safeguard
> & increase collections – photos, etc.)*

> *Then on with the job   Shaw & O'Reilly? Sell car and furniture, etc.
> right away.[1]*

The notes are chilling in their meticulousness of how to plan,
execute and then react after the killing. There can be no doubt that
he was preparing to kill the close female relative in his bid to get
more money to finance his charmed lifestyle.

He hoped that by murdering a relative, he would come into another
large inheritance. Indeed, he was so anxious to come into the cash that
he noted he would have to sell off the victim's car and furniture
immediately. And could the reference to Shaw and O'Reilly in reality
be referring to the English serial killers Shaw and Evans who set out
to rape and kill one woman a week?

His notes also carry a passage headed 'Diary'. In two short
paragraphs, he sets out what must have been his initial itinerary:

> *July 6 – depart Tenerife and arrive London then to Continent (Belgium)
> and then to Ireland.*

> *Aug 4 – arrive Ireland – stay in Connolly's.*

---

1. See Appendix for reproduction of originals.

Close to where the detectives found the notes, were more items which suggested that MacArthur had done more than just research his next crime.

In a white plastic bag, they discovered a folded length of pink nylon clothes line. There was also a piece of the same type of rope, approximately two feet long with a double loop at one end, a knot in the centre and wash knotted at the other end. The bag also contained a 13-amp pin plug, a two-pin plug and round switch together with a phase tester. There was also a roll of sellotape. Another bag contained brown vinyl gloves.

A set of keys found in the room included one which opened a grey cash box which contained an assortment of personal handwritten notes. The detectives also found his passport, an Ordnance Survey map of Co. Meath, three green cravats, all spotted, a white floppy linen hat with a dark band, a knotted dark blue tie with a gold stripe and a dark blue raincoat.

Detectives also wonder about MacArthur's actions in the hours before his arrest. There is no doubt that he intended using the hacksaw blades to saw off the barrels of Donal Dunne's shotgun. Was this to use in a robbery? Or had he intended killing someone later that day? And, if so, who? It couldn't be the female relative referred to in his notes since he planned to electrocute this victim some time later. Perhaps it was Harry Bieling or another friend?

The existence of the notes was to prove invaluable to the prosecution in fighting defence claims later that the accused was insane at the time. How could he be insane when he plotted his crimes so meticulously?

* * *

Malcolm MacArthur is currently incarcerated in Arbour Hill jail in Dublin. In a move which caused enormous controversy at the time, the prosecution only pursued the charge of murdering Bridie Gargan. The killer pleaded guilty and was sentenced to life imprisonment in a trial which lasted just ten minutes. No statement was read out in court nor any evidence given in the trial. The State has never explained why MacArthur wasn't charged with Donal Dunne's murder.

Angry crowds waited outside as he was driven away to prison. It was a very unsatisfactory conclusion to one of the most bizarre and violent episodes in Irish life.

MacArthur has made several attempts to get parole, all of which have been turned down. Such has been the impact of his killings that every month after a particularly serious crime, the jail authorities receive three or four reported sightings of Malcolm MacArthur across the country.

* * *

Soon after the arrest, the Taoiseach summoned Detective Superintendent Courtney and his superior, Chief Superintendent John Paul McMahon, to his home at Kinsealy. He asked them about the circumstances of the case. They told him the facts. Haughey asked if they could have informed him of the seriousness of the developments. Courtney replied no. They had to move fast at the time. He said if the circumstances arose again in relation to any Minister – even Brian Lenihan, the Taoiseach's close friend – 'we would do the same'. Haughey seemed reassured. He then regaled them with stories about Co. Kerry and his island home.

A NARROW ESCAPE

'Well, she's alive isn't she.'
– Larry Murphy.

IT was the summer of 1996. Long before Larry Murphy's photo would be splashed across the front page of every newspaper in the country for one of the most chilling crimes perpetrated in recent times. Jailed for 14 years for abduction, rape and attempted murder – committed in the most barbaric fashion – Murphy would become even more infamous for what he *might* have done. Speculation about him reached fever pitch when it was revealed that he was the focus of inquiries by detectives investigating the disappearances of three women, Annie McCarrick, Jo Jo Dullard and Deirdre Jacob.

All three had vanished within a geographical triangle, and the crime for which Murphy was convicted in 2000 made him a suspect in these Missing Persons cases. So much so that detectives repeatedly visited him in jail to question him about the women. But Murphy remained silent.

In fact, Murphy has little to say to anybody about his crimes. In prison he never discusses with other sex offenders the way he raped and tried to kill a young businesswoman. On the one occasion that he has spoken briefly about his crime, his only remark about his victim showed how little remorse he has: 'She was lucky,' were his words, each one pronounced slowly and deliberately.

* * *

In the summer of 1996, Larry Murphy was a well-respected self-employed carpenter, virtually unknown outside his own small community. On a Sunday evening he returned to his house at Ballinacarrig, Castledermot, Co. Kildare at about 7.40 pm, after spending the afternoon drinking. His wife Margaret was chatting with a close family friend in the kitchen. Murphy asked her if she would like to go out for a drink. She told him she was too busy in the kitchen. He replied that he was going out anyway.

The other woman, who was in her mid-20s, mentioned that she had to see her boyfriend that night. He was picking her up at her home, but she had no way of getting back there. Larry Murphy offered to drive her home.

Murphy and the young woman got into his 1987 Wexford registered car at around 8 pm and headed for Castleroe. They chatted along the way and Murphy mentioned that he had just bought something for his wife. The friend asked if she could see the present.

'He said he would show it to me in a while,' she recalls.

As the car approached the young woman's home, Larry Murphy showed no sign of slowing down.

'He passed by the turn left for my house and continued on a few hundred yards and turned right into the lane which is the back entrance to a farm. When he had passed by the junction I asked him where was he going but he said nothing and continued on.'

The woman pressed Murphy to explain what he was doing but he remained silent. Suddenly, Murphy veered off the main road and sped up a remote boreen. At a fork in the lane, he brought the silver Toyota Corolla to a halt. The woman was petrified. The driver was studying his next move.

'Without saying anything he put his left arm around my shoulder. I cannot remember exactly, but he may have put his right hand on my leg. I was wearing shorts and a T-shirt. I asked what he was doing and pushed him back. Suddenly, he grabbed me with both hands around the throat and pushed me down towards the front seat of the car.

'He said nothing. His expression had totally changed on his face. It was a side of him I had never seen before.

'I got my hand on the door handle beside me and broke his grip on my neck. I jumped out of the car and ran back along the lane towards the main road.'

Larry Murphy jumped out of the vehicle and gave chase. He caught up with the woman and grabbed her from behind. He took hold of her arms and pulled her towards him. His expression had changed.

'Please, please don't tell Mags,' he pleaded.

She was aghast – her best friend's husband had attacked her in broad daylight on a country lane.

'I was frightened and shaking and couldn't believe what was happening, especially from Margaret's husband. I agreed to get back into the car, we got in and he drove me back up home. He pleaded with me not to tell Margaret. When we reached home, I ran into the house, through the kitchen and into the bathroom and locked the door. I was very frightened and upset by what had happened. He came after me and banged on the bathroom door. He asked me to let him in; that he wanted to talk to me.'

In the meantime, Margaret Murphy had changed her mind and decided to join her husband for a drink. She drove to her friend's house to meet him.

Inside, Larry Murphy paced the kitchen. The young woman changed and went out front. She was pale and frightened and still had tears in her eyes.

'Larry said nothing as I passed through the kitchen. I got into the car. Margaret asked me what was wrong as she saw I was crying and was upset about something. I said nothing.'

As his victim explained to gardaí: 'Margaret was told herself by Larry what he had done to me. He said to her he had grabbed me. I guess I didn't give him time enough to squeeze my throat further as I pushed him away immediately and jumped out of the car. After that I hated Larry and things have never been the same between us.' She explained she still remained on very friendly terms with his wife. The incident was never reported to the police.

Larry Murphy had struck, perhaps for the first time, but certainly not for the last. He had chosen broad daylight on a summer's evening to assault a close family friend, a woman who chatted daily to his wife. As he would prove some time later, he was capable of anything.

That summer Murphy's disdain for women would cause one man to remember him. Murphy was in the Glen Lounge pub in Donard when he made a grab at a woman. Trevor Moody, a fitter from Stratford on Slaney, Co. Wicklow, was friendly with the woman's brother. He didn't see the incident but some time later when he was in the woman's company she pointed Murphy out to him. It was enough to stamp Murphy's image in the man's mind – with dramatic consequences.

To some people Larry Murphy looked the epitome of the boy next door. Almost six feet tall, with fair hair and blue eyes, he looked much younger than his 36 years. One person who observed him described the well-built carpenter as having 'boyish looks'. The father of two was described by locals at Woodfield, Baltinglass, where he had built a bungalow, as the 'perfect husband'.

He grew up in the small village of Stratford on the outskirts of Baltinglass, in west Wicklow. Murphy was one of seven children; he had five sisters and a brother. His father, Larry, had worked in the construction industry before retiring with a disability. At 16, Murphy left the Vocational School in Baltinglass, where he excelled at woodwork. Academically, he showed no great capacity for learning and he yearned to start working. His gift with his hands didn't go unnoticed by his woodwork teacher, the school's vice principal, who gave him some work. For six years he worked alongside his former teacher producing salad bowls and other wooden tableware items.

Subsequently, he worked for a number of construction companies and also tried his hand at roofing houses.

Socially, the young carpenter wasn't very adept. Murphy hung around local pubs in Baltinglass, sometimes venturing into Carlow, but wasn't very successful with the opposite sex. The young man's habit of singling women out in a social setting and fixing his gaze on them made those around him feel very uncomfortable. Many described him as a loner, always on the periphery of the group, with an unsettling effect on single women.

Murphy's main pastime was hunting. He owned a 12-gauge shotgun, the cartridges of which were stuffed into the side door pockets of his car. He would go shooting pheasant and foxes in the foothills of the Wicklow Mountains and the remote woodland of west Wicklow. It gave the young carpenter an excellent knowledge of this isolated area.

By the early 1990s, Murphy had set out on his own. He earned a reputation as an excellent carpenter and his services were much in demand. As the amount of work grew, he started charging high rates for his time. But those who tried to bargain with him over prices saw a different side to the quiet tradesman.

'If anybody haggled with him about the price of a job or suggested delaying payment, he'd suddenly get very aggressive. He'd display a level of anger way out of proportion in the circumstances. People reported being frightened of that side of him,' said one detective who later investigated Murphy's background.

In 1994 he married Margaret, who worked in a store in Carlow. They had met in a disco at the Kilkea Castle Hotel.

The couple first moved to a house in Ballinacarrig, Castledermot, Co. Kildare. By 1997 he had completed a large new bungalow for his young family at Woodfield, around three miles east of Baltinglass. He bought a van and was working as a freelance carpenter on building sites all over Leinster, travelling into counties Dublin, Kildare, Carlow and Laois on a regular basis. This pattern of daily travel in the east midlands would arouse deep suspicions amongst detectives about Larry Murphy at a much later stage.

*   *   *

On Friday evening, 11 February, 2000, a young civil servant drove to Carlow town for an appointment. A few hours later at 8.10 pm she left Carlow. She is sure of the time. She was due home by 8.30 pm and checked her watch before getting into the vehicle. The car was parked just a short distance from another car, which was owned by a young businesswoman she had just visited. A man sitting a short distance away in a Fiat Punto car caught her attention.

'I got into my car and then I noticed a man sitting in a car in one of the parking bays opposite where I was parked. His car was facing onto the roadway. It was a blue Fiat. He was alone in the car. I would describe him as 35 years of age with straight brown hair, cut short with a rounded face,' the woman said.

There was something about him that just wasn't right. 'When I sat in my car I looked across at him and it looked to me as if he was fidgety and he kept putting his head down and raising it again for another look at me. He did not open the car door. For some reason I became nervous and I picked up my mobile phone to see if it was on and I put it beside the gear stick. I started the car and drove out.'

Her anxiety was fully justified. Larry Murphy had arrived on the street about 45 minutes earlier. Someone else who had seen him had become equally suspicious of him skulking around the area.

Then minutes later, after locking up, the young businesswoman made her way with the day's takings of £700 to her car parked a short distance away. The same man, by this time out of the Punto, also struck her as being out of place.

'As I walked to my car I noticed a man standing opposite my car on the left-hand side about 20 feet away. I noticed him because there seemed to be a light shining near him. You don't usually see anybody around that area in the evenings. I think he had his hands in his pockets. He looked distracted and he was just walking over and back,' the woman recalls.

It now appears Larry Murphy had been lying in wait for her all along. He had been casing the premises for almost an hour beforehand and had probably visited the area a number of times over the course of a few days, monitoring her movements.

'As I got nearer my car, the man noticed me and started coming over to me. I have central locking in my car, which I had just unlocked. He came around the back of the car. Even though I saw him, I was startled. He said something like "give me money" or "can I have some money?"'

Nothing could prepare her for Murphy's next move. He hit out, striking the woman across the face and knocking her back. The force of the blow broke her nose. She tried to get her balance back and reached out for the car door. In no time, Murphy was on top of her, grabbing her throat with both hands. Almost in the same movement he was pushing her into the small car.

The strongly-built carpenter then shoved the young woman across from the driver's seat onto the passenger side. 'When he got me over to the passenger side he said "Where are the keys?" I said I didn't know. I dropped one set of keys before I was pushed in the car. I still had another set in my hand. He eventually got the keys for the car in the footwell. He was delighted that he got them.'

Murphy's abduction plot was working to plan. Detectives who subsequently investigated the case are amazed at how quickly Murphy moved. One experienced investigator, Detective Garda Mark Carroll, now retired, says Murphy moved with frightening speed.

'It was very unusual the way he took the girl off the street; the way he had the power to take her so fast. He had a lot of physical power. He moved like a rocket, took complete control and threw her into the car. You'd have to think it was planned and rehearsed. You'd have to ask, had he done it before?'

He forced the woman to lay down on the passenger seat and used his elbow to lever her head onto the handbrake. He only lifted his elbow once to release the brake and throw the car into gear. He gave a few revs before working the vehicle onto the road and manouvering just 25 feet away to where he had his small 1997 Kildare registered Fiat hatchback.

All this time, the young woman tried to free herself but Murphy just leaned harder on his elbow, preventing any attempt at escape. Here Murphy showed further evidence of having calculated his every move. Instead of bringing ropes and tape with which to tie the woman up – and which could later be connected to him – he demanded the woman remove her clothing.

He told her to take off her bra. Frightened, she complied and he grabbed it from her. He then used the underwear to bind both her hands. The knot was so tight that the woman's hands began to turn blue and she lost all feeling in them.

'That's when he asked me to give him the money. I told him I couldn't because my hands were tied. He reached into the back seat and grabbed the two money bags from the top of my black bag. I felt numb with shock and fear. I thought he was going to kill me.'

Having checked through the money bags containing £700 cash, Murphy took a headband hanging from the rear view mirror and used it as a gag. To further prevent any escape, he removed both her boots and left them in the car's footwell.

At this stage Murphy got out and walked around to the passenger side. He dragged his victim out and made her stand up, frogmarching her around to the back of his vehicle.

'The next thing I knew the boot was open. He caught me by the back of the neck and pushed me head first with a lot of force. When he put me in the boot I kicked and screamed. I wasn't long in the boot when the car started moving. It was going very fast.'

To drown out the woman's cries for help, Murphy turned his car radio to full volume. Out of Carlow town he set off on a journey which would take them through three counties: Carlow, Kildare and Wicklow.

He drove northeast on the Monasterevin road towards the little village of Kilkea, nine miles away. A mile or so from the River Barrow and a few miles from Castledermot, Kilkea is situated between the main Carlow to Dublin and Carlow to Monasterevin roads. Isolated and dark in the gloomy winter's night, Larry Murphy knew the place well. He should do. It was just a few hundred yards from his wife's family home. It was where, four years earlier, he had attacked his wife's friend.

The journey across the country roads had taken about 25 minutes. The young woman in the boot of the Punto had been thrown around very roughly by the speed at which Murphy was travelling. Underneath her lay Murphy's tools and there was a strong smell of oil and metal in the confined space. In the corner was a little football, belonging to one of Murphy's young children.

There was silence for a few seconds after he brought the car to a halt at the entrance to a field off a small boreen. She could hear Murphy push back the car seat and wind down the seat back. Then he moved around the back of the car.

'I could hear the click of the boot. He pulled me out and pushed me in front of him to the driver's seat and told me to sit down.'

'We were in a field, in a very dirty, mucky dirt track area. I couldn't see any lights nearby. The driver's seat was pushed back and I could see the baby chair in the back seat behind the passenger seat when he pushed me down.'

The woman was still bound as Murphy began to indecently assault her in the front of the car. He removed her clothing and then took down his own trousers and underwear. Over the next 15 minutes or so he raped her violently. Murphy demanded that the woman kiss him during the sexual assault.

After the ordeal, the young woman was terrified that Murphy was going to kill her. 'I felt so numb I couldn't move. I just hoped it would all end. I feared for my life all the time – I thought this is it.'

As best she could, she moved away from Murphy and shunted herself onto the passenger seat. Her assailant was acting as if nothing had happened.

'He asked me if I was married. I lied and said "yeah". I lied because it felt safer and I was so afraid.'

Ominously, Murphy began to tell her about his own life. He revealed he was married with two boys. He wasn't acting like a man who intended releasing her at any stage.

'My hands were blue; the bra was tied so tightly around my wrists and they were really hurting. He loosened the knot and took me out of the car again. I pleaded with him not put me in the boot but he said he had to because I'd start making noise.'

This time Murphy removed the headband from around her mouth and used it to tie her hands behind her back. He used the bra to gag her mouth. He then got back into the car and set off for a new location.

The attacker skirted around the village of Kilkea and headed east towards the N9, the main Dublin to Carlow road. He joined the road for about a mile heading south back towards Carlow before turning off on a small by-road just before the town of Castledermot. Murphy headed back north to the hamlet of Sheriffhill and then east in the general direction of Baltinglass, crossing the main Blessington to Baltinglass road as he did so.

Now he began heading further east towards the army's isolated artillery firing range, the Glen of Imaal, in the foothills of the Wicklow Mountains. At a place called Spinan's Cross, which is not mentioned on most maps, Murphy turned off the small country road onto a dirt track leading to a forestry plantation. He had covered almost 15 miles in 20 minutes. He took the Punto about three quarters of a mile into the forest. The area is known locally as Spinan's Hill, Kilranelagh. Once again, it was a very familiar place to the kidnapper. The bungalow he shared with his wife and two sons was just three miles away at Woodfield.

The young woman in the boot of the car was showing remarkable resilience despite her ordeal. She memorised every twist and turn in the road, the different surfaces and the length of time she was in the car.

'I'd say we were on a main road for a while and then a lot of turns and crossroads. I knew at that stage I was on country roads. I knew that even after having pleaded with him, he still wasn't going to bring me home.'

When the car stopped this time, she was convinced that Murphy was going to kill her. The sound of a fast-flowing brook prompted a terrible fear that he was going to submerge the Fiat in the water while keeping her trapped in the boot.

'The next time we stopped he opened the boot again. I could hear the click. When he opened the boot I could see trees on either side. We were on a dirt track and I could hear water. I thought we were in front of a lake or something. I felt like the car was on a slope. I thought he was going to drive into a river. I had no chance.'

In the dark of the forest the young woman was able to make out a light some distance away, which was later identified as a local bed and breakfast establishment, Kilranelagh House. Otherwise, it was pitch dark.

Murphy took his bound and gagged prisoner out of the boot and brought her to the passenger side of the car, putting her on the seat. He got into the other side of the vehicle and acted as if nothing was wrong. 'Make love to me,' the cowardly attacker said. She pleaded to be brought home. Murphy replied he would.

Once again he launched into a series of sickening sexual assaults, raping her three times and forcing her to have anal and oral sex. The attacks grew more and more violent.

As the ordeal continued, Murphy's mood began to change. He commented at one point that his life wasn't worth living.

'He told me he'd never see his wife and children again. He told me his boys were aged two years and four years and what their names were. He told me his name was Michael, that he was from Baltinglass and that he worked in Dublin. This made me more frightened and made me fear for my life more.

'I asked could I smoke a cigarette. He said yes but I couldn't find them so he turned on the light inside the car. He turned it off really quickly and was looking at the light in the distance.'

Now that she'd had a clear view of his face, the woman's chances of survival were getting slimmer with each passing moment.

Then the woman realised something that was to change her fate. In the course of the attack, the bra used to tie her hands had become loose. The young woman now tried as best she could to work free without her abductor noticing.

Murphy approached her side of the car saying that he was going to put her back in the boot.

Gardaí believe he was heading to a third location. Officers say this was probably where he intended to kill the young woman.

Everything he had done up to now pointed to this. He had not used any items that could be traced back to him. He had given her enough information about himself to allow her to conclusively identify him. Moreover, when he had switched on the interior reading light to allow her light a cigarette, she had a good look at his face.

Using great force he shoved the young victim into the boot of the car and slammed the hatch shut. Stuck in the confines of the boot she finally managed to free her hands. Luckily, and for no apparent reason, he then came back and when he opened the boot again he told the young woman to face inwards.

At last she had her chance. At the point when he opened the boot, she spotted an aerosol can in the corner and grabbed it. She pointed it at his face and pressed the nozzle.

'He was kind of pushing me to turn in. I pressed the top of the can but the spray was broken.'

Murphy was furious and knocked the can of Pledge furniture polish out of her hand and slammed the hatch down. At first, there was no sign of movement. Then a few seconds later he returned to the back of the car with a plastic shopping bag. Murphy, as he had planned all along, was going to kill the young woman.

'When he opened the boot I barely lifted my head. He put a white plastic bag over my head. I remember the bag had red writing on it. He was trying to stop me breathing.'

Using her freed hands, she struggled to pull the bag from her head. It took Murphy by surprise. Despite his strength, the woman put up a fierce battle and with fantastic bravery managed to pull herself out of the boot.

'I kept struggling to get the bag off my head. He took the bag in his hand and put it on my mouth. I thought there was some chemical on it that would knock me out. I felt light-headed and couldn't breathe for a while. I managed to get my right foot over the boot of the car and kept struggling until eventually I had my two legs over and could feel my legs on the ground.'

The terrible pain of Murphy's savage attack and the battle to survive as he tried to suffocate her drained her of energy. 'At one stage I asked if he had a gun because he may as well have shot me, the pain was so bad,' she told investigating gardaí.

Murphy was using such force that the red print from the plastic bag became engrained in her skin and clothes.

With what could only have been seconds to live, what locals have described as a miracle occurred.

Two hunters, Kenneth Jones and Trevor Moody, drove up the forest road with their headlights full on.

Jones and Moody were out hunting foxes when they came on the scene just after 10 pm on the night of 11 February. Jones, a farmer from Donard a few miles to the north, first remembers being surprised to see the registration plate of a car illuminated before him.

'When I got to less than 15 yards from the car a man came out from behind the car and opened the driver's door and sat in. At this stage I said to Trevor: "I know this guy, do you?" Trevor replied: "Yes, I do." I focused in on his face and I was absolutely sure that I knew this man to be a Murphy chap, originally from Randalstown, Stratford on Slaney.'

Trevor had an even better reason to recognise Larry Murphy. It had been four years since his friend's sister had pointed Murphy out to him as the man who had groped her in the pub in Donard.

Both men wondered what the hell he was up to deep in the forest in the dead of night.

Meanwhile, Murphy had turned his car and sped past them towards the forestry entrance. As he drove into the darkness, a red and white plastic shopping bag blew from the rear of the car.

'As soon as this man drove away I saw a girl running away from the car towards the ditch. We both got out and went over to the girl. She was all knotted up in the barbed wire. She was hysterical. She asked me: "Are you with him?" "No," I said, "he is gone." Ken, my friend, shouted that he was getting a torch and she asked if he [Ken] was with him and I replied "No".

'I told her that she was alright and that we would take her wherever she wanted to go.'

Ken remembers the victim being 'in a terrible state, very distraught'. 'We lifted her clear of the wire and we left her standing on the road between us, the three of us walked straight to the jeep. She had blood all over her face. She sat into the jeep and said: "Only for you he was going to kill me. He had a bag over my head, a plastic bag."'

Ken Jones asked if he had hurt her. She told him that she had been raped.

'I said to her that I knew him. I advised her that she would have to go to the Gardaí. We then went to Baltinglass station,' Ken said.

At 10.30 pm, the three gardaí on duty in Baltinglass were facing into a fairly routine period of night duty in the small west Wicklow town. Friday night was busier than most, but still a lot less hectic than the stations in the neighbouring Dublin Metropolitan Region. Garda Peter Cassin was in the public office of the station with his colleague Garda Seamus Murphy. A third colleague on duty, Garda Liam Horgan, from the station in the nearby small village of Donard, had been drafted into the district headquarters.

Garda Cassin saw the three strangers come to the hatch in the public office and he opened it immediately. The two men reported what had happened. Garda Cassin remembers the woman being very distressed.

'She was crying and shivering; there was congealed blood around her nose and mouth. I could see blood all over her teeth. I could clearly see that a bra was tied around her neck,' he told his superiors.

He brought her to the privacy of an interview room. 'During all this time she was trembling and crying. I reassured her that she was safe now and no one could hurt her. After a couple of minutes I sat her down in a seat in the interview room. Again she was crying and shaking with fear. She pointed out to me that her knee was very painful and showed me that it had been badly skinned,' he reported.

As Garda Cassin tried to comfort the young woman, his colleague Garda Murphy got on the telephone and notified senior officers of the serious crimes which had just been committed. Extra gardaí were sent to the town from outside districts and the Detective Unit at Carlow was told of the serious developments and the abduction of the woman in the town just two hours earlier.

The woman gave them the name of her sister who was summoned to the station.

Inspector Patrick Mangan, who was the senior officer on duty at Baltinglass, got to the station as quickly as he could. He alerted the Sexual Assault Unit at the Rotunda Hospital in Dublin and advised them that the rape victim would be brought there later in the night. He arranged for two women gardaí from the Carlow/Kildare divisional headquarters at Naas to come to Baltinglass to accompany the young woman to Dublin.

The investigation had an immediate advantage. The gardaí already had a suspect in the case. Larry Murphy, who lived three miles outside the town, had been identified by Ken Jones and Trevor Moody. But first there were pressing matters to attend to. The scenes of both rapes and of the abduction in Carlow had to be located and sealed off for forensic examination.

* * *

At 8.20 am the following morning, a force of seven gardaí led by Detective Sergeant James Ryan from Carlow and Sergeant Jack Kelleher from Tullow Station arrived at Larry Murphy's bungalow in Woodfield.

Ryan rang the door bell. A man came to the door.

'Are you Larry Murphy?' the detective inquired.

'I am,' came the reply.

'Can we come in.' Murphy nodded before turning his back and walking towards the living room.

Detective Sergeant Ryan told Murphy he was arresting him under section 4 of the Criminal Justice Act for rape. Murphy put his hands up to his head.

'I don't know why it happened. I am terribly sorry,' he claimed.

The detective asked what he was doing in Carlow. 'I was doing a house in Bennekerry with my brother Tom. Why did I do that?'

Murphy asked if he could speak to his wife before the gardaí woke her. He went down the hallway to their bedroom. His wife was still in her pyjamas and was visibly taken aback when she saw her husband surrounded by gardaí.

Murphy beckoned her into the livingroom and sat her down.

'I raped a girl last night,' Murphy finally blurted out.

The admission left his wife distraught and in tears. Detective Sergeant Ryan then tried to explain the presence of the gardaí in the house.

Murphy asked if he could go the bathroom to comb his hair. He was followed by Garda Horgan. The rapist stared at himself in the mirror and murmured: 'Why did I do it?'

Knowing Larry Murphy had a 12-gauge shotgun in the house, the arrest team asked Margaret Murphy where her husband kept the weapon. She told them it was in the bedroom.

'No, it's up there,' said Murphy pointing to the top of a cabinet in the utility room.

Two officers took down the double-barrelled shotgun and ejected a round from its chamber. As they did so, the rapist looked out the back window and said to himself: 'I didn't need to do it.'

Out the back, another group of gardaí had located the 1997 Fiat Punto and another Fiat van and made arrangements for both to be transported by truck to Naas station where both cars would be combed for forensic evidence by members of the Garda Technical Bureau.

Back at Baltinglass Garda Station the suspect was booked in. He was asked to empty out his pockets. From one pocket he pulled £700 cash. 'That's the girl's money,' he said nonchalantly.

He pulled £444 from the other pocket and told them: 'That's my money.'

The gardaí asked where the victim's handbag was. He told them it was in the boot of his car.

Once in the interview room, Murphy told the investigators he was saying nothing until his solicitor arrived. He gave them the names of three solicitors. A lawyer arrived around one hour later and conferred with the prisoner.

During the morning, Murphy was interviewed by pairs of investigators – but refused to give any significant information about the attack. Around noon, Detective Garda Mark Carroll and Inspector Patrick Mangan began to question him. Soon he agreed to hand over his clothing for forensic tests. They gave him a set of clothes that had been sent over by his wife. A short time later, he said he would give DNA samples once he had spoken once more to his solicitor. It was at around 2.30 pm that the real breakthrough came.

Murphy told Carroll, an experienced murder investigator based in Newbridge Station, that he would make a statement about what had occurred the previous night.

With head down, his mood sullen and dour, Murphy began speaking in a low voice. At no point did he show any emotion. He claimed that he abducted and raped the woman on impulse, ignoring the fact that two witnesses had seen him in the area almost an hour before the attack.

He told the two gardaí that he had been working in Greystones before going on to Baltinglass to pay a solicitor for some work he had done. Then he visited his brother and another man in Bennekerry, near Friarstown. He said he decided to stop off for chips in Carlow and parked down a side street.

'I was walking down the path and I seen this girl walking towards me. I had never met the girl in my life. I don't know what came over me. I just flipped. I said to her "Give me your money." She said "Fuck off." I hit her then. She had stopped to open the door of her car. I hit her with my hand on the side of the face. She stumbled back onto the seat in the car. I pushed her over onto the other seat, the passenger seat. I asked her where her keys were. I found her keys on the seat.

'I moved her car over to where my car was. She was sitting in the car beside me with her head on my knee. At that stage I tied her arms. I asked her to remove her bra. I used the bra to tie her arms. At that stage I took her out of her car. She walked out. I told her to get in the boot of my car and she sat in. At this stage I took off up the road. I don't know why I did. I don't know. I suppose I drove for about 20 minutes. travelled out the Athy Road. I stopped at a lane. I raped her. First I took her out of the boot of the car. I put her in the seat of the car. I removed her trousers. I just raped her.'

Murphy went on to tell the detectives about travelling between the two scenes of the sexual assaults, colouring his statement with claims that he had finally uncuffed the woman but failed to mention at any stage that he tried to suffocate her. Without referring in any way to the fact that he was rumbled by the two hunters he spoke about leaving the forest.

'After I left Spinan's I went to Stratford. I went to the Stratford Arms pub and I bought a bottle of whiskey. I drank some of it on the way home. When I got home my wife was in the kitchen. The children were in bed. The bottle of whiskey is still in the car.

'I just went to bed. I threw my clothes on the floor. I slept in the nip ... I was kind of expecting the guards. I didn't sleep much last night.'

Because of the seriousness of the case, the Eastern Regional Commander based in Mullingar, Assistant Commissioner Tony Hickey had at this stage been notified of the abduction and rape. Hickey was also the officer in charge of Operation TRACE, the codename given to the investigation centred at Naas station into the disappearance of six young women in the Leinster area. The Garda Commissioner Pat Byrne had ordered the institution of the inquiry over fears all six had been murdered, possibly by a serial killer.

Hickey took an immediate interest in events in Baltinglass and told the TRACE detectives in Naas to keep a watching brief on events in west Wicklow. The route taken by Murphy was close to where

Kilkenny 21-year-old Jo Jo Dullard vanished in November 1995. It was also not far from where student teacher Deirdre Jacob disappeared on 28 July, 1998.

TRACE stood for tracing, reviewing and collating evidence and had been the mastermind of Byrne who feared there were connections between some or all six missing women. He wanted an outside inquiry team or as he referred to it, a Cold Cases Unit, to reinvestigate the files to seek out possible new connections or leads. Byrne had seen similar units at work in the United States when he trained with the FBI at their academy in Quantico, Virginia earlier in his career.

The decision was also taken to send detectives from the murder investigation section of the National Bureau of Criminal Investigation at Harcourt Square in Dublin to Baltinglass. It was only through sheer luck, officers concluded, that they were not dealing with a murder.

After Detective Garda Carroll and Inspector Mangan finished their interview, two detective sergeants from Harcourt Square took over. Murphy spoke to them about his family life and described in detail the series of sexual assaults. He also pointed out locations on a map where the rapes took place.

At 8.05 pm he was formally charged in the station with rape and abduction. He made no reply to the charges after caution. A special sitting of Baltinglass District Court was organised for that night where Murphy was remanded into custody until the next sitting of Blessington Court.

Gardaí began preparing a file for the DPP to have Murphy further charged with attempted murder. In recommending the charge, the Director was told the accused used extreme violence on the young woman when he first abducted her and broke her nose: 'She is not a frail person in build. It would have taken a considerable blow to stun her.'

The file continues: 'Murphy is a carpenter by trade and is physically well built. In the carrying out of his crimes, Murphy was travelling further away from Carlow, the home of the victim. She was taken to two very remote locations where there was very little opportunity for her to escape. Murphy in his initial actions at Carlow removed her boots. I believe that this action was taken to prevent her escaping and slowing her down if she did manage to get free. I do not believe that he had any intention of ever releasing her.'

The DPP was also told that Murphy had shown absolutely no remorse for his actions: 'It was put to him that the injured girl was going through a lot over what he had done. His reply was: "Well, she is alive isn't she."'

TRACE detectives meanwhile mounted a painstaking investigation into Murphy's background and his movements around the times of the disappearances of the other young women in Leinster.

They turned up interesting information but nothing which could definitively connect Murphy with the missing women. It was discovered that Murphy had been roofing a house in Newbridge around the time Deirdre Jacob disappeared. His route home would have taken him past her house at Roseberry and along the roadway where she was last seen.

As regards the disappearance of Jo Jo Dullard, all the Gardaí could establish was the geographical coincidence between the Carlow woman's abduction and Jo Jo's disappearance. Jo Jo was last seen in a telephone kiosk at Moone, just a few miles from where he carried out the sex attacks. Moone is also only five miles from where Murphy lived in 1995, the year Jo Jo vanished.

Detectives have been unable to find a scintilla of evidence to connect Murphy in any definitive way with the other missing women and searches of his home and neighbouring land have turned up nothing.

The investigation also took officers to Britain to check on the abduction method used by Murphy and in particular his use of the victim's bra as a gag. Despite extensive searches through crime databases at Scotland Yard, no similar *modus operandi* could be found to have been used by other sex offenders in the past.

But for some officers, suspicions about Murphy remain. If only they could identify the third location he was about to bring the young

Carlow woman to, it could throw up vital clues. The only one who knows that location is Larry Murphy.

One line of inquiry the Gardaí are still pursuing is a report that Murphy was friendly with the operator of an illegal dump in Co. Wicklow and that he abandoned a car in the huge tiphead in 1995. According to the report, which came from reliable sources, the car wasn't very old and was in good working order and there was no apparent reason for getting rid of it. Since then, the dump operator has died. However, Wicklow County Council has plans to excavate the site and if the car is recovered it will be forensically examined.

At the Central Criminal Court on 11 May, 2002, Murphy was jailed for 15 years after pleading guilty to six charges of kidnapping, raping and attempting to murder the young woman. Mr Justice Paul Carney also imposed sentences of four years and three years on assault and robbery charges. All the sentences were to run concurrently and date from 11 February, 2000. The judge suspended the final year of each sentence due to Murphy's guilty plea.

In and around Baltinglass, locals believe Murphy's victim's survival was nothing short of a miracle. They point to the fact that the site where the second attack took place is only yards from an ancient holy site, known as St Brigid's Headstone. The small headstone, which was part of an old convent, has been used by local people to cure headaches and illness for generations. The site was a well-known medieval pilgrimage point and was at one time adorned with St Brigid's crosses. One daily newspaper reported how 'locals talk of St Brigid, the patron saint of women, saving the woman's life by sending the two men to intervene. The chances of coming across her at that point are incredible and people are saying it was St Brigid who sent them.'

His victim has since moved from Carlow, and in the summer of 2002 she married her long-term boyfriend.

Murphy is currently appealing the 'severity' of his sentence.

THE TUNNELS

'I have told them basically I did it.
Sorry, it was just a stupid thing that happened.'

– David Lawler, 1996.

ON the evening of St Stephen's Day, 1995, an anxious Stephen
Rynn went to Blanchardstown Garda Station in Dublin to report
that his sister, Marilyn, was missing. The Rynn family were
naturally worried when she failed to turn up for dinner at her
parents' home on Christmas Day.

It was very unlike her not to stay in touch with her family and this
led to much anxiety for her elderly parents and for her brother and
sister. The Rynns were a close-knit family and Marilyn would usually
contact at least one of her siblings or parents on a daily basis. When
she didn't appear for dinner at Stephen's house the following day as
promised, they knew something serious must have occurred. Stephen,
who lived just yards away from his sister in the Brookhaven estate in
Blanchardstown, decided to report the matter to the Gardaí.

Garda Ciaran Noone was on duty in the local station. At around
6.30 pm on 26 December, Stephen walked into the public office
and reported his sister missing. He had not seen her since 8 pm on
21 December and was very worried. Despite making extensive
inquiries and contacting her friends he had failed to locate her. He
said nothing appeared to be amiss at her home.

Stephen expressed concern for her safety, emphasising that it was
totally out of character for her not to make contact and that she had
never acted like this previously. The family were also able to supply a
colour photo which might be of assistance to the police.

The garda took down a detailed description of Marilyn and promised to have it circulated to all Garda stations in the city. The following morning, a description of the missing woman was sent out on the force's teleprinter system alerting officers all over the country to her disappearance.

Not content to leave the matter to the police alone, the Rynns organised for hundreds of 'missing person' posters, featuring a photo of their sister, to be distributed around Dublin. The posters described Marilyn as 5ft 5ins/5ft 6ins in height, around nine stone in weight, with permed brown curly hair and piercing brown eyes. She was believed to have been wearing a green-coloured three-quarter-length single-breasted coat with a black fur collar, a black knee-length skirt, a red blouse and black shoes when she went missing. She wore a gold neck-chain to cover substantial scarring following an operation for goitre some years earlier.

Over the next few days the disappearance featured prominently in daily and evening newspaper stories alongside photos of Marilyn. The concern of the Rynn family helped convince news editors in the various papers that this was something more than a run-of-the-mill Missing Persons report. Such reports come into newsrooms from the Garda Press Office on an almost daily basis. These mostly concern teenagers who run away from home and return within days. Others relate to people feeling depressed in the days leading up to their disappearance. But this case was different. The missing 41-year-old had a steady job as a civil servant in the Department of the Environment. She had not been depressed at the time of her disappearance. There appeared to be no reason whatsoever for her to vanish.

Officers in Blanchardstown were conducting behind-the-scenes investigations into the mystery. A team under Inspector Eddie Quirke was piecing together the woman's last known movements and their inquiries were discussed at a daily conference at the district headquarters at Cabra Station.

They discovered that on 21 December, after she finished work at the National Roads Authority in St Martyn's House, just off Baggot

Street in Dublin's south city centre, Marilyn and a group of friends from the office went to O'Reilly's pub on Tara Street. The venue, a newly-opened public house in the arches beneath Tara Street DART station, was chosen as a gathering point for the group before travelling on to their Christmas party at the Old Shieling Hotel across the city in Raheny.

At around 7.30 pm the group headed off to the hotel. Marilyn remained there until about 2 am. She met a work colleague from the Department of the Environment on the way out and told him she was going to walk into Raheny village to get a taxi into town. He walked with her and suggested she should head in the Howth direction because it would offer a better chance of getting a cab. They walked for a short period along the Howth Road where he flagged down a passing taxi. She got in alone and sat in the back passenger side seat. He later told gardaí that Marilyn was sober and did not appear upset or worried. The man shortly afterwards got his own taxi and travelled in the opposite direction towards Sutton.

The next positive sighting of Marilyn was at Eddie Rocket's American-style diner on O'Connell Street at around 2.50 am where she bumped into another work acquaintance and they had a brief chat. The man was with a group of people. She told him she was going to get the 3 am Dublin Nitelink Bus home to Blanchardstown. The Nitelink buses, which were introduced to cater for the thousands of revellers out celebrating Christmas, ran throughout the city up until the early hours. Marilyn was still alone at this time. There were no sightings of her after that.

* * *

Marilyn Rynn was the second eldest in a family of three. She came between Stephen (43) and Rosaleen (37). She was born on 19 December, 1954, to Stephen and Christine Rynn who lived at Rossmore Road in Ballyfermot. Prior to her disappearance she maintained almost daily contact with her brother Stephen, his wife Catherine, and their children.

She was single and lived alone at her home on Brookhaven Drive which she purchased nine years earlier on the strength of a £20,000 mortgage. Marilyn was a very popular member of staff at the National Roads Authority section of the Department of the Environment where she was employed as an Executive Officer.

Marilyn's superiors regarded her as a highly-efficient worker. She was punctual and had an excellent attendance record. While quite a private person, she was very sociable with her circle of friends at work and well-liked amongst her colleagues. She drank a little but did not smoke and often went out for the night with her colleagues at the Department and other friends in the Central Statistics Office. It was not unknown for her to 'go on the tear' with the girls on special occasions, have breakfast and then turn in for work. Although this was very rare.

Neighbours described her as pleasant and friendly although she was not one to engage in long conversations. Despite extensive investigations the Gardaí identified few male friends and certainly nobody with a grudge against her.

Marilyn often used the Nitelink service to return home late at night and then walked between Blanchardstown village and her home via a badly lit laneway known as 'The Tunnels', Kelly's Lane and Tolka Valley Road. She felt safe in her own locality and was not put off by the dangers posed by the lack of public lighting on the route.

* * *

By Friday, 29 December, with no contact from Marilyn, the missing persons probe shifted up a gear. A special incident room was set up at Cabra Garda station. More press and radio appeals were organised and the investigation was now taken over by local Chief Superintendent Jim McHugh, based in Santry divisional headquarters, and Superintendent Michael Carty, Cabra. While no great progress was being made in locating Marilyn, the police were getting what they believed to be an accurate account of her movements on the night of 21 December and the early hours of 22 December.

But soon their inquiries would lead them down a cul de sac. It would be something which would hamper the investigation for a vital eight days and prevent detectives establishing what had really happened to Marilyn Rynn.

The preliminary investigations indicated that Marilyn had arrived home safely sometime in the early hours of 22 December. This assumption was mainly based on three statements given to gardaí.

The first was from an old friend of Marilyn's who lived in the country but had arrived in Dublin for a few days over Christmas for her husband's office party. She said Marilyn rang her at her mother's home at around 9.30 am on the 22nd. The woman was quite sure of the conversation and said Marilyn had even made arrangements to see her that night. Marilyn told her to make sure to call her at the Department of the Environment 'before knocking off for the day'.

Two young neighbours of Marilyns also told of seeing the civil servant leave her house shortly after noon that day and get the No 38 bus into town. Another woman thought she saw her shopping in Penneys department store on Mary Street on that day. As a result, the Gardaí assumed that Marilyn was still alive on the morning of 22 December.

This assumption prevented them from ordering a full-scale search for a vital number of days. In fact, Marilyn had been brutally raped and murdered several hours before, but the Gardaí would not realise this until 7 January.

*   *   *

As with all major investigations, senior officers had ordered telephone checks to see who may have been in telephone contact with Marilyn in the days before her disappearance. A check of all the outgoing calls from her home was carried out to find out the last time Marilyn had called anybody. On 5 January, Telecom Éireann reported back to the investigation team at Cabra. The printout of calls had a major bearing on the direction of the Garda hunt.

It established that, in fact, no call was ever made by Marilyn Rynn to her friend from the country. Indeed no calls from anywhere in Dublin had been made to her friend's home during the crucial period between 9–10 am on the morning of the 22nd when the woman believed Marilyn had called. The police were also able to find out that no calls whatsoever were made from Marilyn's home at Brookhaven Drive, Blanchardstown, on the three days of 21, 22 and 23 December.

This information substantially altered the course of the search. It meant the last definitive sighting the Gardaí had of the missing woman was at 2.50 am on the night of her Christmas party when she spoke briefly to a casual work acquaintance in Eddie Rocket's diner on O'Connell Street. The only definite clue the force had to go on now was that Marilyn had caught the 3 am Nitelink bus service to Blanchardstown from Westmoreland Street. If this was so, she should have arrived in Blanchardstown village around 3.30 am, where she would have gotten off the bus and probably gone through a local park, known as Tolka Valley Park, to get home. At night the area is badly lit and visibility is very poor.

Based on this information, a conference was held at Cabra station on 6 January. It was decided that the evidence revealed by Telecom Éireann warranted a full search of fields and open areas adjacent to the Brookhaven estate. The search commenced at first light the following morning, a Sunday.

After a number of false starts the Gardaí were finally on the right track.

The search of Tolka Valley Park began at 8 am on 7 January and involved a team of gardaí from the 'Kilo' District which comprises Blanchardstown and Cabra stations. They were backed up by members of the force's Dog Unit based at Kilmainham. The search was concentrated in a wooded area of the park, adjacent to the Tolka River.

The area is bounded on one side by the Blanchardstown bypass and on the other by several housing estates including Edgewood Lawns, Brookhaven, where Marilyn and her brother Stephen resided, Greenridge Court, Ashling Heights and Corduff Cottages. During the hours of darkness there is no public lighting system in operation within the park confines. The floor of the valley is about 60ft below the public footpath and is densely overgrown with gorse and bushes. Tolka Valley Park is regularly used by locals as a short cut to Blanchardstown village and during the day is a hive of activity with young children playing and residents exercising or walking their dogs.

Less than one hour into the planned search the attention of the Garda team was drawn to a cluster of undergrowth out of sight of the public footpath. It was the excited barking of a Garda alsation which guided them to the spot. The scene which greeted them was something which will be remembered for a long time by every member of the search team. Concealed beneath bushes they found the naked and bruised body of a woman.

The body had lain there for the best part of a fortnight and there were no recognisable facial features. The victim's clothes had been strewn around the scene. The deceased was still wearing a gold chain. In close proximity to the body they found a woman's black shoe. Not far away, concealed behind a disused drainage pipe, were items of clothing, including a green coat with a black fur collar, a black skirt, a red blouse and a handbag – the items Marilyn was wearing when last seen at Eddie Rocket's. Such was the horror of the scene that the gardaí who attended it were later offered trauma counselling.

Within a short time, Garda numbers at the scene swelled as members of the Technical Bureau arrived from Headquarters to conduct a forensic examination of the scene and detectives from the Serious Crime Squad were summoned to provide backup assistance. The Gardaí were now dealing with a murder inquiry. It was obvious from an early stage that robbery was not a motive in the killing. Marilyn still had some of her jewellery when found and there was £240 in her handbag.

The discovery of the body on Sunday morning led to a frenzy of activity in Tolka Valley Park. The Assistant Commissioner in charge of the Dublin area, Pat O'Toole, visited the scene along with the local divisional commander, Chief Superintendent Jim McHugh. The two men who had been leading the missing persons inquiry, Superintendent Michael Carty and Detective Inspector Derek Byrne, both from Cabra, were also at hand. A host of specialist detectives from the Technical Bureau, including photographers, mappers, ballistics experts and a fingerprint team joined the search team. Inevitably, the national media arrived on the scene, including a television crew from RTÉ. The story was the top item on *Six One* television news that night and a front-page story in all the dailies the following morning.

Much of the painstaking work which often decides the course of a murder investigation remained to be done at Tolka Valley Park. The search team who found the body had immediately preserved the scene, ensuring the whole area was sealed off pending the arrival of a pathologist and the Technical Bureau. It would take nine days before the police completed their examination of the area.

The State Pathologist, Professor John Harbison, arrived late on the morning of 7 January and carried out a preliminary examination of the body in a bid to establish a possible time of death. This was inconclusive because of the degree of decomposition. He directed that the body be removed to the morgue at nearby James Connolly Memorial hospital where an autopsy would be conducted. The pathologist supervised the removal of the body.

At Cabra Garda station, a 1970s purpose-built station situated on the Navan Road, a conference of detectives was scheduled for 3 pm. Around 40 officers attended the meeting to discuss how the investigation should now progress. The general feeling was that the Gardaí were dealing with a sexually-motivated murder and that robbery could be ruled out as a motive.

Several team leaders were appointed to carry out door-to-door inquiries in the area and a Detective Sergeant was given the job of

Exhibits Officer in charge of identifying and storing all items found at the scene, some of which would be very important in any criminal trial.

A decision was also made to involve the Forensic Science Laboratory of the Department of Justice from the outset of the inquiry because of the importance of finding DNA samples which could connect the killer with the body.

Back at the scene, the expanded search team was finding more and more of the victim's personal items. They were spread over a large area, giving the impression that the killer had thrown them in a variety of directions. Two keys were located on waste ground at Greenridge Road which is adjacent to the scene. They were identified as belonging to Marilyn and one of them fitted her front door. Her second shoe was found in undergrowth some distance away along with tights, a comb, an earring, a perfume bottle, a purse, a make-up pouch and a wristwatch, which was badly damaged.

Late in the evening of 7 January, Professor Harbison issued his preliminary report on the cause of death. He found that the victim had been strangled. The killer had used both hands to choke Marilyn. There was no evidence that he had used rope or any other form of ligature to carry out the killing. The police suspicions that the motive was sexual were confirmed when the post mortem found bruising on the fronts and insides of both thighs and around the genital area. The autopsy report stated that this strongly suggested that the victim had been raped.

Moreover, there were visible signs of a struggle with bruising on both arms. 'Small, mostly vertical scratches on the lower abdomen and on the fronts of the thighs could have arisen from contact with thorn bushes but were scarcely prominent enough to have been caused by dragging the deceased any appreciable distance over ground,' the findings said.

Unfortunately, the victim could not be identified from visual examination because of the degree of decomposition which had occurred in the two weeks between the disappearance and discovery of the body. Therefore, the investigation team tried to get a positive identification using dental charts. They called in Dr Hugh Barry, a consultant oral surgeon at the Dublin Dental Hospital, who compared dental features on the body of the deceased with charts supplied by Marilyn's dentist. His comparison yielded a positive result. This was further confirmed when blood samples provided by Marilyn's parents yielded a DNA match, proving beyond doubt that the victim was their daughter.

The murder hunt team received a major boost on the evening of Monday, 8 January. An examination of samples taken from the body by scientists at the State Forensic Laboratory based at Garda Headquarters in Phoenix Park revealed the presence of semen, believed to be that of the killer. Significantly, the scientists were able to get a successful DNA match from the sample.

In effect, they had found the genetic fingerprints of the killer. All the police had to do now was find a suspect in the case whose DNA matched the sample being stored in the Forensic Laboratory. The decision to call in the laboratory at such an early stage was already paying off.

The huge attention being given to the investigation by the newspapers generated an overwhelming response from the public. It resulted in the incident room receiving dozens of phone calls about possible suspects and suspicious movements on the night of the killing. Each call had to be followed up by detectives and where the callers gave their name, officers sought a written statement. In the bulk of cases the information yielded no tangible results.

The murder was highlighted on RTÉ television's *Crimeline* programme on Monday, 15 January, when viewers saw a reconstruction of Marilyn Rynn's last known movements. Chief Superintendent Jim McHugh appealed for any information, no matter how trivial. Dozens of calls followed the broadcast, including ones where callers nominated suspects, but again nothing concrete emerged.

On the Pat Kenny radio show, Superintendent Michael Carty asked listeners if they had seen anybody acting out of character in the area. Householders were asked if a family member or friend had been washing clothes in the early hours for example. Again the police were casting a wide net in a case where the crime was random and they had no prime suspect.

The radio appeal drew a large response, including one from a woman who was suspicious of her husband's movements on the night in question. Upon checking his background the investigation team was satisfied that he was not involved – he was a garda who had been working at the relevant time. *Crimeline* featured the murder again on its broadcasts of Monday, 12 February and 11 March.

In the Blanchardstown area, a large force of uniformed officers, backed up by the Crime Task Force[1], continued door-to-door inquiries. Almost 1,900 homes in the Brookhaven area and adjoining estates were visited by the police who asked about any suspicious activity in the early hours of 22 December.

In Westmoreland Street, just off O'Connell Bridge in the city centre, where the Nitelink bus for Blanchardstown sets off, late night travellers were questioned, as were those stepping off at Blanchardstown village. In all, 200 people were interviewed in this fashion.

Eventually, the Gardaí extended their door-to-door inquiries to 1,700 more houses in estates around Blanchardstown in a determined effort to get a trace on Marilyn Rynn's killer.

Back at the murder hunt headquarters in Cabra, Detective Inspector Derek Byrne and his team were drawing up a list of possible suspects. Byrne, a young officer who had spent most of his career in the Kilo district, knew most of the offenders on his patch. Many of the officers under his command had spent dozens of years between them in the District Detective Units (DDUs) based at Blanchardstown and Cabra. They were well acquainted with most

---

1. A uniformed branch of the force which provided a quick-action response to public order problems and robberies in the division.

of the sex offenders in the area and would have put away a lot of them down through the years.

Rapists, recently released sex offenders, psychiatric patients and drifters with a record for violent offences were among the possible suspects they would have to investigate. Within a few weeks they had drawn up a list containing more than 300 names. It would ultimately total more than 350 men. Even the Gardaí themselves were shocked that they could come up with such a large number of names from such a small section of the city.

Having compiled the list, the investigation team decided to go in search of the men on the list and seek their co-operation in the inquiry. Because of the existence of a DNA sample which would help trace the killer, each individual would be asked to provide a blood sample to match against the one held by the Forensic Laboratory. However, under the Criminal Justice Act, such a sample can only be obtained voluntarily and the police have no power to demand that a suspect provide one. Even in a case where the police have one prime suspect, that person can refuse to co-operate in handing over a bodily sample.

In the vast bulk of cases, the men involved were willing to give their blood, anxious to have themselves ruled out of such a vicious crime from an early stage. In all, more than 330 individuals gave blood voluntarily. In a further 15 cases, the suspects were arrested and gave hair samples rather than blood, while another three men gave hair samples voluntarily. Hair, just like saliva, can give examiners a satisfactory DNA profile. At the Forensic Lab, two scientists, Dr Maureen Smyth and Dr Geraldine O'Donnell, were co-ordinating the analysis of samples coming in from the Gardaí. But the sheer number being sent to them for testing was beginning to cause problems and the investigation soon faced another hitch.

By the middle of March, the DNA department at the lab had only tested ten samples and in the process cleared the same number of suspects. A further 12 blood specimens were in the process of being analysed but dozens more lay in wait. The procedure was proving extremely expensive and infuriatingly slow for the fledgling department, which came under the overall direction of Dr James Donovan, as Chief State Forensic Scientist.

Late in March, the Garda authorities approved a special budget to allow samples for DNA testing to be sent to police laboratories in Britain and Northern Ireland. On 4 April, 1996, the first specimens were handed over to Brian Irwin of the Forensic Science Agency of Northern Ireland based in Carrickfergus. The cross-border cooperation would soon begin to bear fruit.

* * *

Thousands of people were interviewed in the first two months of the murder inquiry. But as progress in the case began to slacken and fewer leads were coming in, Chief Superintendent Jim McHugh, who had overall responsibility for the inquiry, ordered his officers to go back to the Brookhaven estate and neighbouring developments once more to see if any of the residents could recall anything about the night of 21 December and the early hours of the following morning. The foot slogging brought officers to a total of 1,880 homes.

Telecom Éireann technician, David Lawler, was one of the householders who was visited a second time. His house at Edgewood Lawns, Blanchardstown, was not far from the murder scene at Tolka Valley Park and was one of the first visited during door-to-door inquiries in the early days of the Garda hunt. Two uniformed officers interviewed him for their standard questionnaire form and asked him where he was on the night of the rape and killing. Lawler told them he was at his office Christmas party at the Central Hotel on Exchequer Street in the city centre. He said he walked home, not getting in the door until about 4.45 am. In response to a number of other routine questions he told them he did not know Marilyn Rynn and had not seen her on his travels. In due course the questionnaire was one of hundreds returned to the Incident Room at Cabra.

On 13 January, as the Gardaí retraced their steps, Sergeant John Carr from Cabra station interviewed the 33-year-old technician again at his home and took a written statement from him.

Lawler repeated what he had told the two gardaí who had called to the house the previous week about the Telecom Éireann Christmas party and his long walk home to Blanchardstown. In the statement he also said he went to a takeaway restaurant on Dame Street, not far from the taxi rank opposite the Bank of Ireland building. He spent about 45 minutes in the takeaway before trying to get a taxi home. The taxi queues were extremely long and he decided to get the Nitelink bus but just missed one and went to Aston Quay where he again failed to get a taxi.

Lawler began to go into greater detail with Sergeant Carr and told him how he continued along the quays until he reached Heuston station and turned from Parkgate Street into Phoenix Park. He continued through the park, through Castleknock village and into Blanchardstown village via the area known locally as 'The Tunnels', finally arriving home at 4.45 am.

Asked if he had seen anybody en route or noted anything peculiar, Lawler told the officer that as he passed Justin's shop in Blanchardstown village he saw a woman near a car who walked down Old Corduff Road through The Tunnels. He walked about 150 yards behind the woman who was wearing a knee-length dark coat. He thought that she may have been smoking. Some distance along the way he saw a younger man, who was taller than himself, walking fast in the opposite direction to him. Other than giving a description of the younger man, aged in his 20s, Lawler remarked that there was nothing else unusual about the journey home.

'When I got into the house I stuck on the kettle for a cup of tea and I looked at the clock on the cooker. It was 4.45 am,' he claimed.

On 27 February, the Gardaí contacted David Lawler for a different reason. It was simply routine. Because he said he was out on the night Marilyn Rynn was killed they asked if he would be willing to give a blood sample to eliminate him from inquiries. He readily agreed and signed the required form of consent before a doctor took the specimen.

Back in the Incident Room, as detectives sifted through the statements which were pouring in, the man and woman David Lawler encountered in The Tunnels had taken on a major significance. Despite the thousands of people interviewed, the investigation team had not come across this young man before and nobody else had mentioned him.

It was a loose end which could lead to something or it could just be another false line of inquiry. Either way it was important to find out. After discussing it with the Garda Press Office, the murder hunt team issued a press statement seeking information about the woman David Lawler encountered in The Tunnels. Anybody who thought they fitted that description or who might have known the person was asked to come forward.

On 25 March, 1996, three months after Marilyn Rynn was so brutally murdered, the Gardaí finally found their mystery man. It was no surprise it took them so long, the 6ft 4ins tall man whom David Lawler had seen walking fast against him lived several miles away in Kilbarrack.

The mystery man turned out to be a 21-year-old who had attended a work function in the Clonsilla Inn pub on Thursday night, 21 December. At 2.45 am, after the function ended, he and two friends got a taxi to one of their homes at Ashling Heights, Blanchardstown, where they chatted for about half an hour. Around 3 am he left for Blanchardstown village where he hoped to get a taxi, but first he had to go through The Tunnels. The young man told Gardaí that he felt nervous walking through the pitch-dark laneway and started to run. He remembered passing a woman coming in the other direction and felt a little more comfortable on seeing her and slowed down to a fast walking pace. While he could not describe her in any great detail, he recalled passing a man further on. After that he got a taxi in the village to his girlfriend's home in Coolock.

Detectives began trying to corroborate the young man's statement and soon established that what he was telling them was the truth. His girlfriend and other witnesses were able to support his alibi.

The woman whom he described, however, despite an appeal in the press and on television and radio, was never found. Given what the new witness had said, detectives began working on the assumption that the woman he passed in The Tunnels was Marilyn Rynn and the man was David Lawler. But if this was so, there was a crucial time gap between when the witness says he passed along The Tunnels and the time given by Lawler.

Major consideration was given to the statement by the young man that he passed through the area around 3.45 am and arrived at his girlfriend's house in Coolock at 4.40 am in the taxi. He said he checked his wristwatch at that time. Detectives thought his account quite credible.

On the other hand, David Lawler said he arrived home at Edgewood Lawns at 4.45 am on Friday morning and confirmed the time by saying he noticed it on the family's cooker clock. But what was niggling the investigation team, particularly Detective Garda John Lyons, was that Lawler said he left his work function at 12.30 am and went for a takeaway, which put him leaving the city centre around 1 am. It meant it took him three hours and 50 minutes to walk home.

But if the new witness was right and he did meet Lawler around 3.45 am, then the Telecom Éireann worker should have completed the short journey home in five to ten minutes at 3.55 am and not 4.45 am.

It was decided that Detective Lyons' hunch about the time difference should be followed up. It was time to speak to David Lawler again and ask him about the crucial time difference of almost an hour. In the meantime, Superintendent Michael Carty decided Lawler's blood specimen should be given priority testing at the Northern Ireland Forensic Laboratory.

*   *   *

In the Greyhound bar in Blanchardstown village, David Lawler was commonly known to regulars as 'Jesus' or 'God'. The 33-year-old earned the nickname from his shoulder-length hair and long beard. In the estate where he lived, neighbours described him as quiet and withdrawn. But the pub patrons knew a different man. He was the life and soul of the party.

On St Patrick's Day 1996, almost three months after Marilyn Rynn's murder, he had his hair and beard shaved off for charity and photos of the event were distributed amongst the locals.

Lawler was born in Baltinglass, Co. Wicklow, on 18 September, 1963. Upon finishing school he joined the Department of Posts and Telegraphs, which later split into two semi-State organisations, An Post and Telecom Éireann. Lawler became an employee of Telecom Éireann. In 1989, he married Evelyn Kelly and they had one child, a boy, a year later. That same year they bought their first home at Edgewood Lawns.

At work, colleagues knew him as a fairly-efficient worker. Unknown to many of them, however, he regularly disappeared when he should have been working. As a technician, he had his own van to travel to different jobs and made full use of it for other reasons. Once, he drove all the way to Galway in the Telecom van on a drinking binge. There were also several other unaccounted for escapades in the State van.

In fact, heavy drinking took over Lawler's life and severely interfered with family life. People began to notice the way he ignored Evelyn and their son and concentrated on meeting his pub pals. When he would return from work, he would often just lie on the couch watching television or fall asleep, hardly communicating with his wife. Then it would be off to the pub for a few pints, ignoring the stresses and strains of raising a young child.

Things came to a head once when Evelyn opened a particularly high telephone bill, which even took into account the subsidy

Telecom workers enjoyed. Mrs Lawler contacted the phone company and was told the exorbitant rates were accounted for by frequent calls to telephone sex lines. When she confronted her husband about the matter and asked if there could be some mistake, he admitted using the expensive sex lines.

Apart from drink, there was one other passion he enjoyed. David Lawler was an early Internet subscriber and spent hours in front of the computer in an upstairs bedroom, accessing a host of sites, some of which would be of particular interest to the Gardaí.

* * *

In late July, the investigation team at Cabra received the news they had been waiting for. Dr Geraldine O'Connell contacted Detective Inspector Derek Byrne with the news that the forensic centre in Carrickfergus had made a positive DNA match. The blood sample for David Lawler which had been sent to the laboratory matched the semen sample found on the body of Marilyn Rynn. The Gardaí couldn't believe the news. They finally had their man.

A conference was hastily arranged to discuss what should be done next. It was attended by all the senior officers involved in the case. The decision taken was that a surveillance unit from the Serious Crime Squad (SCS) would keep Lawler under observation for a few days while more sophisticated DNA checks were made. It was also concluded that the team should examine Lawler's background more closely by making some discreet inquiries.

Another conference was held on the evening of 5 August at Cabra. The definitive results they required from the DNA fingerprinting had come through, putting Lawler firmly in the frame. The team would move early the following morning.

Just before 9 am on 6 August, several armed detectives from Cabra and Blanchardstown stations, along with the SCS stakeout team, who were more acquainted with keeping tabs on the city's organised crime bosses, waited outside the murder suspect's home at Edgewood Lawns. They watched as he got into his car to go to work. A short distance away, on Church Road, the squad pounced. Detective Inspector Byrne rushed over to the suspect's vehicle and ordered him to step away from the car. He told him he was arresting him under section 4 of the Criminal Justice Act for the murder of Marilyn Rynn between 22 December 1995 and 7 January 1996. The man the Gardaí had been seeking for the last nine months was taken in the back of a patrol car to Cabra station.

* * *

During the course of his detention, Lawler was questioned by two experienced interviewers, Detective Sergeant John Dennedy and Detective Garda Jim Clinton. Within a short time, Lawler admitted to them that he had raped and murdered Marilyn Rynn at Tolka Valley Park in the early hours of Friday, 22 December. He made several written statements outlining the events leading to the brutal killing. He claimed that he was overcome by an uncontrollable sexual impulse. But before he would agree to confess in writing, Lawler insisted on telling his wife and family first. Gardaí were dispatched to bring his relations to Cabra station.

All were shocked when told why he was arrested. They had absolutely no idea.

'I have told them [the Gardaí] basically I did it. Sorry, it was just a stupid thing that happened'.

The colour drained from their faces.

According to Lawler, he first accosted the victim as she arrived at Greenridge Court.

'I was walking up behind her. I would have been 100 yards possibly 150 yards behind her. I went up through the two tunnels and this woman turned left towards Greenridge Court. On the pathway I grabbed this woman, at first it was a bear hug trying to push her into the park but she started to shout. I don't know what she shouted so I put my hand over her mouth.'

He forced her off the pathway into the bushes below. During the course of the confrontation they both slipped down a grass embankment into the floor of the valley. There he forced Marilyn to strip off her clothes and raped her.

After the attack he said the woman said she was cold and he told her to put her jacket on. He went on to claim that when the victim said she recognised him he panicked.

'She said to me that she knew who I was. I had long hair and a beard so I was fairly distinctive. I panicked at that stage and that's when I strangled her.'

He tried to strangle her from behind but she put up a fierce struggle. He pinned her to the ground, got on top of her and strangled the defenceless woman with both hands.

'I tried doing it from behind at first but she was struggling and I could not get a hold of her. I pushed her down and got on top of her and strangled her with my two hands around her neck. The first thing I thought of was "stupid, stupid, stupid".'

She went limp and he believed she was dead. Lawler told detectives he then dragged the body further into the undergrowth to hide it from the public path. He tried to cover his tracks, gathering up all her clothes and hiding them in a disused pipe.

'I scattered some of the stuff out of her handbag that I had collected up the pathway and I scattered this around the place when I was leaving. I tried to make it look like a robbery.'

He sneaked home in a circuitous route, walking along wasteground and using trees for cover against being spotted. He discarded more of Marilyn's personal items as he went. Once at home, just before 5 am he put his clothes, which were filthy from the attack, into the washing machine and took a cloth to his runners.

'I just sat there for a while. I then went up to the bathroom. My wife came down the stairs and called me. She asked me what had kept me. I told her I could not get a taxi and I walked home. She asked me about the washing machine being on and I said that my jeans and jacket got wet and I decided to wash them.'

The following day he went sick from work but his absence was never noted.

Lawler also admitted that he felt he had outwitted Gardaí when they asked him for a DNA sample. He told of how he had accessed a DNA website on the Internet and had learned that DNA samples were only good for up to two weeks. He felt safe giving a blood specimen, believing that any bodily fluids or hair samples left at the scene would be useless to the police who had not discovered the body for a fortnight. But what he could not have known was that temperatures for December were the lowest for years, freezing the semen at the scene. According to the Met Service, the period 24–29 December was a severe cold spell with sharp to severe ground frost each night and air temperatures were sub zero. It was the coldest December for 14 years. It was a lucky throw of the dice which allowed a genetic fingerprint to be drawn from the evidence at the scene.

On the evening of his arrest, Lawler agreed to show three officers, Detective Inspector Byrne, Detective Sergeant John Dennedy and Detective Garda Jim Clinton where he had hidden more of the victim's personal items. A further search of the area uncovered several items, including her video membership cards, address book, blood donor card and VHI membership card along with a black mascara brush.

That night, Lawler was brought before a special sitting of the Dublin District Court charged with the rape and murder of Marilyn Rynn. The District Judge ordered that he be remanded in custody for one week to Mountjoy prison. He was later granted bail in the High Court on condition that he live with his parents at Baltinglass, Co. Wicklow, not apply for a passport and sign on daily at the local Garda station.

Three days after his arrest, detectives went back to his home where they took away Lawler's personal computer and accessories. The items were taken to the Computer Section of the force's National Bureau of Fraud Investigation based at Harcourt Square.

During the course of his interrogation, the accused had drawn a map of how he accessed the DNA website on the Internet for

Detective Garda Clinton. Using this, Detective Sergeant Paul Gillen from the Fraud Section was able to get into the DNA site.

The detectives also discovered from this examination of Lawler's computer equipment that he had downloaded a vast quantity of pornography from the Internet, including a lot of paedophilic pornography. A deeper background investigation into Lawler also unearthed evidence that he was a transvestite. Lawler, the hard man in the gang at the pub, frequently liked to dress up in women's clothes.

* * *

At the Central Criminal Court on Monday, 26 January, 1998, David Lawler was jailed for life after he pleaded guilty to Marilyn Rynn's murder. Peter Charleton SC, prosecuting, said Ms Rynn was a 'highly-respected and liked public servant'. He said, 'She was accosted by the accused who assaulted her pursuant to a homicidal and sexual impulse. He strangled her having dragged her to a more private place.'

Mr Justice Kevin O'Higgins told Lawler he had pleaded guilty to murder for which there was only one sentence, mandatory life imprisonment.

After the court case, the man who led the murder inquiry, Superintendent Michael Carty was interviewed on RTÉ television by the station's legal affairs correspondent. The officer paid tribute to all the investigators involved. All angles had been pursued and the killer was caught by dogged police work and cooperation from the public. 'It was a textbook murder inquiry,' he said.

THE GREEN VAN

'Sure, anybody's fingerprints could be on that bicycle, even mine.'
Man questioned about the murder of Bernadette Connolly, 1970.

THE abduction and murder of little Bernadette Connolly, a 10-year-old girl from Co. Sligo, has never been solved. Several suspects were identified by the Gardaí and thousands of men fingerprinted in a bid to catch the young girl's killer, but to no avail.

Despite the horrific nature of the killing, the Gardaí were frustrated throughout the case by a lack of co-operation from a number of vital witnesses. The men involved appeared to know a lot more about Bernadette's disappearance than they were willing to tell the police.

Suspicion also hung over a local monastery. In the Ireland of 1970, the Church was still very powerful and held in high esteem. The Gardaí were slow to accuse members of any religious community of wrongdoing, no matter how serious. Nevertheless, during the investigation into the murder of Bernadette Connolly, the Gardaí were perturbed by a wall of silence erected before them.

Detectives were particularly anxious to trace the whereabouts of a monastery van that was seen on the day the schoolgirl disappeared. The vehicle was spotted on the road by a number of people around the time she was last seen alive. But no one from the local St Joseph's Passionist Retreat at Cloonmahon, known locally as the Monastery, who owned the van, admitted driving the van around that period. It is something which has never been adequately explained.

The age-old problem of sectarian distrust was also something which would rear its ugly head during the investigation.

More than 30 years on, the case has taken a new twist. Some witnesses who were reluctant to come forward during the initial inquiries have now passed on dramatic new information.

* * *

It was a miserable spring day. Showers coming in off the Atlantic lashed the Co. Sligo countryside. In the townland of Lisanoona, near Collooney, on Friday, 17 April, 1970, Mrs Maureen Connolly telephoned her friend, Ellen Molloy. Both women discussed arrangements for going to bingo that evening. During the course of their conversation, Mrs Connolly asked her friend, who lived closer to town, to purchase some fish in Collooney. She said she would send her daughter, 10-year-old Bernadette, along to collect the purchase later.

Bernadette had not been feeling well all week. On Wednesday and Thursday she had been off sick from school with an upset stomach. However, according to her dad, other than the odd patch of sickness she was a normal, healthy child. 'She was forever dancing and hopping around the place. She was a very lively little kid.'

It was Friday afternoon. The weekend lay ahead and the young girl was in good form. When her mother asked her to collect the fish, she got her bicycle and set off on the one-and-a-half-mile journey to Molloy's house. The time was 4.30 pm. It was a route she had travelled several times before.

The Connolly's home was situated on the Collooney to Boyle road, about three miles from Collooney. The Molloys lived in Lisaneena, which is situated just off the main road. The Lisaneena Road connects the two main routes from Collooney to Boyle and Tubbercurry.

In her haste, Bernadette overtook 12-year-old Oliver Flynn, who was about 100 yards from her house travelling by donkey and cart down the country road. She shouted 'Hello' as she pedalled past. Oliver's mother, Mrs Kathleen Flynn, was travelling behind her son on a bicycle. She remembered it had been a particularly bad day. At the time Bernadette passed them by it was raining very heavily and the young girl had the hood of her anorak pulled over her head.

'She was cycling hard at this time and it was raining a fairly heavy shower. I didn't pay much attention to Bernadette as her mother had been talking to me earlier at about 2 pm and mentioned that she was sending Bernadette to Collooney for messages,' Mrs Flynn recalled. The Flynns were the last known people to see Bernadette alive.

By 6 pm that evening there was no sign of her. Her mother became concerned and when her elder daughter Ann, aged 13, came home from school she sent her in search of the younger girl. Ann borrowed a bicycle from their next-door neighbour and cycled off towards Molloy's house. She kept a good lookout for her sister, checking gateways and neighbours' houses along the way. She did notice a bicycle in some bushes just off the road but did not pay it any great attention.

On arrival at Molloys, she discovered that Bernadette had never arrived there. Some of the family members were watching television coverage of the return of the Apollo 13 space mission and the astronauts' splashdown in the Pacific. Initially, Ann thought the Molloys were joking when they said Bernadette was not there. When she realised they were serious she became extremely anxious.

With the help of Patricia Molloy, who was 13, they retraced the route which would have been taken by Bernadette. They returned to the spot where Ann had earlier seen a bicycle in the ditch. There, on the Lisaneena Road, just off the Boyle Road, they found Bernadette's bicycle.

The spot was just half a mile from Molloys. The bike lay inside a roadside fence. At the side of the road they found Bernadette's purse. The purse was soaking wet and had obviously been left in the rain for some time. There was still some money in it. The two teenagers were now very worried. They picked up the bicycle and placed it against a tree. Then they cycled off towards Ann Connolly's home to report the ominous news.

On the way they met Gerry Connolly, Bernadette and Ann's father. They told him exactly what they had seen. The girls got into the car with him and drove to the spot where they had found the bicycle. There Mr Connolly noticed a man's footprints and those of a child in the mud. It was enough to set off alarm bells in his head. By now extremely anxious, he drove to Collooney and the local Garda station where he reported his daughter's disappearance to Sergeant Tom O'Brien.

An immediate search of the area was organised. Locals, backed up by a few gardaí and priests and brothers from the Cloonmahon Passionist Monastery, spread out along fields to look for the young girl. Around 8 pm, the Garda Superintendent from Sligo, Superintendent Long, visited the scene. What he learned made him very suspicious.

By the following morning, Saturday 18 April, there was still no sign of Bernadette. The search teams had worked on into the early hours with no success. Bernadette appeared to have vanished without trace. At this stage Superintendent Long decided to call in the expertise of the Murder Squad at Garda Headquarters. Although almost universally known as the Murder Squad, the unit was officially called the Investigation Section of the force's Technical Bureau and was led by Detective Inspector Dan Murphy. It was called in for all major crimes around the country where local officers needed backup.

The Connolly case came at around the same time as the Gardaí were investigating the capital murder of one of their own colleagues, Garda Dick Fallon. He was shot down at Arran Quay in Dublin by a Republican terror gang – styling itself Saor Éire – during a bank robbery. This inevitably limited the amount of resources which could be applied to the Sligo investigation.

When the team of detectives from Dublin arrived at the scene, the search was extended. A team of ten gardaí, 30 local people and members of the Passionist Fathers covered the route which Bernadette was likely to have taken. They paid particular attention to two lakes, known as the Toberscanavan Loughs, which lay just off the roadway where her bicycle was found. Members of the Garda Sub-aqua Unit were also summoned to the scene to trawl the lakes while tracker dogs were used to comb woods and bogland in the area.

Fr Brian D'Arcy, a member of the Passionist Order and now well-known from his appearances on Irish television programmes, such as the Late Late Show, and from his own Sunday newspaper column, was in Cloonmahon Monastery at the time of Bernadette's disappearance and assisted in the search. He was a 24-year-old trainee priest and knew her family well. 'It was a very tough traumatic time for the family and for the whole community,' recalls Fr D'Arcy.

'I remember Bernadette well as a great wee Irish dancer and her father I knew through the Gaelic club. A lot of effort was put into finding her. We were out the whole night and every day on the bogs looking for her but we never found anything,' he says.

During the investigation the small community lived in fear of the abductor striking again. 'Everyone was in a real deep state of shock that something so unspeakable could happen in the town. There were all sorts of rumours at the time which divided the community. Over 30 years on and it is hard to remember the exact details of what happened but you always wonder did you miss something,' he added.

By Sunday, as fears grew about the safety of the little schoolgirl, the search party swelled to more than 100-strong volunteers who were helping gardaí and members of the civil defence. They were briefed by Detective Sergeant John Courtney from the Murder Squad on what to look out for, such as signs of fresh clay or disturbed earth. All outhouses, lock-ups, disused wells and septic tanks were to be checked.

In the meantime, detectives were trying to locate anyone who travelled along the route Bernadette took around the time she disappeared. They managed to find 14 people who had used the road close to the critical time of 4.30 pm. These included salesmen, farmers and people visiting Cloonmahon Monastery. Despite the fact that most of them had travelled the road, the only ones who had seen Bernadette were Oliver and Kathleen Flynn, the mother and son she had overtaken 100 yards from home. It was a very worrying time for Bernadette's parents.

* * *

The Connollys had only returned from Britain five years earlier and they purchased the cottage at Doorla, Collooney at that time. Gerrard was a plumbing and heating contractor and had built up a good business in Sligo. He was originally from the area and his parents owned a pub in the neighbouring parish of Lackagh, but he had emigrated to England in 1951. He met his wife, Maureen, there.

Born in Moyvane in north Kerry, she had been raised in England from the age of two. At the age of 15, she returned to Moyvane and worked in Co. Limerick for a short time. In 1954, having returned to England, she started going out with Gerrard and they married two years later.

Their eldest daughter, Ann, was born that same year and three years later, Maureen gave birth to their second child, Bernadette. In 1962, the couple had a son, Thomas. Gerrard moved home to Ireland ahead of the family in August 1964 and once he had found a house they joined him.

Bernadette, who was near-sighted, wore glasses and, like other children in the area, attended a youth club run for the under-16s at Cloonmahon Monastery. The club organised stage shows as well as dancing and music lessons for the youngsters. The activities brought the children into regular contact with most members of the Passionist Order based there.

* * *

As the chances of finding Bernadette safe and well diminished, Detective Inspector Murphy's team decided to run time tests with the co-operation of the 14 potential witnesses who had travelled her route on 17 April. The Inspector wanted to place them as they had been on the road in relation to one another and in relation to the missing girl on the night of her disappearance. The re-enactment took place precisely one week after she had disappeared.

Ann Connolly was enlisted to cycle the two possible routes Bernadette could have taken to the Molloys' house. Based on the time tests, Detective Inspector Murphy and his team established that Bernadette had left her home at just after 4.29 pm. She reached the entrance to Cloonmahon Monastery at 4.33 pm and may have passed through the grounds for a shortcut. According to the re-enactment, the youngster could also have passed close to three men who were working in fields along various parts of the main road in the area at that time, although they all contended that they never saw her. The men's statements would become controversial some time later when friends told the Gardaí that two of the men had admitted seeing something on that day.

Back at Collooncy Station, the investigation squad made an important discovery.

The examination of Bernadette's bicycle had thrown up a vital clue. Members of the Technical Bureau discovered a fingerprint on the upper crossbar. While the mark was of poor quality, it exhibited enough characteristics to enable a match to be made with any suspect.

Based on this breakthrough, the Gardaí decided that everyone who passed by the area around the critical time, as well as men who lived in neighbouring townlands, would be asked to undergo fingerprint examination.

As is normal in an investigation of this type, the Gardaí also identified known sex offenders in the area along with patients recently released from mental hospitals. They drew up a list of 45 such individuals and checked their movements on the day of Bernadette's disappearance. Each was asked to give fingerprint samples and all were completely eliminated as suspects. There was absolutely nothing to link any of them with the scene of the crime and most had firm alibis.

In all, a total of 513 sets of prints were taken. All had negative results.

* * *

Detective Inspector Dan Murphy, who was one of the force's most respected investigators, decided to try concentrating on another aspect of the case.

Murphy, originally from Milford, Co. Cork, joined the Technical Bureau as a young detective from Clondalkin station in Dublin. It was a station which was to produce two other notable investigators, John Courtney, who would himself one day head the Murder Squad and John Paul McMahon, who later reached the rank of Deputy Commissioner.

Dan Murphy was admired within the detective branch of the force and investigated several of the country's most famous crimes. He would eventually become the Detective Chief Superintendent in charge of the Technical Bureau. The Connolly case, however, was one of the first major inquiries he headed and would prove to be one of his most frustrating cases. On the Sligo case with Murphy was a young detective, Paddy Culligan, who would later become Commissioner. A Sligo garda, Sean Doherty, was also one of the dozens of local officers assisting. He would later become a controversial Minister for Justice.

Murphy decided to concentrate on unaccounted-for cars seen in the area at the time of Bernadette's disappearance and which remained untraced. Four witnesses had seen a green van. A large black car was also seen. Appeals were broadcast on radio and television and published in the newspapers asking the owners to come forward but there was no response to the appeals. It is likely, however, that some of the descriptions of the various vehicles may have been duplicated.

A check was made of all green vans registered in Co. Sligo. In the days before computerisation, this was a long, painstaking job, which involved checking through paper records. Meanwhile, the Gardaí also decided to mount a surveillance operation in the Lisaneena area to try and identify any green vans which passed through. Those which were spotted were then followed and their drivers questioned.

A similar operation was mounted for large black cars. All their registrations were taken down and the drivers traced, and then interviewed. Lists of vehicles which left the country by car ferry on 18 April were also obtained.

Checkpoints were mounted on all the main routes around Lisaneena and at the entrance to Cloonmahon Monastery. Officers questioned the drivers and their passengers and asked if they had passed by the area the previous Friday. Those who had were then interviewed at length but nothing tangible came from this line of inquiry.

As the investigation continued, Detective Inspector Murphy's team began to pay more attention to a green van owned by the Monastery. Run by the Passionist Order, the religious community was made up of priests and brothers as well as student priests and monks. On the day Bernadette disappeared, there were 22 members of the order present along with three farm workers.

In particular, the Gardaí were anxious to find out where the green van was at the time the young girl went missing. The dark green Ford Escort was one of two vehicles owned by the order, the other was a Morris 1000. Both were at the full disposal of any member of the order.

The Gardaí soon discovered that the Ford Escort van could not be accounted for between 4.30 pm – when it was returned to the Monastery by one of the priests – and 7.55 pm.

Interest in this van increased when a service station attendant in Co. Sligo said the Monastery van pulled up at petrol pumps between 7 pm and 8 pm on the 17th. James McTiernan named one of the members of the Order as the driver. The attendant said he remembered the event clearly as it occurred at the time the astronauts were out of the capsule after successfully splashing down in the ocean – a reference to the return of the Apollo space capsule.

The cleric was interviewed about this claim and denied going for petrol on that day, although he did say he purchased petrol there on a morning previous to the 17th. Both men were brought face to face and the Order member remained unshakeable in his insistence that he did not drive the van that day. Likewise, the attendant was equally adamant. He said he could remember the event quite clearly as the cleric had seemed short-tempered and had blown the horn seeking service.

There was another peculiar twist to the case. When statements were initially taken from members of the Passionist Community on 28 April about their movements on the critical day, none of them could recall seeing that member of the Order in the Monastery between 6 pm and 8 pm.

However, when the Gardaí went back to conduct further interviews in May, two members of the Order told detectives they could recall seeing him in the television room watching the splashdown.

That brother is still alive and to this day denies James McTiernan's version of events. 'I had nothing to do with Bernadette Connolly's murder. I was at the petrol station just getting petrol,' he maintains 30 years later.

Asked about why the petrol station attendant would say he was there, he replied. 'I'm saying that Mr McTiernan was wrong. I differ with him on times.'

As the hunt continued, the Passionist Monastery offered support to the grief-stricken Connolly family. A recently-ordained priest from Cloonmahon Monastery became a regular visitor. The priest, Fr Columba, even moved into the Connolly home to comfort the family in their nightmare.

When Gerry Connolly lost his glasses, Fr Columba read his letters of sympathy for him and delivered them to the Garda station in Sligo. He brought the heartbroken family to Knock to say a private Mass. Over the subsequent weeks, the small family endured a living hell, waiting and hoping for news. For most of the time, Maureen Connolly lay heavily sedated in her bedroom.

Fr Columba, who was in his early 20s, was a strange choice by the Order to assist the family. Gardaí saw him as a highly-strung individual and felt he was not being very co-operative with their investigation.

Indeed, what the Connollys could not have known was that Detective Inspector Murphy's team regarded Fr Columba as a suspect. They were not satisfied with his account of his movements on the afternoon Bernadette disappeared. It would also transpire that he had a bizarre view of what might have happened to Bernadette.

Interviewed almost 30 years later about the murder, just before his death, Fr Columba gave a staggeringly confused and incomprehensible account of what he believed could have happened. He maintained that a covert security forces operation may have been involved.

'In my gut feeling I think it was the security forces,' he said. 'I heard that there was a consignment of guns for the IRA coming to the area of Cloonmahon around the time she disappeared. I have always had my suspicions. I've never talked to anybody about this. I would say the child was kidnapped in order to get the area searched for arms and things went wrong. I think the security forces could have abducted the child,' the priest said.

Fr Brian D'Arcy was friendly with Fr Columba, who died in 2001, and believes his story to be crazy.

'Columba was given to joking a bit,' he said. 'His heart was as big as a mountain but his recollection of reality had a lot to do with his imagination. Put it like this; he wasn't the most prudent of men. I never thought Columba was guilty, absolutely not. I thought his IRA story was a load of bullshit,' Fr D'Arcy told a Sunday newspaper.

He says he remembers that Columba was in the television room with the other clerics watching the splashdown at the critical time. 'As far as him being in the television room, I remember him being there.'

Soon after the murder, Columba was sent on the missions to Botswana. Fr D'Arcy visited his fellow priest in Africa.

'I stayed with Columba several times in Botswana and we celebrated our Silver Jubilee in Africa. When he died last year he practically had a state funeral. I couldn't make it there myself but I always felt sorry for him and particularly for Brother [name withheld – the cleric whom petrol pump attendant James McTiernan said was getting petrol for the green van on the day of the disappearance] who was under suspicion by the police.'

The Gardaí felt that Fr Columba knew a lot more than he was saying and that he could hold the key to Bernadette's whereabouts. The investigation team had no proof, however, of anything to connect him with the crime.

* * *

The police had their hunches but they had no firm evidence. By mid-May the searches had been wound down. Hundreds of acres within a three-and-a-half-mile radius of the spot where the bike was found had been walked, lakes were searched and 44 houses and sheds were entered but not a single clue was found to indicate what had happened to the little girl. Almost 2,000 people had been questioned and statements taken from more than 500 of them.

The investigation team also enlisted the help of the RUC and police in Britain. There was a fear that Bernadette may have been kidnapped by someone she met while the family lived in Birmingham. Despite inquiries by the British Police, they didn't come up with any results.

Eventually, at the end of May, the Missing Persons case was completely wound down. Nevertheless, in a report sent to Garda Headquarters, the local Superintendent admitted having some doubts about the co-operation he had received from the clergy at Cloonmahon. According to his report, 'each member of the Community was interviewed and detailed statements were taken from them covering their movements of 17 April. These statements have been checked and verified as far as it is possible for the period 4 pm to 6 pm.

'There does, however, still remain a certain mystery surrounding the van for that afternoon. To this date, none of them admit to using the van between 4.30 pm and 7.55 pm and not one of them can say that they saw the van at the Monastery during that time.'

Luck was not on the side of the police. Early in the investigation, they got a report of a fresh grave being dug at a bog near Boyle. A search team went to investigate but only managed to find an uprooted tree. This discovery meant the Gardaí did not search this particular spot again. The body of Bernadette Connolly lay just 100 yards further up the road.

*   *   *

On 4 August, Mrs Margaret O'Connor was working in the bog at Limnagh, near Boyle, Co. Roscommon. She detected a very bad smell in the air but did not pay it much attention, believing it to be a dead animal, and carried on with her work. The following day she returned to the bog with members of her family.

'I was standing on the road and I again got a terrible smell. It was so bad that I thought whatever was causing it couldn't be far away, so I looked around to see if I could find it. I walked up on the bank between the road and the plantation, this was on the left-hand side as you go towards the Ballymote to Boyle road. I walked along the bank for a bit. Down in the drain I saw what appeared to be a skeleton. I saw teeth and bones. I didn't know what type of skeleton it was but I thought the teeth were not those of an animal. I immediately thought of Bernadette Connolly who was missing from Collooney.'

Mrs O'Connor told her husband about the find and they reported the matter to the police.

Sergeant John Cuffe from Boyle arrived at the bog to investigate the discovery. He was left with little doubt that it was the remains of a child. Moreover, three miraculous medals pinned to the victims vest helped confirm the identity. Bernadette Connolly had been wearing them at the time she went missing.

The scene was about 15 miles south east of where Bernadette's bicycle was found four months earlier. The Limnagh Road, or as it is known locally, the Limnagh Line, is a sand road about two-and-a-half-miles long which links the Boyle to Collooney road with the Boyle to Ballymote road. It was about four miles from the town of Boyle. It could be reached by a myriad of minor roads from the spot where Bernadette had disappeared without ever having to travel on a main road.

At 9 am on 7 August, the Assistant State Pathologist Dr RB O'Neill viewed the body at the scene. It was in an advanced state of decomposition. Both legs and the right arm were missing. All that remained were the skull, neck, rib cage, part of the spine and left arm. A lot of the victim's clothing was missing, including her underwear, shoes, glasses and a signet ring. All the missing clothing was from below the waistline.

The body was taken to the mortuary at Boyle District Hospital where Dr O'Neill carried out a post-mortem. The pathologist confirmed the body was that of a young girl of between 10 and 12 years old. Unfortunately, due to the state of the body, he was unable to determine the cause of her death.

The finding of the body meant that the investigation, which had been wound down in mid-May, was now resumed with great vigour. It was no longer just a Missing Persons case. Detective Inspector Dan Murphy's team arrived back in Co. Sligo. They were now dealing with a murder inquiry.

The crime shocked the whole community and there was great revulsion that a young girl should have her life terminated in this manner. The Gardaí spared no effort in their attempts to track down her killer.

A full search of the bog, involving the force's Dog Unit, was carried out in an effort to find the rest of Bernadette's clothing. Not far from where her body was found, the Gardaí discovered her weather-beaten anorak. There was a pink stain on the right sleeve of the coat, which officers believed could be significant. The anorak was sent off to the Institute for Industrial Research and Standards in Dublin for analysis. The stain turned out to be a form of fungus which was irrelevant to the inquiry.

The Murder Squad decided that every male over the age of 15 years in the area bounded by the Boyle to Collooney and Ballymote roads would be interviewed to account for their movements on 17 April.

This included the towns of Boyle, Ballymote, Collooney and the villages of Ballinafad, Castlebaldwin and Drumfin. Uniformed officers called to each household. Statements given by the men were checked out by detectives.

Later, the area would be enlarged to encompass a slice of the north-east covering 380 square miles, with the spot where Bernadette's bicycle was found at its centre. Every man living in this geographical region was interviewed and his fingerprints taken. It was a task of momentous proportions, involving scores of detectives from the Sligo/Leitrim and Roscommon/Galway East divisions. Men who had left the area since 17 April were also contacted and asked to account for their movements and to give their fingerprints.

Taking prints enabled cross-checks to be made against the fingermark found on Bernadette's bicycle months earlier. By 28 August the force had accumulated 2,324 sets of fingerprints from men in counties Roscommon, Sligo and Leitrim, which came within the 380-square-mile area. None of them matched the sample lifted from the bicycle frame.

Inspector Murphy and his team of officers, including Detective Sergeant John Courtney, began to re-examine every single statement taken during the course of the earlier Missing Persons inquiry. They were looking for inconsistencies, time gaps, peculiar explanations, anything which would demand further attention.

The team was still very suspicious about the movements of the Monastery van. Nobody had yet adequately explained where it was around the time Bernadette went missing. Yet four witnesses had seen such a van on the road at the critical period. But on 17 April, before the squad had the chance to re-examine the Passionists' accounts, two new leads arose. Each had the potential to solve the case.

On 25 August, Sergeant Tom O'Brien from Collooney Station met a man in the village. They were chatting casually and in the course of the conversation the murder of Bernadette Connolly came up. The mass taking of fingerprints was the talk of the locality and for miles around. It had generated much controversy and led to fierce speculation about who could have killed the young girl. The man spoke to Sergeant O'Brien about the fingerprints and how the experts were now closer to taking samples from people in his townland. He remarked: 'Sure, anybody's fingerprints could be on that bicycle, even mine.'

Curious, the Sergeant asked him how this could be so. The man explained how he had once put the bicycle in the back of his car and his prints could therefore be on the frame. It was enough for the officer to report the matter to his superiors.

The following day they asked the man for his fingerprints. The prints were then checked by Technical Bureau experts against the mark taken from Bernadette bicycle. They got a match. The print on the bicycle was more than likely left by the right finger of the man who spoke to Sergeant O'Brien.

On 27 August he was interviewed by Detective Inspector Dan Murphy and Detective Sergeant Courtney. The man involved was very worried about the circumstances in which he found himself.

He told the two detectives how he had carried the bike in the boot of his car. Certain aspects of his statement had to be checked out and several people were interviewed in an attempt to verify the story.

It was a protracted affair which involved speaking to some of the people involved a number of times. This aspect of the inquiry dragged into September. However, for the investigators it proved a dead end. The man was able to account satisfactorily for his movements of 17 April, 1970. The Gardaí were satisfied he had carried the bike in his car.

It was a frustrating time for the murder hunt team. Despite the various appeals, they were no closer to catching the killer. Apart from the fingerprint match, which they were now certain had been left some time prior to Bernadette's disappearance, there were no new leads. Again they began re-checking statements. In particular, the accounts of two men who were in the area on that day appeared to be sketchy and were deemed worthy of further analysis.

The men had been interviewed on several occasions over the first few days of the inquiry and were asked about their movements and what they had seen. Soon after, a letter was received from them at Collooney Station. The substance of the letter was that they had seen a dark-coloured car or van parked on the Lisaneena Road, at the spot where Bernadette Connolly's bicycle was found. They said the car was parked there around 4.55 pm. The men were then re-interviewed but would not elaborate further on the statement.

A few weeks later, on 27 June, one of the men was talking to a friend and mentioned to him that he had seen 'the Monastery van' on the afternoon of Bernadette's disappearance. Unprompted, he told the friend that the van had gone along Lisaneena Road towards Tubercurry Road, turned and come back. When asked why he had not told this to the Gardaí, the man just shrugged his shoulders. Why should he when others wouldn't, he responded. The friend notified the Gardaí of the conversation.

On 18 September, a visitor to the man's house also reported a similar conversation. The man told him how he had seen the green van from the Monastery on the day Bernadette disappeared. The Gardaí decided they would have to confront the man about what he had said to two people, information he had left out of his statements to them.

However, the Gardaí met a brick wall. The man denied that any such conversations had taken place. Detective Inspector Murphy's team now decided to take a new approach. They confronted the man with the two people he had spoken to and who had reported his references to the Monastery van to the Gardaí. At this stage he agreed the conversations had taken place but denied ever mentioning the green van. The two other men, however, remained adamant that he had.

Despite several attempts by third parties to get him to speak to the Gardaí, the man steadfastly refused. When asked at a meeting with one of the third parties why he would not be more forthcoming, he is reported to have said: 'I have my reasons.'

On 9 October, in a final bid to clear up the matter, he was brought to Boyle Garda station where he was interviewed by detectives. Again, he denied having ever said anything about seeing the green Monastery van.

He was not the only one to hold back however. The investigation team believed another man also knew more than he told them. This man is reported to have told a relative that he saw a car or van stopped 'for a nice while' and a man crossing the fence near where this vehicle was parked – close to where Bernadette's bike was found. Again, both men were brought face to face and the man denied his earlier account.

Detectives, however, remain convinced that the men know more than they told them. They are mystified as to why this is so. Some believe that in the Co. Sligo of the time, any accusation against the Church could stir up awful resentment. They believe that at least two of the men did not wish to spark off rows between people in the community, which was a tightknit cross-denominational one. To level any allegation against the Church could have sparked off sectarian distrust in an area close to the border, where just a few miles to the north, religious intolerance was at its height in 1970.

* * *

By 16 October, 1970, when no breakthrough was made in the murder inquiry, resources began to be directed elsewhere.

At the time, the bulk of the investigation team's suspicions still surrounded the Monastery van. One of the senior Gardaí at the time reported to his authorities: 'A certain amount of suspicion lay on the Cloonmahon Monastery van, which is a dark-green Ford Escort. This van is not satisfactorily accounted for during the period 4.30 pm to 7.55 pm. Since the investigation resumed, suspicion has hardened towards the Monastery van having been on the Lisaneena Road on that afternoon.'

The officer continued: 'We are not entirely happy about the Cloonmahon Monastery van. However, in the absence of more tangible evidence, there is relatively little else that can be done by way of inquiry regarding this van, irrespective of what our feelings are.'

As soon as his report arrived in Garda Headquarters, the investigation team was asked for a second copy. Somehow, this copy ended up in the hands of members of the Irish clergy. As a result of its contents, some senior members of the Passionist Order, which incidentally holds the chaplaincy to the Garda Siochána, refused to greet or acknowledge Detective Inspector Dan Murphy or some members of his team for years afterwards.

This attitude towards members of the investigation team changed with the appointment as chaplains of inspired priests such as Fr Ralph Egan and Fr Hilarion Cleary years later.

* * *

The passage of time has done nothing to bring us closer to the positive identification of Bernadette's killer. Instead, the number of suspects in the case has increased by at least two in the past three decades.

Over the years the murder has attracted more attention in the media. In particular, the murders of Holly Wells and Jessica Chapman in Britain in 2002, which bore striking similarities to Bernadette's disappearance, have caused the killing to be highlighted once more.

In late 1999, possibly prompted by the renewed publicity, a vital new witness came forward. His information could have major consequences for the inquiry in terms of identifying the killer.

The new witness was, just like Bernadette, 10 years old in 1970. A short time before Bernadette went missing, he was cycling between Ballygawley and Ballintogher on the Collooney to Dromahair road, about three miles from Collooney. He remembers that a van passed him out and stopped 20–30 feet ahead of him. As the young boy cycled towards the van he became a little apprehensive. Just as he was about to pass it out, a man lurched at him and attempted to grab him.

The schoolboy cycled harder and just managed to evade the tackle. But it made a lasting impression on him and he consigned the van's registration to memory. When he finally approached the Gardaí to tell them of his experience, he told officers that when he related what had happened to his father, he was told not to tell anyone about it. However, the incident preyed on his conscience for years, particularly in light of the renewed interest in Bernadette's murder. He passed on the full registration of the van.

This lead has given an impetus to a new investigation which was established at the request of the Connolly family. A small team of detectives at Sligo station, led by Assistant Commissioner Kevin Carty, are looking at the new information and analysing thousands of documents compiled during the original inquiry. In particular, they are trying to ascertain the reasons some suspects were identified and others eliminated.

Detectives at Sligo checked the vehicle index that was passed on to them and found it belonged to a Scottish man who worked in the area as a television repair man in 1970. When gardaí checked with the Scottish authorities about his current whereabouts, they learned he was listed on the UK's Sex Offender Register and had only recently been released from prison. The man, who is now in his late 70s, has several previous convictions for sexual assaults on young boys and served a number of long jail terms. It has also emerged that he was questioned by gardaí during the original inquiry but eliminated as a suspect from the investigation.

When a detective travelled to Edinburgh to speak with him, he agreed to meet the officer in a police station for interview. He conceded he was in the Collooney area at the time of Bernadette's disappearance. But he said he could not recollect anything about the girl's murder. He told the officer that his recollection of events back then was 'hazy'.

Whether the paedophile's presence in the Collooney area in April 1970 is a total coincidence or the vital breakthrough is difficult to establish. Did he, for example, given his history of assaults on boys, mistake Bernadette for a boy because she wore a hood over her head from the rain?

Unfortunately, the passage of time means alibi witnesses in this case will now be extremely difficult to find. And even today's sophisticated DNA technology gives detectives little to go on. 'The delay in finding Bernadette's body means that any samples the killer left were destroyed by the weather and decay. It means, unfortunately, that there are no blood or other samples which we can cross-check with a suspect,' said one of the investigators.

Gardaí intend to travel to Edinburgh again to re-interview the new suspect.

While this is the strongest lead, it is not the only one. Three years after Bernadette's murder, detectives questioned another British paedophile, Bob Reynolds. Reynolds, who arrived in Ireland in April 1970 to write for a fishing magazine, was arrested in 1973 for the abduction and rape of a nine-year-old girl in Castlebar, Co. Mayo. Reynolds was arrested in Co. Cavan and jailed for six years.

Retired detective John Courtney remembers that Reynolds was ruled out of the inquiry when he could not be placed in Collooney at the vital time. John Courtney says Reynolds was questioned at length but could not be tied into the investigation. More recently, in September 2002, officers at Sligo have begun looking into a statement from a man who, for the first time, claims he saw Reynolds in the area at the time.

While detectives are pursuing this line, they do not believe it is as strong as the Scottish lead.

*   *   *

The disappearance and murder of Bernadette Connolly is still a mystery. The emergence more than 30 years later of two new suspects, one of whom is an active suspect, has led to the investigation being re-opened. The chances of the killer ever being charged with the crime, however, remain slim.

There are still a lot of unanswered questions about the goings on at Cloonmahon Monastery on the day of the murder. Some people in the locality still know a lot more about the disappearance than they have ever said. The emergence of two people with new leads at this stage shows there is still a lot more information out there. Many of the individuals who hold the key to finding the killer remain alive and as long as they do, it is still possible that Bernadette's murderer, whether alive or not, will be identified.

The inquiry was one of the biggest of its day. Perhaps if the case had occurred in contemporary Ireland, there would have been more pressure to pursue and arrest suspects, something which perhaps the police felt they could not do at the time – although it did not affect the thoroughness of their investigations. One thing is for sure – some people know a lot more about the case than they have ever told the police. In withholding information they assisted in keeping the circumstances of Bernadette's death a mystery.

The case is still spoken about in the north-east. Children who pass the area where she went missing are often asked to say a prayer to Bernadette by their parents.

* * *

Detective Chief Superintendent Dan Murphy died in service on 12 June, 1984. The Bernadette Connolly mystery still very much troubled him in the period before his death. Murphy told friends and colleagues he had a strong idea who killed Bernadette. Indeed, he told one senior colleague of a plan he had put in place to interview Fr Columba once more in the autumn of 1984. He felt that the priest held the key to solving the case. The Chief Superintendent felt confident he could yet crack the case. Unfortunately, he died before his plan was implemented.

MURDER IN THE CURRAGH

'I still held out hope that Joyce was alive until a garda officer arrived on my doorstep with tears in his eyes and I realised that Joyce was gone.'

– Ray Quinn.

BEIRUT in the 1980s was synonymous with violence and war. Kidnappings were almost a daily occurrence at one point in the conflict and gun battles raged between the warring Christian and Muslim factions. At the height of the civil war, the Irish United Nations battalion based in south Lebanon regularly made the capital out of bounds to its soldiers.

Ray Quinn was an army officer based at the UN headquarters at Naqoura. It is a small seaside town right on the border with the former Israeli-controlled area of Lebanon and then an official crossing point into Israel proper. Like many officers posted abroad on missions longer than six months, Ray had brought his family to the Middle East. Rather than live in the war zone of south Lebanon, the Quinns rented a home in northern Israel, which for the most part had been spared the violence which raged across the frontier in south Lebanon. It meant that Ray could visit his wife Joyce and their children on a regular basis and enjoy the Mediterranean lifestyle on offer in Israel.

When they travelled home to Ireland, the flight was normally from an airport in Israel. On one occasion, however, Ray remembers that there was a good deal on offer on a flight out of Beirut. Against their better judgment, perhaps, Ray and Joyce travelled with their two young children to Beirut on the northern highway, which hugs the Mediterranean coastline for most of the journey to the capital. It's a scenic journey but at that time it was also a fairly dangerous one.

As they drove into the outskirts of Beirut, Ray saw a young man dashing out of a building. He was closely followed by two men armed with AK47 assault rifles.

The gunmen fired several bursts of gunfire in the direction of the youth. At such close range, Ray believes that they must have killed the young man.

At the UN headquarters in the city, a sniper had opened fire and peacekeeping staff were put on red alert. The couple booked into a hotel and were given a room on the ninth floor. In the early hours they were awoken by the sound of a ferocious explosion. Their young son David was jolted awake and screamed out in fear. Soon after, the city echoed to a long gun battle which lasted most of the night. Ray later learned that the fighting had been a spontaneous eruption of hostilities between the staffs of the Iranian and Iraqi embassies.

The Quinns got a flight out of Beirut without any further incident the following morning. They reasoned that having survived that violent night in the Middle East, life back home in the Co. Kildare countryside would be very pleasant indeed.

How wrong they were.

*   *   *

The love affair between Joyce Wickham and Ray Quinn is the stuff of fairytales. The dashing young army officer and the beautiful and vivacious young woman. They were childhood sweethearts, who both grew up in the Navan Road area of north Dublin. Joyce was a schoolfriend of Ray's sister Ann and a regular visitor to the Quinn household. The Quinns owned a supermarket on Ashtown Grove, off the Navan Road, and while working in the shop Ray often encountered the pretty young Wickham girl buying sweets on her way home from school.

Later, in their teens, Ray set up a blind date for Joyce with one of his schoolfriends. But the teenager soon saw his mistake. Joyce looked radiant on the night and the young Quinn boy became quite envious. That evening he concluded that she was the girl for him.

It was 1969 and Joyce had just turned 17 when they officially began dating. Four years later they were married. It was the perfect match. Ray had joined the Defence Forces as a cadet officer around the time they started dating and was commissioned in 1969. Coming from an army family she knew all about the demands and uncertainties of military life. Joyce's dad, Commandant Tommy Wickham, was killed by a Syrian soldier in a shooting accident while serving with the UN on the Golan Heights two years earlier.

Before their marriage, Joyce worked for the Bankers Institute on Nassau Street in Dublin, later getting a job with the Blood Transfusion Service Board.

As a young lieutenant Ray was transferred to Mullingar and Joyce gave up her job to move with him. Two years later the couple moved to Kildare for his next posting. Apart from one year spent in Britain where the young officer underwent a gunnery staff course and Ray's occasional posting to the Middle East, the Quinns lived in Co. Kildare.

In June 1990, Ray returned from a tour of duty in south Lebanon. During his absence, the couple had discussed Joyce returning to work. With Ray abroad and the children at school, life in the Kildare countryside could be quite lonely. They eventually settled on the idea of buying a small shop in Milltown, Co. Kildare. Then known as 'Milltown Stores', it was the only shop in the tiny village situated just a few miles from the famous Curragh Racecourse.

It's hard to imagine a more peaceful setting. At one end of the village lies a section of the Grand Canal spanned by a high, narrow humpback bridge. Traffic coming from the racecourse direction passes over the bridge where immediately on the left there is a picturesque canalside public house. A few yards further up on the left is the new one-storey primary school with a large playground facing onto the roadway. At a T-junction the Curragh road meets the main Kildare road and the shop is directly opposite. It's a narrow building, fronted by a large glass pane and doorway. Immediately to the right is the Milltown Inn public house, a long, modern, red-brick building with a car park to the front. Further to the right are a few private homes before the village meets the countryside again. On the other side of the shop is the village church and graveyard. Large, dark, nineteenth-century gravestones crop out of the slightly risen site. The cemetery in the middle of the village gives the place a solemn feel. It's more in keeping with a small English village. Further on towards Kildare a few more houses lie on the left side of the road before the small spread of well-kept one-storey homes of the Millview local authority estate can be seen. In recent years the expansion of Dublin has led to an inevitable increase in the volume of traffic through the small community.

From the outset Ray was determined he would not become too involved with the business. He joined the Defence Forces to get away from his own family shop and had no interest in getting back behind a counter. Apart from helping raise the £44,000 loan to purchase the property, the shop was now entirely Joyce's responsibility.

By now the couple had two girls and a boy. Joyce adored the children. After the eldest, Nicole, was born, Joyce had gynaecological problems and though doctors decided against a hysterectomy she was warned that she would probably not give birth again. When David was born five years later, the Quinns' only son was as good as a miracle. 'A lovely fat little baby,' Ray recalls. Lisa, their second girl, followed a year later.

Apart from the separations necessitated by foreign military missions, the Quinns lived pretty much an idyllic life. They were a two-car family with a beautiful bungalow at Moorefield, outside Kildare town, which they built in 1986. Joyce's business was doing very well and Ray was studying at the College of Industrial Relations every Monday and Wednesday night to further his military career. She was very popular with the locals, always ready to listen to customers' problems. And for those who occasionally couldn't afford to pay for their groceries, she was willing to extend credit.

The women of the village had great respect for their new shopkeeper. 'Joyce Quinn was so patient with the kids. The way they'd go in with 30p and want 5p worth of this, 5p worth of that. She had the patience of a saint,' said one.

Another woman remembers that: 'Joyce would let fellas who were on the dole get their cigarettes on tick and they could fix up on dole day. She was a very kind woman.'

By 1995 the Quinns had managed to pay off the bulk of their loan. In a few more years they planned to sell off the shop and use the proceeds to buy a holiday apartment in Tenerife.

On the morning of Tuesday, 23 January, 1996, Ray got up as usual at 7.15 am to drive to work in Dublin. He was a commandant in the Army's Operations Department, acting as liaison officer with the Gardaí. Whenever the police needed a helicopter, the assistance of the Navy or the armed back-up of the Army, they would contact Commandant Quinn.

The couple had a brief chat before he got on the road shortly before 8 am. 'Remind me to go to bed tonight,' she told Ray as she pulled on her clothes. 'I'm so tired.'

Around 7.30 am Joyce had woken David (15) and Lisa (14) for school. Their elder sister Nicole (21) had left for work earlier on the 7.15 am train to Dublin.

After dropping the children off to catch the school bus, Joyce continued on to Milltown to open the shop. It was a typical day in Milltown, with the usual stream of customers in and out of the business they had renamed The Store. After school, David and Lisa called in to their mother at 4.45 pm. David collected some ham, crisps and a bar of chocolate for his lunch the following day while Lisa stayed in charge of the shop. It was customary for Joyce to leave one of the children to deal with customers while she brought the other teenager home and began to prepare dinner.

That evening Joyce drove her son into Kildare where she paid her mobile phone bill. The phone had been a present from Ray at Christmas. A few months earlier she had got two punctures when her car had hit a pothole returning from Dublin. She was stuck on the side of the road and had to walk some distance to a house to phone her family. The incident worried Ray, who was always security conscious. He bought the phone specifically in case something similar happened again. He programmed several numbers into the speed dial of the little Ericsson – 3 was for Kildare Gardaí, 4 home, 5 his office, while 6 and 7 were for his mother and Joyce's mother.

While on holidays in Florida a few years earlier he had also bought his wife a can of pepper spray as a defensive weapon. Shooting the spray into the eyes of an assailant would be enough to temporarily blind the attacker and give a victim enough time to escape. After all, dealing with the Gardaí on a daily basis and seeing some of the violent crimes they had to investigate, the army officer thought that you couldn't be too careful.

Having done some shopping, mother and son returned home where she prepared dinner. Joyce had planned roast pork and potatoes for the evening meal. She put the food in the oven, instructing David to turn down the temperature after an hour before she made the six-mile journey back to the shop to relieve Lisa. It was the last time her son would see her alive.

At 5.40 pm Ray arrived at the shop before his wife had returned and went inside to chat with Lisa. He went back outside to read one of the newspapers and listen to live updates on the car radio of the Budget announced a short time earlier in the Dáil by the Minister for Finance. Joyce arrived about 6 pm and they discussed the day's happenings.

'She gave me instructions about putting on the vegetables for dinner at home and said that the roast was already in the oven. She told me there was already a *Star* newspaper at home and I asked her to bring the *Independent* and *Herald* home if there were any left over. We spoke for a while and I suddenly noticed it was about 6.15 pm and I was due to collect Nicole at 6.20 pm.'

Almost directly across the road near the primary school on the junction which leads to the Curragh, Kenneth O'Reilly was watching. One neighbour remembers passing the 22-year-old as he skulked around the schoolgate. O'Reilly explained that he was looking for a £5 note. In reality, the unemployed butcher was probably ensuring the school gate was open for when he returned there later that night in Joyce's car.

In contrast to the busy lifestyle the Quinns led, O'Reilly was one of life's misfits. He had given up his job as a boner in a meat factory in Kildare and spent his days watching videos. Gardaí now suspect he also spent much of his time fantasising about Joyce. He lived at home with his parents just 400 yards from the shop. He was a regular customer at The Store and Joyce even extended him credit. Two weeks earlier she had entered his name on the 'tick' book for a few pounds worth of shopping.

Ray Quinn, who was accompanied by Lisa, picked Nicole up at the railway station and arrived home around 6.35 pm. Ray changed out of uniform and began working on a panic button and alarm system for Joyce's sister Barbara, who lived in Dublin with her teenage children. He took the parts in from the boot of the car and laid them out on the mat in front of the stove in the breakfast room. Soon the place was a mess and he moved the whole operation out of everybody's way into the study.

'I was engrossed in the work but remembered I had to cook the vegetables. It was around 6.50 pm because I remember thinking they'd be ready in half an hour, when Joyce was due in. Joyce had the potatoes and carrots already prepared.'

Time flew by and the next time he looked at his watch it was 8.15 pm. 'I went into the kitchen to see why nobody had called me for dinner. Nicole told me that Joyce hadn't arrived home and that she had switched off the cooker.'

The family's nightmare had just begun.

It started with the typical feeling most people get when somebody is unduly late. All scenarios are lived out – a car crash, a mugging or worse. In most cases the person has simply stayed chatting with friends or got delayed in traffic. When they return they are surprised and wonder what all the fuss is about. Unfortunately, for the Quinns this would not be the case.

At first, Ray thought Joyce must have had a breakdown. 'I tried to contact Joyce on the mobile phone. I assumed the car had broken down or she had a puncture. I was surprised she hadn't contacted me on the mobile phone as this was the whole purpose of getting it.

'When I rang I got the answering service saying the customer I was trying to ring was temporarily out of range. At that stage I assumed the phone wasn't switched on or hadn't been fully charged.'

Getting increasingly worried, Ray decided to go in search of his wife. He drove back to Milltown. He went into Kildare and out past the Cill Dara Golf Club directly to the village.

'There was no sign of her car. I went into the Milltown Inn and phoned home to see if she had arrived as there are a number of alternative routes from Kildare town she might have taken and I could have missed her on the road.'

Nicole answered and said that their mum had not returned. Ray retraced his steps back to the house in Moorefield and became more concerned. He got back to the house before 8.45 pm.

The family speculated where their mother might be. It was suggested she could have gone to the cash and carry or to the mobile blood bank, which one of them thought may have been in the Keadeen Hotel that day. Again Ray tried the mobile phone but got the same recorded message.

'I drove into Newbridge to the Keadeen but the blood bank wasn't there. Again I phoned home from the Keadeen to see if Joyce had returned. She hadn't. I went down to Dunnes Stores but the shopping centre was closed. I went on to Cox's cash and carry which was also closed,' says Ray.

The family were becoming frantic.

This was totally unlike Joyce. First of all not to have told them she was going somewhere and then not to contact them. Ray drove back to Milltown, hoping she may have returned to the shop.

'I tried the shutters on the shop but they were locked and the shop and the backroom were in darkness. I went into the Milltown Inn and phoned home again. I asked Nicole to phone Joyce's mother and sister to ask them if Joyce was with them or was due to visit them, which would have surprised me because my understanding was that she was coming directly home.'

At 9.45 pm he returned to the family home at Moorefield where everybody was now deeply alarmed.

A short time earlier, Ray had a brief moment of hope. 'I met a car similar to Joyce's being driven by a fair-haired woman. I was so sure it was Joyce's car that I turned around and came home and expected to see it in the driveway.' But it was not to be.

'When I got back Nicole told me she had managed to contact Joyce's mother and her sister Barbara and neither of them were expecting to see her.'

The family made the difficult decision to call the Gardaí.

Ray undertook to ring the local station. He gave a description of his wife – 5ft 6ins tall with fair, medium-length hair and wearing a long mid-thigh pullover, black leggings/ski pants and white runners. He described the car she was a driving – a dark Citroen AX, 1991 with a KE registration.

'I impressed on the garda that this was serious. He said he would send out a description to the cars and stations at Athy, Newbridge and Naas.'

Ray and his son David got in the car and drove around Kildare, the Curragh plains and back into Milltown. David had brought his torch and shone it into gateways and fields as they past. It was around 11 pm when they got into the village.

David directed the torchlight into the shop to check for any sign of his mother but they could see nothing amiss.

'David went into the graveyard. I could see the light among the headstones as he crouched around for traces of his mother. I called on him to come out. He came out and insisted on going into the schoolyard across the road,' Ray recalls.

David remembered it was around 11.30 pm when he met back up with his father at the churchyard gate.

'I asked could I have a look in the grounds of Milltown National School. I jumped over the wall at the old school and I walked to the rear of the new school. Dad also jumped the wall and checked around the front of the new school.'

Then came the discovery they had both been dreading.

'I noticed Mam's black Citroen. I called Dad and he ran around.'

Ray remembers the moment distinctly.

'I recall David giving a moan and crying out: "There's mum's car." He shone the light in and we could see the cash register at an angle on the backseat with no money in it. All the doors were closed. I opened the driver's door and David opened the passenger's door.'

In the dark it was impossible to detect the bloodstains on the dashboard and seat which would become apparent the following morning.

Ray ran into the Milltown Inn to ring the Gardaí. A staff member and three customers came out to help in the search while a distraught David continued to look for any clue as to what had happened to his mother.

As he searched along the perimeter fence of the school he found Joyce's black and grey handbag in a hedge. It had been hastily dumped in the ditch with envelopes spilling out of it.

At about that time a garda squad car pulled up. The officers asked everybody not to touch anything. They asked if they could get access to the shop across the road. Neither of the Quinns had keys – the second set of keys to the shop had gone missing a few months earlier.

They forced a back window and David got into the shop. Everything inside was intact and there was no sign of intruders or a struggle. As David got back out the alarm went off. He silenced it and joined his dad outside.

The gardaí advised that there was nothing more that Ray and David could do so late in the night and suggested that they return home. All kinds of thoughts were running through their heads as they made the journey home to a house without Joyce. No one really slept that night. The family stayed up until about 4 am, trying to reassure each other.

They made the necessary phone calls to family, friends, the Gardaí and army colleagues. It was a traumatic night, a terrible mixture of worry, anxiety, tears and apprehension.

* * *

The Gardaí continued their searches during the night and the national newspapers were notified of the growing fears for Joyce Quinn. The following morning the *Irish Independent* carried a story headlined: 'Missing Woman Search As Car Found.' It told how: 'A Garda search was underway early today after a Kildare businesswoman disappeared under suspicious circumstances. Gardaí are concerned for the safety of the 44-year-old married woman who disappeared after locking up her shop in Milltown, Co. Kildare last night.'

At first light the family were joined by several uncles from both sides of the family. A large group of locals, numbering about 100, many of whom had heard about the disappearance on radio, also gathered to help search for Joyce. They formed into groups in the front car park of the Milltown Inn, right next to Joyce's shop.

The army authorities arranged for a few platoons of soldiers from the 3rd Infantry Battalion based at the Curragh to join the search operation. Shortly before 10 am, Superintendent Gerry Moran from Kildare Station organised the searchers into groups of eight. He carried printed search routes on a clipboard and consulted an Ordnance Survey map propped up against the back windscreen of a car.

Earlier Ray arrived looking grey and haggard, with fresh mud on his Wellingtons from searches during the morning. Someone handed him a mobile phone. Friends gathered protectively around him. Others kept a respectful distance.

A few minutes after 10 am, 80 soldiers dressed in combat uniforms spread off across the fields, joined overhead by two Air Corps helicopters. The mood amongst the searchers was downcast. Everyone feared the worst.

GUILTY

Ray Quinn peeled away from the search parties to return home to do a radio interview to appeal for anyone who may have seen his wife to make contact. He also wanted to speak directly to the person who had taken Joyce and plead with them not to harm her. As he prepared to go on air around 11 am, a senior garda arrived at the house. Chief Superintendent Sean Feely broke the news everyone dreaded.

Joyce's body had been found half an hour previously.

Two neighbours discovered the semi-naked body during a search of commonage 100 feet off the Milltown-Kildare Road opposite Cill Dara Golf Club. She had been murdered.

* * *

Around 7 pm the previous evening Joyce had locked up The Store as usual. As she drove out of the village towards home, it appears Kenneth O'Reilly was on the roadside thumbing a lift. O'Reilly had been watching Joyce's movements most of the evening. When he saw her pull down the shutters and lock the front door he put his plan into action. He was carrying a small bag, in which he had hidden a boning knife from his days at the local meat factory.

Milltown is the sort of country place where you don't pass people on the road, especially if you know them. It appears Joyce may have stopped the car and offered the 22-year-old a lift.

Nobody will ever know precisely what happened during the next hour, but about two miles down the road O'Reilly admits he asked Joyce to stop the car. When she did he lunged at her with one of the butcher's knives, stabbing her close to the heart. He then drove the car behind a clump of furze in the Curragh, ripped off her clothes and raped the dying or already dead woman.

At some stage around the time Joyce was killed there was an attempt to make a phone call from her mobile. Perhaps Joyce was desperately trying to contact her husband or, during the struggle, one of the speed dial numbers was pressed. Either way the call never connected.

* * *

News of the murder caused a national outrage. All the daily newspapers carried pages of coverage of the killing. The homicide had come at a very sensitive time for the Rainbow Coalition Government already facing serious criticism of its track record on dealing with crime, particularly because of the increasing levels of gangland crime. The murder also came just weeks after the rape and murder of Dublin woman Marilyn Rynn. A day earlier two elderly men were found murdered in separate incidents in Co. Kerry and Co. Galway. The previous week an 81-year-old woman was viciously beaten by two men who ransacked her home in Cork.

In the Dáil, Justice Minister Nora Owen was under enormous pressure from the Fianna Fáil and Progressive Democrats opposition benches to reassure the public about the increasing incidents of violent crime. In Garda Headquarters, the Commissioner Patrick Culligan and his advisors were struggling to cope with the media frenzy.

No one was more aware of the crime situation than Joyce's bereaved husband. A distraught Ray Quinn described to the nation his own and his family's anguish. 'I still held out hope that Joyce was alive until a garda officer arrived at my doorstep with tears in his eyes and I realised that Joyce was gone,' he told a national newspaper.

'We are distraught. The whole family is in agony and by speaking out I hope that perhaps some other family will be spared the ordeal that we are experiencing at the moment.'

As if coping with Joyce's murder was not enough, difficulties in getting a pathologist to the scene meant her body would be left lying out on the bitterly cold Curragh Plains for another night. The Gardaí were waiting for the arrival of State Pathologist, Professor John Harbison and couldn't move the body. Professor Harbison's arrival was delayed because he was attending the scene of another killing.

Ray Quinn remembers that sheer exhaustion set in that night. All the grief, anger, worry, fear and questions had taken their toll and the family was left mentally and physically exhausted. 'The body makes you sleep even though you don't want to. I awoke the following morning and thought it had all just been a nightmare. I looked around for Joyce and there was a shape in the bed and I thought "great", the nightmare is over. But when I examined closer it wasn't Joyce's face at all. It was a different shape and features. David had crept into the bed during the night. The poor little fella was missing his mother and needed to be with someone. It brought home to me the full magnitude of what had happened and the nightmare we were living.'

Within a few hours of the discovery of the body, the garda investigation team felt they were dealing with a killer from the locality.

Detectives reasoned that the fact that the murderer brought the car back to Milltown was highly significant. It showed he had a good knowledge of the area and had gone to the trouble of working out an escape route. The key to the murder, they decided, lay in the village.

The murder hunt team began to focus on getting statements from villagers about their movements at the critical time. The shop's closing time of around 6 pm was also one of the busiest periods in the day for The Store. It was the only grocery shop in the general area and there was always a last minute rush as people called for essentials like milk and bread before settling in for the night.

The Gardaí decided to concentrate on talking to the dozen or so people it was estimated visited the shop just before closing time. They soon identified three of the shoppers who were anxious to help detectives any way they could. These three witnesses were able to tell the investigation team the names or descriptions of the others who had called into the shop.

Significantly, one person leaving the shop remembered seeing Kenneth O'Reilly. 'One of them remembered being about to cross the road when O'Reilly passed by. He was walking away from the shop,' recalls experienced investigation member Detective Garda Pat Donlon.

'Another witness 40–50 yards down the road met him again. This time, however, he was going towards the shop,' Detective Donlon recalls.

O'Reilly's name was beginning to feature in the inquiry.

The crucial piece of information would come a short time afterwards. Door-to-door inquiries continued in the village and local residents were encouraged to give statements accounting for their movements and giving details of anything suspicious they may have seen on the night Joyce was murdered.

At least one person remembered a man who spoke with a foreign accent. In the early part of the investigation, newspaper reports featured the stranger as a possible suspect. Within hours of the articles appearing the man was cleared from the inquiry.

As the mundane process of questioning villagers continued, a crucial third witness emerged.

He remembered seeing O'Reilly inside the wall of the old primary school almost directly across from the shop shortly before it closed. O'Reilly mentioned that he was looking for a dropped £5 note.

O'Reilly had now been seen by three different people at three different locations around the shop at the critical time.

As the investigation team based at Naas station began to pay more attention to Kenneth O'Reilly, the Quinn family were dealing with Joyce's funeral arrangements.

On the night of Friday, 26 January, 1996, the remains of Joyce Quinn were received by her heartbroken husband and three distraught children at their parish church of St Brigid in Kildare town.

As snow and biting cold wind swept around the chapel in the town centre, relatives, friends and shocked neighbours gathered to pay their respects to the 44-year-old mother. Joyce's mother, Patricia Wickham, was overcome with grief as she prayed for her daughter.

Parish priest Fr Matt Kelly said words failed to comfort at a time like this 'but our hearts go out to Ray, Nicole, Lisa and David and Joyce's mother'. He said it was 'now a sad world where the innocent frequently suffer. This was surely so in Joyce's case. She was much loved by all who knew her. She was vibrant, kind and caring. The grief of the community at the tragic death is obvious. The pain and loss of her family is almost beyond comprehension.'

Back at Naas, a small team of officers discreetly began looking into O'Reilly's background. What they discovered didn't make him look like a hot suspect. Other than one minor traffic offence, he had never come to Garda notice before.

'He appeared to be a very normal person; very quiet. He had never come to the notice of the small community and was not known as a miscreant in the neighbourhood. All you could say about him was that he was something of a loner,' Detective Garda Donlon says.

Indeed, O'Reilly appeared to be as shocked as everyone else by the rape and murder of the local shopkeeper. He spoke to friends and neighbours about the killing and expressed horror that such a crime could occur in their small community.

Gardaí also discovered that on the night of the killing O'Reilly had been drinking with his girlfriend in one of Milltown's two pubs between 9 and 10 pm. Later, the couple travelled to Newbridge where they shared a Chinese meal.

'His general movements and attitude made us wonder whether he had committed such a dreadful crime,' a member of the murder hunt unit remembers.

*   *   *

Six days into the inquiry, however, the investigation team made the decision to arrest O'Reilly. He had been placed at the last location Joyce was seen and was probably the last person to see her alive.

On the morning of Tuesday, 30 January, a team of detectives arrested Kenneth O'Reilly at his home in the Millview local authority estate in Milltown. He was detained under section 4 of the Criminal Justice Act which allowed for him to be held for up to 12 hours. While he was taken in a patrol car to Naas Garda Station a search team combed the house. Under his bed officers found several sharp boning knives, including one with bloodstains.

At the station O'Reilly was taken to an interview room and asked about his movements on the night of the killing. Gardaí asked if he had been stalking Joyce Quinn and whether he fancied her.

The two interviewing detectives were surprised a short time into the questioning when O'Reilly admitted he was in the car. They pressed him further and he then told them how he carried out the actual murder. He said he forced Joyce to stop the car at the Curragh to allow him out. Then he lunged at her with a knife, stabbing her close to the heart. He drove the car off the road into a secluded area. He had chosen the spot carefully. During the winter months it is almost impossible to drive off the road onto the Curragh Plains without getting bogged down. O'Reilly had obviously marked out the route beforehand.

The murder trial later heard from the prosecuting barrister that O'Reilly 'left the car and had sexual intercourse with the deceased who may have been dead at the time, we don't know.'

After the rape attack he dragged Joyce from the car and stabbed her in the neck, dumping the body in furze bushes.

He threw the murder weapon into the dense undergrowth, he claimed. The murder complete, he drove the car in the darkness back to Milltown, concealing the little black Citroen behind the school building. After getting out of the school grounds he called on the man who had earlier seen him inside the wall of the old school building. He told the man not to worry he had found the £5 note.

O'Reilly was acting as if nothing had happened. Keen to get rid of Joyce's phone, he hid it in a cistern in the men's toilet of a local pub.

O'Reilly was brought before a special sitting of Bray District Court and charged with the murder but not the rape of Joyce Quinn. The court was told that when the charges were put to him, O'Reilly replied 'sorry'. At the back of the court for the three-minute hearing sat his mother and father, Elizabeth and Michael O'Reilly. Judge Thomas Ballagh remanded the accused until the following day's sitting of

Newbridge District Court, when a crowd of 200 gathered outside. Most of the crowd stood silently as O'Reilly was led away from the court building in a high-speed convoy.

Gardaí spent a week searching for the weapon O'Reilly claimed to have discarded near the murder scene and eventually found a knife with a five-inch blade hidden in furze 150 yards from where Joyce was murdered.

The murder weapon was shown to all members of the Quinn family to see if they recognised it. This was Garda procedure and was done in case the killer claimed he had not brought the knife with him but had found it in the car. None of the family had ever seen the knife before and it had certainly never been in Joyce's car.

On 7 October, 1997, O'Reilly pleaded guilty to the murder and was sentenced to life imprisonment. Up to the last minute it had been expected the killer would fight the case every inch of the way and time had been set aside for a full trial. O'Reilly, however, escaped being charged with rape and sexual assault.

Ray is still furious O'Reilly was never charged with Joyce's rape. It means that whenever the killer is released his name will not appear on the Sex Offenders Register. 'He went out with the intention of having his way with a woman and making sure there was no evidence afterwards. That is factually what happened but still his name will not go on the Register and that is an injustice.'

In sentencing the murderer, Mr Justice Fergus Flood told O'Reilly he had no discretion whatsoever, which meant that he had to hand down the statutory sentence for the crime, which is life imprisonment.

O'Reilly's barrister, Paddy McEntee submitted that there was no reason for any outline of the facts of the case to be given in court because a mandatory sentence was to be imposed.

This view, however, was contrary to the wishes of the Quinns, who wanted the public to know the evil acts O'Reilly had perpetrated. Indeed, the comments in court were another example of the way the Quinn family felt sidelined by the lawyers and court procedures.

Contrary to the views of Mr McEntee, Ray Quinn had gone to enormous lengths to ensure that the details of the awful death his wife had met would be told. He met with the prosecution barrister to ensure that the details would be revealed to the public.

Court buildings are heartless places at the best of times. For the relations of a murder victim they must be enormously intimidating. No special arrangements are made for them. Moreover, relatives have no automatic right of audience with the prosecution team. There isn't even a section of the court set aside where they can sit. Often it is left to a caring individual garda or gardaí to make arrangements for them. At different stages in the proceedings, Ray Quinn was forced to sit within arm's reach of his wife's killer. Naturally, it did occur to him on occasions that his army training would have allowed him exact the ultimate revenge, but it was never more than that, a fleeting thought.

Ray also had to fight tooth and nail to get the Chief State Solicitor's Office to keep the family up to date on the progress of the prosecution. He became something of a campaigner as he tirelessly wrote to the Minister for Justice and Director of Public Prosecutions to ensure that they kept him informed of developments.

A relation of another murder victim knew exactly the trauma the Quinn family was experiencing. A sister-in-law of Patricia O'Toole, who was murdered by Sean Courtney in the Dublin Mountains, was an enormous help to the Quinns. She described in detail what they should expect during the course of the case, the lack of interest by the Courts Service in their plight, the physical layout of the courts and the dearth of information. It was the kind of insight the Courts Service and the prosecution authorities should have offered but did not. To this day they still do not provide such information.

Fortunately, the army authorities and the investigating gardaí did all they could to assist the family in their hour of need. Ray was given the opportunity to serve abroad for one year with the United Nations in Cyprus, in which case he could bring his three children with him. It was the kind of space the family needed to cope with their terrible loss and trauma.

The delays in getting a trial date, however, and again a complete lack of information from the legal system, meant the family's departure date had to be put back on several occasions. Luckily the army authorities always facilitated the postponed hearings, allowing the family to depart for Cyprus after the case eventually came to trial.

'The year in Cyprus did a lot of good to help ease the trauma,' says Ray. In the years since the family returned the two youngest children, David and Lisa, have returned to further education and the couple's eldest daughter Nicole has married and now lives not far from the family home. Ray has been promoted to Lieutenant Colonel and holds a senior position as Chief Instructor at the Defence Force's Staff School in the Curragh. He is grateful to his army colleagues for the support they gave during the ordeal. 'The Army have been magnificent. People stop calling after a few weeks but the army guys, they are still calling years later.'

An oak tree, planted by the family, now stands at the spot where Joyce's body was found.

AN UNWILLING ACCOMPLICE

'Just shut your mouth and mind your own business.
We are going on a message.'

– John Cullen, 1983.

HELEN Murray found it difficult to sleep in the early hours of Sunday morning, 16 January, 1983. She had gone to bed around midnight but at 2 am she was still awake. Outside she could hear neighbours returning home. Two hours later she was still awake when she was startled by a sudden noise from the adjoining terraced house.

'Oh, Jesus,' she heard neighbour Carmel Prendergast scream.

Helen Murray knocked on the dividing wall to let her neighbour know she had heard. It was a procedure they had practised down the years. If one of them took ill or had an accident her neighbour would acknowledge the other's cry for help by banging on the bedroom wall and immediately going to her rescue. But when she reached the front door Helen was surprised to find Carmel Prendergast already dressed and standing outside.

'There's a fire in Lynch's house,' Mrs Prendergast said pointing to the artisan building next door.

The two women knew they would have to act quickly to save their neighbours. They could see the bright orange glow of flames through the front window. The house was an inferno. While Carmel Prendergast shouted into the house in a bid to rouse the occupants, her husband Sam ran down the street with Helen Murray to alert other neighbours to the blaze. Within minutes Hammond Street in Dublin's south inner-city was frantic with activity as residents considered how to rescue the four women who occupied No. 15.

Sam Prendergast realised almost immediately the gravity of the situation. He smashed a pane of glass in the front door of the blazing house and pushed open the door.

'There was a lot of smoke in the room and the stairs at the back wall of the living room were blazing fiercely. I only got half way across the room when the heat and the flames forced me back,' he said.

'My wife, who had come down to the house, then told me that Dolores Lynch was at the window of the back bedroom. When I heard this I ran out through Bob McDonald's house with Bob and around to the back of No. 15.'

The two men climbed over a back wall and onto the roof of the kitchen extension of the burning house. They could see the figure of Dolores Lynch silhouetted by the flames. They tried to pull her through the small rear window but it proved an almost impossible task.

'Dolores was very black from the fire and I found it very difficult to get a grip on her,' Sam said.

The two brave men were joined by another neighbour Kevin Murray and after what seemed to be about five minutes they managed to drag her to safety.

'Sam, help my mother,' were her first words.

Kevin Murray remembers tending to the fire victim on the roof as they waited for an ambulance crew to arrive. 'Don't let me die,' she said. 'Get my mother out.'

With the help of firefighters, they managed to lower her down onto a carrying sheet and 34-year-old Dolores was rushed off to nearby St James's Hospital.

The inferno had completely gutted the tiny two-storey home.

Later in the morning, with the blaze under control, firemen ventured upstairs. In the front upstairs room they found the body of a woman kneeling between two beds covered with a blanket. It was Dolores' mother, Kathleen, aged 61 years. She had tried to protect herself with the blanket but had received burns on 90 per cent of her body. A second dead woman was found in a sitting position behind the door of the same front room. It was Dolores' aunt Mrs Hannah Hearne who was 64. She had suffered burns to 70 per cent of the body surface. She died from smoke inhalation.

Dolores, who suffered first and second-degree burns covering 70 per cent of her body, died from her terrible injuries that afternoon.

* * *

It appeared to be a tragic accident. The three women, along with some friends, had been playing cards early into the morning. There was an open fire in the kitchen. The theory was that a stray spark could have caused the fire after the women retired to bed. Another daughter, Kathleen, who also lived in the house, was out babysitting at the time and escaped the horror.

'I don't know how it could have happened. A lot of my aunts and cousins were in the house for a card game that went on until about 2 am,' she told a newspaper reporter.

Gardaí mounted a guard on the house to preserve the scene for technical examination. No. 15 was a typical artisan dwelling coming right out onto the footpath. It was one of 25 terraced red-brick houses on Hammond Street, inhabited in most instances by the same families for generations. None of the houses had a rear entrance. They had no back gardens and only a tiny yard, used mainly to store coal.

By Monday, 17 January, suspicions about the cause of the inferno began to grow in some quarters. To some officers, it no longer looked entirely like an accident. Ballistics expert Detective Garda John Fitzpatrick carried out an examination of the shell, and contrary to the common belief, discovered that the seat of the fire was not around the kitchen grate. He found that the fire broke out at the end of the stairs beside the back downstairs window. The window was unlocked.

Local detectives recalled a fire at the same dwelling the previous April. Mrs Kathleen Lynch had returned to the house around 3.40 am on 25 April, 1982, and found a packet of firelighters ablaze inside the front hall door. The lighters had been pushed through the letter box and extensive damage was caused to the floor coverings and walls as well as to gas and electric fittings. Mrs Lynch's daughter, Dolores, was asleep upstairs at the time, totally unaware of the fire. Luckily, nobody was injured and the flames were quickly brought under control.

The family believed a 21-year-old man from the south inner-city with whom they had had some trouble was responsible for the incident. Detectives interviewed the man at the time but he denied any knowledge of the arson attack. The suspect was released without charge.

However, despite this abundance of circumstantial evidence and suspicions by several officers, the Garda authorities still insisted on treating the fire and three deaths as accidental. The reasons for this are hard to comprehend but it would be another four days before they would consider treating the case as arson.

The first real break came with the results of tests at the Forensic Science Laboratory. They indicated the presence of paraffin in debris taken from around the stairs. More important information began to come to light in the days that followed.

* * *

Like all police forces, the Gardaí cultivate informants in the underworld, the vice scene and even in business. These confidential sources are sometimes paid but more often than not receive no monetary reward. They are invaluable in providing an understanding of the workings of the criminal world, explaining feuds between various gangs or individuals and providing insights about the underworld's suspicion as to who is responsible for certain crimes.

Detective Garda John Gallagher, based in Fitzgibbon Street district, which covers areas of the north inner-city, came into possession of information in this way.

It indicated that John Cullen, a pimp with a reputation for extreme violence, had set fire to the house with the intention of murdering Dolores Lynch. His sole reason was one of revenge. He wanted to kill her because she had given evidence against him in an assault trial several years previously.

Gallagher's information was corroborated by other criminal informants who contacted two other Special Branch gardaí. The officers attached to the quick action response Special Task Force had received the same report from their own separate sources. It all fitted in with a heartless slogan daubed across a wall at St James's Hospital in silver paint: 'Dolores Lynch is a rat.' Suspicion that the women had been murdered grew.

One week after the three deaths, a major case conference was held at Kevin Street. Detective Superintendent John Reynolds and Detective Inspector Mick Connolly from the Dublin Metropolitan Area (DMA) South Central Division were joined by senior members of the Murder Squad. They included Detective Superintendent John Courtney along with dozens of officers from the local detective and uniformed branches, the Central Detective Unit and Special Branch.

* * *

The intended victim of the cold-blooded arson attack, Dolores Lynch, was the second eldest of four daughters. She was born on 10 February, 1948, at Hammond Street in an area known locally as Blackpitts. After attending school at Warrenmount Convent, she began working with her mother in a local factory at the age of 14. She left after just six months.

Her home life was a troubled one which eventually led to Dolores leaving home and, ultimately, becoming a prostitute. Without any accommodation or money she worked the area around the Grand Canal on Dublin's southside. It was here she came into contact with John Cullen, the hardman pimp.

Despite her profession, she was always a little religious. She was one of the few street women who said the rosary at the Legion of Mary house, which provided shelter for the prostitutes. The group dedicated itself to saving the souls of 'fallen women'.

On two occasions Dolores took a group tour to Lourdes. She also visited the Vatican and had an audience with the Pope. Dolores did her best to go straight but as one garda who knew her said: 'She did have some lapses every now and then.'

Dolores eventually quit life on the street and became a wardsmaid at St James's Hospital. She turned to religion more and more and shortly before her murder went on pilgrimage to Lough Derg.

She became very involved in the feminist movement and participated in several marches. After the rape and death of ex-prostitute Teresa Maguire in 1978, Dolores wrote to the then Minister for Justice, Gerry Collins, calling for changes in the law relating to prostitution. The former vice girl had been beaten with an iron bar when she refused to have sex with her attacker. The letter criticised the Minister for not meeting a delegation: 'The girls who make their living on the streets of Dublin are very annoyed and disappointed that you have refused to meet us in the company of the Council for the Status of Women to hear our point of view about the injustice we suffer in the courts,' Dolores wrote.

On one occasion, she narrowly avoided being sent to prison for soliciting when she promised the judge she would get a job. Dolores went to work as a chambermaid in the Montrose Hotel in Dublin but would still visit her old colleagues down by the canal at night.

But it was an event two years earlier, when Dolores was still on the game, which would eventually lead to her murder.

Around midnight on 11 May, 1976, she was with three other girls, Catherine, Alice and Marian, in a Kentucky Fried Chicken restaurant at Upper Baggot Street. They sat at the window and were clearly visible to anybody passing by. John Cullen and another man walked into the fast-food restaurant. Cullen walked over to the group and asked them where the cigarette machine was. One of the group told him it was at the counter.

Cullen bought a can of 7-Up while his friend walked to the door to prevent anybody coming in. Dolores later told the police of the events which unfolded.

'He turned to me and without warning hit me on the head with the can of 7-Up. He then asked me if I knew him. I did not answer him and he hit me again with the can of 7-Up. I then said that I did not know him. He then kicked me in the tummy and I doubled up. He kicked me in the eye and chest. He continued to hit me with the can until he drew blood.

'He also turned me around to face [the man] and said, "If you know him on Friday you will get it."[1] The man at this point said, "You will be dead." He kicked me and hit me several more times. Before he left he again said if I went to court on Thursday or Friday that I would be killed stone dead. Then they left and remained outside for about 20 minutes. We had to stay until some customer came into the restaurant before we could get out of the place as we were scared to leave.'

Little did Dolores know that Cullen, an evil man, meant every word of it. He was a man riven with hate who used violence against anyone who ever crossed him. After the vicious assault, Dolores Lynch was taken to St Vincent's Hospital where she received 10 stitches for the injuries to her head. Her right eye was so badly hurt it remained closed for five days.

Despite the ordeal and subsequent intimidation, Dolores still gave evidence against the man and subsequently against Cullen for the assault on her. On 6 December, 1976, Cullen was sentenced to three years in prison for the attack. The man got 18 months for assault. Dolores' determination to give testimony against the pimp tormented him in jail. During his term inside he plotted and schemed a way of getting back at her.

* * *

Cullen, the father of three children, was born on 30 October, 1950. All his adult life he was involved in the vice trade. Garda crime reports describe him as a 'well-known pimp'. He is known to have used strongarm methods to frighten prostitutes and collect as high as 80 per cent of their earnings. He received his first criminal

---

1. Reference to an upcoming assault case in which Dolores was a witness.

conviction at the age of nine, going on to amass a total of 20 for housebreaking, larceny, receiving stolen property and loitering, along with two vicious assaults, including that on Dolores Lynch.

On one occasion, when he found one of his prostitutes, whom he was seeing at the time, in bed with a friend of his, Cullen erupted into a rage. He broke her arm and she had to receive 30 stitches to her head. Another example of his uncontrollable violence came a year before the fatal fire. In January 1982, Cullen walked into a flat in Ballymun where his girlfriend and prostitute Lyn Madden were talking to two other men. Cullen was overcome with a jealous rage and lashed out at one of the men.

The victim told gardaí: 'When Cullen came in I saluted him. I don't know if he answered me, I did not take much notice of him. Suddenly I saw stars and everything went red. I was staggering towards John Cullen when I saw him lunging towards me with a knife in his hand. He stabbed me with the knife under my right arm. After a few seconds everything came into focus again and I saw Lyn Madden lying at the kitchen door. The upper part of her body was out in the hallway and John Cullen was bent over her trying to stab her with the knife but she was trying to hold him back with her legs – kicking him away.

'I got up off the floor and tried to get Cullen off Lyn Madden and she got away. I saw her run off down the hall. Cullen attacked me with the knife and kept slashing me. Most of the time he was slashing me on the arms and head.'

The male victim, who was a friend of Cullen's brother, managed to barricade himself into a room but the pimp tried to kick down the door. After a few minutes when things quietened down, he checked to see if the coast was clear. But Cullen was still in a mad rage.

'The next thing I saw was John Cullen coming from the kitchen with two knives in his hands, one of them a breadknife. He attacked me with the two knives. I was lying against the wall helpless. I collapsed on the ground and he kept slashing down at me with the knives ... All I could hear was Cullen shouting: "He's dead, I'll fucking kill him." I crawled back into the toilet and I was lying on the floor,

I was losing an awful lot of blood. I had my head against the door and Cullen kept trying to get in.'

The pimp was eventually dragged away from the toilet door. He fled the scene but was later charged with assault. Unfortunately for Dolores Lynch and her family, he got out on bail. Over the next 12 months his obsession with Dolores would fluctuate. At times he would be consumed with hatred for her, then on occasions others would be the target of his temper.

Less than four months after the vicious stabbing incident in Ballymun flats on 25 April, 1982, he tried for the first time to burn down Dolores' family home. Cullen stuffed lighted firelighters through the letterbox but fortunately the blaze was spotted by her aunt.

The Lynches unwittingly blamed another man for the incident and John Cullen never figured in the subsequent investigation. After that, Cullen would periodically place their home under surveillance for several months at a time.

* * *

Lyn Madden was born in Cork in 1944. She was taken to England at the age of seven by her mother when her parents broke up. After a row with her mother, she became a prostitute in Leicester at just 16 years of age. She was also on the game in Birmingham before moving to Dublin with her boyfriend and two young sons in 1966. Later, he moved back to England with one of the children. Between 1974 and 1980 she accumulated ten convictions, mostly for soliciting, but two were for conspiracy to defraud and receiving stolen property.

Lyn was a friend of Dolores Lynch. She was also very close to John Cullen. She first came into contact with John Cullen in 1980. Madden was having trouble with her boyfriend at the time. One night he tried to break into her flat and as she escaped over the balcony, she fell and broke her ankle. The boyfriend stabbed her five times with a scissors. In hospital she was visited by other women on the game, one of whom brought her boyfriend, John Cullen, along. Within a few weeks, Cullen had recruited Madden as one of his own vice girls. She replaced another woman whose arm he had broken a few weeks earlier. Lyn Madden initially saw him as her saviour.

Shortly after leaving hospital, a neighbour in Coolock attacked her 18-year-old son with a hurley and smashed the windows in their flat. She told Cullen what happened.

'He told me to go up the stairs and ask the fellow to pay for the window he had broken and he walked up behind me with a hammer from my flat. When the fellow came out to the door I asked him was he going to pay for my windows and he said, "No, why should I?"

'As soon as he said that John Cullen pushed me aside and struck this fellow on the head with the hammer. He was bleeding very badly and I thought he would die. Cullen was holding him over the balcony for a while and one of the neighbours said the police were coming and an ambulance arrived in a short time.'

After that, he moved in with her in a flat provided by the Corporation in the Ballymun complex. He usually stayed there into the early hours of the morning before returning to the family home in Kilbarrack. His obsession with Lyn's friend Dolores soon came to the surface however.

'He was paranoid about her and told me he was going to kill her for getting him three years in prison and taking his kids away from him. He always said she should pay for it.'

Cullen also told Lyn Madden about his first attempt on Dolores' life: 'One night he came to my flat and told me he had been around to Dolores' place last night and had set fire to it but the fucking thing went out,' she recalled. But far more serious trouble lay ahead for Lyn Madden.

On Saturday, 15 January, 1983, Lyn Madden was at home around 6 pm when Cullen arrived. She was alone in the flat. Her son had gone to Liverpool to a soccer match. The couple stayed up watching videos until about 3 am. Suddenly he ordered: 'Get dressed.' Madden was in her dressing-gown and asked where they were going.

'Just shut your mouth and mind your own business. We are going on a message,' was the reply. Before leaving he took her son's jacket from the hallway and put it on.

Cullen's trial in the Circuit Criminal Court for the vicious Ballymun stabbing was only days away and she felt he was going to stake out the victim's house in Rathfarnham. He had previously proclaimed that he was going to burn down the house and regularly sat outside the man's home for hours. It was part of the intimidation techniques used by the thug.

Within a short time, however, she knew Rathfarnham was not their destination.

They drove from Ballymun into the city centre and at Clanbrassil Street, in the Liberties, Cullen turned off onto a side street and parked the car on a slope near a group of houses on St Alban's Road. From the glove compartment he took a pair of gloves and slipped them on. He went around to the boot and grabbed two plastic bottles filled with petrol and a blue holdall bag belonging to Lyn Madden. The zip on the bag was broken and it was held together with a safety pin. It contained a hammer, a Stanley knife, some kitchen knives and firelighters, all taken from her flat.

'Get out,' he told his accomplice.

'What's in the bag,' she asked.

Pointing to his nose he told her: 'Mind your own fucking business.'

The couple walked down the deserted street. They weren't alone for long. Cullen panicked when he saw a woman coming towards them. He hadn't noticed her at first because she was dressed in dark clothes. He pulled Lyn close and began kissing her. The young woman, aged about 25–30 with red hair, smiled at the couple and passed on.

They continued on and at Clarence Mangan Road, Cullen began counting off the houses. The street backed onto Hammond Street. At a gap in the terrace of houses was a wall with two doors leading into the back gardens. He ordered her to stand guard.

'Right, now listen, I'm going over the wall here. Watch the lights in this house. If the lights come on, whistle. Watch the road for cars. If you see a police car and it comes on top, get a taxi home,' he said, handing her a £20 note.

'But John I can't whistle.'

'Well then, shout but don't shout my fucking name.'

The pimp clambered over the wall, careful not to cut himself on the broken glass dotted along the top. Seconds later, one of the doors in the wall slid open. Lyn Madden walked into the back garden while Cullen slowly made his way to the back wall of another house – 15 Hammond Street, the home of Dolores Lynch. Soon afterwards he returned taking the carving knife, Stanley knife and hammer from the blue holdall bag and went off again.

Cullen had been trying to perfect an incendiary device for some time and had experimented with several. He had even added sugar to the petrol to give it a greater blast.

Madden recalls: 'After a few minutes he came back again and told me the back window was open and he didn't have to force it. He put the hammer in the bag and took two plastic containers full of petrol from the bag. There were two firelighters taped to both of these containers and there were matches with red tops stuck in the firelighters.'

In the darkness of the back garden, using the street lights for guidance, he took the filters off two cigarettes and attached the broken cigarettes to two matches which had been stuck into the firelighters. The idea was to light the cigarette which would slowly burn down to the match, igniting the firelighters and then the petrol. It would give the arsonist enough time to get safely away by the time the device exploded.

'Come down to the bottom of the garden with me,' he ordered his companion.

Cullen then jumped onto the back wall of Dolores Lynch's home, careful not to cut himself on the chicken wire spread along the top. With several kicks he managed to flatten the security wire. The lights were on in the upstairs of No. 15 but he was undeterred. He pulled up the rear window. Dolores, her mother and aunt were inside.

Using a lighter he ignited the cigarettes and placed the fused firebomb inside. Confident of his work, Cullen slowly pulled the window closed and climbed onto the kitchen extension. In doing so, he dislodged a slate, sending a rumbling noise out into the night air. Cullen immediately lay down flat on the roof. He looked down at Madden. She shook her head. He scrambled onto the ground and both of them took off towards the back gate onto Clarence Mangan Road.

'When I got out onto Clarence Mangan Road, I heard a woman screaming and the sound of glass breaking,' Lyn Madden later remembered. She later told a friend the voice was that of Dolores Lynch crying: 'Get my mother out.'

* * *

On the journey back to Ballymun, John Cullen laughed out loud. He was ecstatic. 'I hope it was the right house,' he joked.

But the psychopath's joy at the horror he had caused did not affect his cunning judgement. He was now desperate to discard anything which would connect him with the fire. On the route back from Hammond Street, he threw the gloves he used out the car window in Phibsboro. Back at Lyn Madden's flat, he began to strip off all his clothes. He threw everything onto a newspaper spread out on the floor. He bundled the paper up into a ball and disposed of it in a rubbish chute in the hallway.

Cullen then told Lyn Madden to put on the kettle. He was thirsty and wanted a cup of tea.

'What was all that about?' she enquired.

'Let's put it this way, if it's the right place you will know all about it tomorrow. If not, all well and good,' he replied. Then he had a bath. Around 5 am, he returned to his wife in Kilbarrack.

By now, the frightening significance of what had occurred was beginning to dawn on Lyn Madden. She knew it was Dolores Lynch's house which had been consumed in the fireball. The fact that she had been an accomplice in the attack and the possible murder of one of her friends left her completely traumatised. She took a few valium tablets and went to bed. That evening she tuned into the 6 pm television news. At first, there was a feeling of relief. But it was followed by utter devastation.

'The first thing I heard was about a judge getting shot in the North. The second was about a fire in a house in Dublin where two elderly women died and the 34-year-old daughter of one of them died later. I think it was Charles Mitchell who read the news and he said Miss Dolores Lynch. I knew immediately it was a friend of mine, Dolores Lynch, that John Cullen had killed.'

Around two hours later he arrived in the flat, took off his jacket and shoes and lay in the bed beside her.

'I'm glad I got the right house,' he boasted. 'I'm just glad she is dead.'

Later in the evening, it struck him that the clothes he disposed of early that morning would not be collected until the following day. At around 10 pm, he told Lyn Madden to gather up the bundle. They were going to Portrane, on the north Dublin coast, to dump the clothes over a cliff. He said he wanted to get on the road before the Gardaí started checking for car tax around pub closing time.

'We drove out to Portrane and he was low in petrol and he got £5 worth of petrol there. We drove up to the cliff top by the houses where the car park is. There was a car parked there with a couple in it. We sat in the car for a while and they drove off. We both got out of the car and he asked me to give him the plastic bag of clothes. The jumper was old and he tore it up easily. He asked me to give him the knife which he had brought out in the car and he cut up his jeans with that.

'He then walked down over the rocks and I followed him until the heel of my shoe got caught in the rock and he told me to stay there. I walked back towards the top of the cliff. As I was waiting, he came up behind me and I thought he was going to push me over.

'He took what was left in the plastic bag and went back down again. He returned in a few minutes and we drove back towards Ballymun. When we reached the knacker's camp at the top of Coolock Lane which we had turned off the Swords Road to do, I threw the plastic holdall bag out the window near the camp.'

A few days later, when they went to see Lyn's daughter in Belfast, the car's seat covers were discarded near Dublin Airport.

*   *   *

John Cullen believed he had carried out the perfect murder. His confidence was misplaced. His involvement in the triple murder would not remain secret for long. He had made mistakes and was continuing to make more.

His first blunder was bringing Lyn Madden along. She was already beginning to confide in friends on the vice scene about what had happened. One of them, Geraldine, visited Lyn the day after the arson attack. 'Elizabeth [Lyn] said to me that her nerves were gone. I told her that Dolores Lynch, who we both knew, was dead. She just nodded her head, signifying that's why her nerves were gone.'

By Saturday, 22 January, Cullen himself was openly hinting at his involvement in the murders. Late that night he picked up prostitute Geraldine along the Grand Canal and drove her back to her flat where he raped her. It was a particularly violent and degrading sexual assault in which he carried out several acts of perversion including urinating and defecating on the woman. During the night, he asked the woman if she knew who was responsible for starting a collection among the prostitutes for Dolores Lynch's family.

'He said they had an awful cheek making a collection for her. He said he was glad she was dead and he wanted to know did she die screaming,' Geraldine said.

Cullen seemed to be in a rage when talking about Dolores and repeated several times: 'I'm glad she's dead, she deserves to be dead, anyone who rats deserves to be dead.'

He also made reference to the arson attack.

'If you want to get rid of someone, you don't shoot them because you can trace bullets. You don't stab them, you burn them. That way you burn all evidence as well. He said you don't use matches to start a fire because matches go out, so if you light a firelighter and hold it for a few minutes it won't go out,' Geraldine recalled. The secret was

– 241 –

out. It was only a matter of time before the Gardaí got to hear of Cullen's boasts.

The Gardaí picked Geraldine up soon afterwards. She told them everything she knew about the case. But knowing Cullen's reputation for violence, she demanded 24-hour armed protection. It was granted.

* * *

At dawn on 26 January, armed detectives from the murder hunt team descended on John Cullen's home at Mount Olive Road, Kilbarrack. They had a warrant to search the residence and his car, a red Datsun. The warrant issued under the Offences Against the State Act specified that the police believed he was responsible for the arson attack at 15 Hammond Street.

Gardaí banged on the door and it was answered by Cullen's wife Judy. Detective Sergeant Kevin Ward, who led the raid, read the warrant to her while other gardaí rushed through the door and up the stairs. Cullen was in the front bedroom pulling on his socks when the gardaí came in. Ward put his hand on the pimp's shoulder and told him he was arresting him under Section 30 of the Offences Against the State Act.

Simultaneously, two other teams of gardaí were searching the homes of two prostitutes. One of them was that of Cullen's girlfriend, Lyn Madden. Detective Inspector Thomas Ibar Dunne from the Murder Squad led the unit which raided her home at Coultry Road, Ballymun. She too was put in the back of a patrol car and taken to Kevin Street station. The early morning swoops had gone without a hitch. Now it was time to see what the suspects had to say for themselves.

* * *

Cullen and Madden were held in separate interview rooms. During the day he was questioned by teams of two officers led by Detective Inspectors Mick Connolly and Gerry McCarrick. When told he was being held in connection with the deaths of three women at

Hammond Street and asked where he was on that night he told the police: 'I was in bed.'

He vehemently denied being involved in prostitution, knowing Dolores Lynch or even knowing where Hammond Street was. When Inspector Connolly asked him what he knew about the fire, Cullen said, 'I don't know nothing about it and I didn't hear anything about it.' He added: 'I went to bed at my normal time, say 12 midnight. I stayed in bed all night.'

In another room a short distance away, detectives were having a little more success. After a period in which she denied knowledge of the incident, Lyn Madden began to break when she heard her friend and colleague, Geraldine, had already told the police everything she knew. Lyn asked to see Geraldine and it was arranged.

Following their meeting she made a statement implicating John Cullen in the three murders. It was a major breakthrough. She acknowledged that she went with John Cullen in his car and was present when he set fire to the house. However, she claimed she did not know at the time that Cullen had set out to kill Dolores.

Gardaí continued to question Cullen in relays. Around 10.15 pm, Detective Sergeants Pat Lynagh and Tony Hickey took over from Detective Gardaí PJ Browne and Tom Byrne. Lynagh told the killer that Geraldine had made a statement to the effect that he had told her he had burned down the house. Cullen immediately denied even knowing Geraldine, the woman he had raped just a few days earlier. Eventually, he agreed he did know her but not very well. He told the detective he didn't believe she would make such a statement.

The following morning he was equally shocked to hear Lyn Madden had also made a statement. A Detective Sergeant read it out to him. His reply was equally surprising and revealing.

'That's all true. It couldn't be invented, there's too many facts in it. The only thing is I didn't tell that I could have burned the wrong house. I'll tell the whole truth myself when I see her.'

That afternoon, both women admitted in front of him that they had made the statements, implicating him. Later that evening when asked if what the women had said was true, he responded: 'More or less.'

Detective Gardaí John Mulligan and Tom Mulligan interviewed him that night. 'What's the maximum sentence for malicious wounding?' he asked.

'I don't know exactly,' replied Tom Mulligan.

'I'd take a bow for the malicious wounding if I thought I wouldn't get more than two years.' Asked what he meant, he told the two officers: 'Well, I'd take a bow for the fire.'

Just before 11 pm that night, he was charged with the murder of Dolores Lynch and the arson attack at Hammond Lane.

* * *

After Cullen was charged, Lyn Madden had to be taken into protective custody by the Gardaí because of continuous threats to her life. Two of the murder team, Detectives Tony Sourke and Brendan Billings, heard that she was living in fear of Cullen in her flat shortly after leaving Garda custody. Some of Cullen's friends planned to push her off a high-rise balcony. The Gardaí kept a watch on the flat to prevent anyone breaking in. But even that did not stop her from feeling under threat. She stayed the night in Ballymun Station – the only place she felt safe.

The following morning she arrived back in Kevin Street station and gave the Gardaí an even more detailed statement about Cullen. She outlined to Detective Inspector Dunne how the crime was committed, and how they stood around at the back of Dolores' house.

This information led Detectives Sourke and John Ridge to find parts of a firelighter and cigarettes from Cullen's firebomb discarded near houses on Clarence Mangan Road.

Three female gardaí had to be assigned to escort and protect Lyn Madden. Even while on remand, Cullen, from his jail cell, tried to buy her and other witnesses off with money. When this did not work, he issued threats and officers believe this worked against one particular witness.

In the first trial, the jury failed to agree on a verdict. In the second trial, the jury convicted him of the murder of Dolores Lynch and

Cullen was sentenced to life imprisonment at the Central Criminal Court. Despite an extensive search, his clothing was never found at Portrane. Neither were the gloves he discarded in Phibsboro. Lyn Madden has since left the country.

Describing Cullen's motive for the crime, Detective Superintendent John Courtney, who led the inquiry, says: 'There is no doubt about the motive for this calamitous crime. It was a result of a grudge engendered in the poisonous mind of a pimp who lived for a number of years off the immoral earnings of unfortunate girls of different creeds and nationalities.

'John Cullen brutally assaulted Dolores Lynch in 1976 and she, in the face of his evil intimidation, was brave enough to go to court and give evidence against him. Cullen did not forget and always said she would rue the day. His memory lasted a long time until he accomplished his goal in the early hours of Sunday, 16 January, 1983, and fulfilled his revenge.'

In her book *Lyn: A Story of Prostitution*, co-written with journalist June Levine some years later, Lyn tried to explain why she hadn't exposed Cullen earlier.

> Not once in that night had Lyn considered stopping him or running from Cullen. She had seen too much of his violence. She certainly could not have prevented what happened. As for running away, even if she had made it out of the garden without getting her skull caved in or the butcher's knife between her shoulder blades, where could she run to? He had the keys to the flat. No matter when she would have gone home, he would have been there on the bed, smiling, waiting. She wished that she hadn't heard the screams. She couldn't stop them in her head.' [1]

* * *

John Cullen is currently incarcerated in Portlaoise jail, where he is housed in the Dublin gangland corridor.

---

1. June Levine and Lyn Madden, *Lyn: A Story of Prostitution*, (1987), Attic Press: Dublin, p.19.

Epilogue
THE SACRISTAN

THE vast majority of killers featured in this book have been incarcerated for the best part of their sentences in Arbour Hill prison in Dublin.

The jail's notorious reputation comes from the prisoners who are housed there rather than conditions within its walls. Arbour Hill – which lies just off the north quays not far from Heuston station – has the least harsh regime of any closed penal institution in the country. Most of those held within its granite walls are inmates serving life sentences or offenders who cannot be detained in any other jail because of the nature of the crimes they have committed.

The fact that all are 'lifers' leads to a certain stability within the complex. Unlike other penitentiaries, each prisoner has his own cell. Until recently, both of the longest-serving prisoners in the State, John Shaw and Geoffrey Evans were housed there along with Malcolm MacArthur, Larry Murphy, Michael Bambrick, Frank McCann and David Lawler.

On being convicted of murder following the deaths of Elizabeth Plunkett and Mary Duffy in 1978, Shaw and Evans were visited at the prison by a senior Department of Justice official. He called them into the Governor's Office where he told them in no uncertain terms that they would never again see the light of day. Both men turned pale after the official delivered his pronouncement and did not leave their basement cells for three weeks afterwards.

In 2001, 23 years after their conviction, Shaw applied for a transfer to Castlerea jail in Co. Roscommon. His request was granted. He is one of a number of killers and serious sex offenders who in recent years sought to be moved to the modern jail, located in the grounds of a former mental hospital. Prison officers expected him to seek to return to Arbour Hill within a few months but he has indicated that he wishes to stay in Castlerea. Up to his transfer, Shaw had worked in the prison carpenter's shop and was described as a good woodturner.

His friend and fellow killer Geoffrey Evans remains in Arbour Hill. Staff describe him as a loner. While he does sometimes communicate with fellow inmates, he prefers the solitude of his cell. During his time there he has worked in the library, where he was in charge of videoing material, and in the kitchens. Most recently, he was assigned to general cleaning duties.

In 2000, Malcolm MacArthur was transferred from Arbour Hill to the Training Unit of Mountjoy jail. At the time, the move was met with an outcry in the national media as it was seen as a prelude to release. More recently, in September 2002, the parole board recommended that he be sent to the open prison at Shelton Abbey in Co. Wicklow to prepare for permanent release.

This decision was met with dismay by the families of Bridie Gargan and Donal Dunne. At the time of publication, the Government had yet to decide whether to conform with the parole board decision.

In Arbour Hill, MacArthur was described as 'haughty and aloof.' One officer commented: 'He feels superior to everyone else and looks down his nose at the staff. He doesn't like interference.' Staff hold the same opinion of him in the Training Unit. MacArthur only began seeing psychologists when it became part of the conditions of going before the Sentence Review Group to seek parole.

Michael Bambrick is described as one of the weirdest inmates in the jail. Until recently he refused to wash and never cleaned his cell. The years, however, have taken their toll and Bambrick has begun to integrate into the prison population and has finally started maintaining bodily hygiene. He works in the prison Braille Shop with, amongst others, Frank McCann and David Lawler.

McCann, like MacArthur, has never settled into the prison routine. He keeps within a tight circle of inmates, which includes Lawler.

Both see themselves as being in charge of the Braille Shop and give instructions to the 20 or so other inmates working there. 'McCann sees himself as superior to other prisoners. He is "uppity" with staff and fellow inmates alike,' observed one prison officer.

Larry Murphy works in the prison Joiner's Shop. Staff describe him as a 'model prisoner'. The master carpenter made the podiums for the 2003 Special Olympics. He speaks openly with staff and inmates alike but has always refused to talk about his crime or speculation that he was involved in the disappearances of women in the Leinster area.

Another 'model prisoner' has been Sean Courtney, who was transferred to the Training Unit at Mountjoy prior to his imminent release. Respectful towards staff, he is always careful about his appearance. He was the jail sacristan in Arbour Hill where he maintained the chapel. Prior to this, he was a typesetter in the printshop, a job he took over from MacArthur. At one stage, he printed material for the Army.

One prison source described John Cullen as a 'pure animal'. Cullen is a disruptive inmate held in Wheatfield jail in the Clondalkin suburb of Dublin. He has spent the bulk of his term of his imprisonment in Portlaoise jail where he mixed with inmates in the Dublin gangland wing of the institution. At one stage he was moved to the Training Unit of Mountjoy but was not deemed suitable for the low-security regime and was transferred to Wheatfield. In Portlaoise he earned a reputation for constantly trying to stir up trouble with prison officers and other convicts. While exercising in 'A' Wing of Mountjoy he bit off another inmate's ear. 'Cullen is a born killer. He always has the potential to kill. He is one of the people whom staff members never turn their backs on,' a source said.

APPENDIX

MacArthur's handwritten notes found by Gardaí when he was arrested.

1 heavy fuse to be temporarily installed and then removed
— or tape (cloth to be put between tape and clothes)

4 leather straps — each with a bolt in it dividing it in 2

A gag —   1 screwdriver   [— to wear gloves always
A blindfold   1 phase tester   — no prints
                  1 pliers :

Additional rope for tying up — accm's chest   [All to be taken
Two black bags for taking equipment away.   away — dispose

Electric fire with faulty plug attached — adaptor
left in wall — plug on, jury adaptor, plug pulled out. More of
my finger prints — make sure bars on handle
+ body of fire. Take away one of two fires if it appears there are too many
unplugged. Body in 10.1 chair. non unplugged electric fire.
Fire to be left behind floor for scene.

Shock gadget — rigidly fixed bar (bribery) —
wooden frame (skating car)   with handle
long wire with plug + taped switch. single live wire ...
to handle and a wire connected to one end of bar
switch on it. — Hair(s) + bar wet for main
only contact. Dry hand(s) at end.

Metal tray on lid for bare feet and for a little water
for contact. water run from river tray to the cord socket
contact. Dry feet at end — socks perhaps — no shoes
in a wall plug :

gun, disguise, rubber gloves to be set free later
perhaps no disguise & removing the car, money for ...
scenario. —

Wait for a while to ensure that death is final.
During this time take a few very important items (certain small photos in my possession. Make an inventory of other important items to so that I can check on their presence? even 5 ensure for the journal

Letter(s) from me left in prominent place —
on table or in or beside her address book, on
telephone directory (if an envelope then tear out
the string) — put her prints on the letter
+ envelope. — giving my address + telephone
number for a certain length of time. etc .

on it Returning giving that up address + wait for message.
Then give instructions to R. Bellasty + hurry ones
to take charge. (Death Cert) (New suit, paper, — times,
+ grave flowers clean out grave? — inform a few of her
friends + New Byrne (Safeguard + increase collections. — photos etc.)
+ collect.

Then on with the job: —
Shaw + O'Reilly.
Sell car + furniture etc. right away.